ELEANOR ROOSEVELT

First Lady of American Liberalism

Lois Scharf

TWAYNE PUBLISHERS • BOSTON
A Division of G.K. Hall & Co.

To David, Laura, Bonnie and Gary

Copyright 1987 by G.K. Hall & Co.
All rights reserved
Published by Twayne Publishers
A Division of G.K. Hall & Co.
70 Lincoln Street, Boston, Massachusetts 02111

Twayne's Twentieth-Century
American Biography Series No. 6

The Roosevelt genealogy is adapted from **World of Love: Eleanor Roosevelt and Her Friends, 1943–1962** by Joseph Lash and is reproduced by permission of Doubleday & Company, Inc.

Copyediting supervised by Lewis DeSimone
Produced by Janet Zietowski
Typeset in 11/13 Goudy by Compset, Inc.

Printed on permanent/durable acid-free paper
and bound in the United States of America

First Printing

Library of Congress Cataloging-in-Publication Data

Scharf, Lois.
Eleanor Roosevelt : first lady of American liberalism.

(Twayne's twentieth-century American biography series ; no. 6)
Bibliography: p.
Includes index.
1. Roosevelt, Eleanor, 1884–1962.   2. Presidents—
United States—Wives—Biography.   3. Liberalism—
United States—History—20th century.   I. Title.   II. Series.
E807.1.R48S34   1987   973.917'092'4   [B]   87-17725
ISBN 0-8057-7769-5 (alk. paper)
ISBN 0-8057-7778-4 (pbk. : alk. paper)

CONTENTS

FOREWORD

For the last thirty years of her life, Eleanor Roosevelt was the most famous and at times most influential woman in the world. The editorial cartoonist "Herblock" of the *Washington Post* once depicted a scene of an immigrant mother and son aboard a ship sailing past the Statue of Liberty. In the cartoon's caption the little boy says, "Of course I know who that is. It's Mrs. Roosevelt." She had many popular titles and nicknames, most of them affectionate, some derogatory, a few vicious, but Eleanor Roosevelt's most widely used appellation was "First Lady of the World." That title, which she never used herself, encapsulated both the main source of her fame and influence and her ironic position among twentieth-century American women.

Much of Eleanor Roosevelt's fame and influence resulted from her marriage to Franklin Delano Roosevelt. From 1905 until her death in 1962, she was the wife then the widow of the man elected to four terms as president of the United States. It seems doubtful that she would have achieved a stature anything like she did without her husband's position. Still, in contrast to every other first lady, it is easy to imagine her establishing a significant public position for herself if she had remained single, had been widowed in early adulthood, or had married a man who never entered politics.

Her choice of friends—Frances Perkins, who served as secretary of labor in F.D.R.'s four administrations, and Caroline O'Day, who served in Congress from 1935 to 1943—are instructive as both comparisons and contrasts. Even before her husband's election to the presidency, Eleanor Roosevelt played an active role in the Democratic party, and it is quite conceivable that under different circumstances she could have received a cabinet appointment or run for elected office. As first lady, she soon made herself much more than the president's wife. She became his troubleshooter and fact finder in a number of policy areas, and she initiated concerns on her own. She developed a constituency among liberal activists, social workers, and some politicians that was a distinct element of Roosevelt's New Deal coalition. Her advocacy of racial justice was carefully tempered and totally symbolic while her husband was alive, but even those small gestures earned her the enmity—frequently to a near pathological degree—of many white Southerners, who remained loyal to the Democratic party and devoted to the man in the White House. Conversely, she gained the often grudging but sometimes heartfelt admiration of upper-middle-class women, female college graduates, and old-style feminists, who usually had little use for her husband and his party.

Eleanor Roosevelt's prominence and political power were, as Lois Scharf demonstrates in this incisive biography, as ironic as they were genuine. The product of late–nineteenth-century high society, Eleanor Roosevelt always retained some of the limitations of her upbringing. She never learned to cook or type or clean house. She never earned her own living or, even after her husband's death, really made her way on her own. Although she possessed a strong social conscience and deep philanthropic urges from an early age, she never thought of going to college or pursuing a career. Likewise, even though the upper-crust social whirl bored her, she evidently never considered doing anything other than making her debut, going to parties, and marrying a suitable partner from her own social class. Eleanor Roosevelt, the shining figure of fame and champion of liberal causes, remains inseparable from her patrician, sometimes snobbish roots. First and last, she was the "first lady."

The irony of her public life runs deeper still, as Scharf makes clear. Eleanor Roosevelt's early shyness would probably have kept her from venturing beyond self-effacing charitable work if two tragedies had not befallen her in her thirties. One was her husband's crippling by polio in 1921, which forced her to attend meetings and make speeches for him. Even before that, the discovery of F.D.R.'s love affair with her secretary, Lucy Mercer, had shattered the emotional foundation of her marriage, robbed her of the only sustained love she had ever known, and forced her into stoic self-reliance. The hard-driving public person and tireless champion of the downtrodden emerged, not from the happiness and trust of a close, supportive marriage and family, but from the need to endure wounds and bring forth good from disappointment. As Scharf deftly shows, Eleanor Roosevelt not only drew bitter strength from her new role, but she also suffered in her relations with her children and closest friends. She became an admirable, awe-inspiring, yet complex, conflicted person. Behind her fame and influence lie a fascinating person who, in spite of her privileged background, embodied some of the most profound struggles of American women in the twentieth century.

John Milton Cooper, Jr.

PREFACE

Within days of Eleanor Roosevelt's death, cartoonist Bill Mauldin drew his memorial tribute. Three cherubic faces peek from behind their respective clouds. "It's her," one of the angels announces. Mauldin did not have to create a visual image of her or even identify her by name. At home and abroad, anyone who saw the cartoon knew whom the angels welcomed. Eleanor Roosevelt was the most famous and influential woman of her time.

Eleanor Roosevelt was a practiced politician and an articulate spokeswoman for views that marked American liberalism in the middle third of the twentieth century. The manner in which she met the changes and challenges of her complex, often battered world personalized the experiences of a generation of Americans. Together with her husband during his three terms in office and then during widowhood, she became symbol and substance of efforts to create a humane social order and a peaceful international community in the wake of depression and wars, both hot and cold. She appealed to the most positive qualities of human nature and to an enlightened, caring government to build a just and secure world. That she became so beloved and admired testifies to the appeal of her messages to those who listened.

In the years following her death, revelations about Franklin Roosevelt's infidelity and her own passionate friendship with a female journalist cast doubt on the quality of her marriage and political partnership as well as on the nature of her intimate relationships. Writers reexamined the private side of Eleanor Roosevelt and discovered an emotionally scarred woman. But her inner turmoil never inhibited—in fact, often provided the springboard for—her public triumphs. It was, nevertheless, a sad paradox that this woman who was so acclaimed for her steadfast commitment to humanitarian aspirations should have remained a despairing human being.

Without ignoring her personal agonies, this biography focuses on the public figure and the political culture in which she moved. But it also draws on recent scholarship in women's history. The female sphere of love and support and the vital women's movement of the early decades of the century provide the context and underpinnings for Eleanor Roosevelt's singular accomplishments. These special features of the female experience, combined with her incredible self-discipline and iron will, enabled Eleanor Roosevelt to achieve her unique status.

This book also draws heavily on the work of scholars and biographers who have mined the published record and sifted through Eleanor Roosevelt's vast manuscript collection at the Franklin D. Roosevelt Library. Tamara Hareven wrote an early biography before the private papers were opened, and her work remains eminently useful. Joseph Lash wrote two volumes of definitive biography and collected two additional volumes of personal correspondence. Bernard Asbell's edition of letters between Eleanor Roosevelt and her daughter carries superb insights as well. I am also grateful to the scholars who contributed to the centenary anthology, *Without Precedent: The Life and Career of Eleanor Roosevelt*. The archivists at the FDR Library and the Park Service personnel at the Hyde Park mansion and the Val-Kill cottages were extremely helpful.

Few manuscripts fail to benefit from the comments of colleagues. Ann Warren and Marian Morton read this work early, quickly, and critically, and they offered support when it was needed most. Winn Wandersee and David Van Tassel have left constructive and face-saving marks. And Cathy Gorn made it possible for me to undertake, and complete, the book. I am most grateful to John Cooper for his careful reading and constant encouragement as well as to Anne Jones and Cecile Watters of Twayne for working miracles on some murky prose.

My husband, Victor, endured the trials and disruptions that accompany writing, rewriting, and rewriting again. The final version is dedicated to my children: to Bonnie and Gary, who had the good sense to put many miles between themselves and this project; to Laura, who read the first draft first, with the eye of a fine critic and the tact of a loving daughter; and to David, who patiently—and occasionally impatiently—guided me through the unfamiliar territory of the word processor. I love them all.

PROLOGUE
CHICAGO, 1940

On a late July afternoon, a twin-engine American Air Lines plane landed at Chicago's city airport. James A. Farley, postmaster general of the United States and chairman of the Democratic party, stood near the runway waiting for the plane to come to a stop. Newspaper reporters and radio commentators huddled around him. Outside the airport terminal, a large sedan, a motorcycle escort, and fifty Chicago policemen also waited.

Once the aircraft halted and the ground crew set the stairs in place, Farley bounded up to welcome the passenger. Eleanor Roosevelt, accompanied by her son Franklin, Jr., emerged and greeted Farley warmly. Before she took a step toward the group, a reporter thrust a microphone at her and began to fire questions. At Farley's suggestion, she agreed to an impromptu press conference, and the sizable group snaked its way to the terminal building and the upstairs office of the airline. With uncharacteristic gravity the nation's first lady told the eager reporters that she did not know how she would spend the next few hours since she was not yet familiar with the events scheduled for the Democratic National Convention that evening.

The previous day Democratic delegates to the 1940 conclave had done what no party had ever done before or, after 1947, would ever do again. They nominated a president for a third term. Franklin Delano

⌐ ɔsevelt had not openly sought renomination, but neither had he discouraged supporters. Eleanor Roosevelt believed he should have made specific efforts to prepare a successor for the office, but when she pressed the point, he just smiled and replied that people had to prepare themselves once he had given them the opportunity. Although she thought that FDR's dominant position and overbearing presence created insurmountable obstacles for potential nominees, she eventually agreed. Eleanor Roosevelt believed that opportunity was the single requisite for any individual's achievements.

Foreign affairs overwhelmed presidential hopefuls. Because the military situation in Europe during the spring and early summer of 1940 deteriorated dramatically with the fall of France to Nazi Germany, the prospects of Democrats who vied for the nomination failed to gain momentum. The urge to keep his hand at the helm and provide leadership in a world tottering on the edge of military and political disaster proved irresistible to Roosevelt. Even much of the public opposition to breaking with the two-term political tradition hallowed by Washington and Jefferson vanished in the wake of the ominous events overseas.

Once having decided upon his course, however, FDR still refused to seek delegate support. Nor did he signal his intentions to presidential hopefuls looking for clues to his plans. He was no more open with the public, sharing his new resolve with only a small close-knit clique of aides that did not even include his wife. But by mid-June, the first lady had watched and listened carefully enough to conclude what path her husband had chosen. Later when a reporter asked if she had known her husband was planning to run again, she replied that she had not known, "at least not from him."[1]

FDR was determined to maintain the impression that he was being drafted, that there was a ground swell of support for him from the party faithful and the American people. Delegates filtered into Chicago in a muddle over the lack of direction from the White House, their confusion compounded by the fact that the chairman of the party wanted to be the standard-bearer himself. Jim Farley was one of those who genuinely opposed a third term, who sought the nomination, and who felt personally aggrieved at the treatment he had received at the hands of the president and his aides. He reflected the uncertainty and suspicion delegates brought with them to the convention site.

When the political gathering finally opened, Secretary of Labor Frances Perkins telephoned FDR from Chicago because she was so disturbed by the confusion and ill feeling his waffling candidacy perpetuated. The first woman to hold a cabinet post, she was an able, trusted adviser and an astute judge of prevailing political winds. She had no doubt Franklin Roosevelt would be renominated, but "one had doubt as to the good will with which it could be done." She begged him to fly to Chicago to salve hot tempers, but he refused. "How would it be if Eleanor came?" he offered. "You know Eleanor always makes people feel right. She has a way with them."[2] But having offered to send the first lady in his place, the president and the labor secretary temporarily set the suggestion aside.

After the delegates had written their platform and turned to the process of nominating a presidential ticket, Roosevelt sent a message reaffirming his contention that he had no desire to be a candidate again and that all delegates were free to nominate whomever they chose. The vast gathering responded with a moment of stunned silence and then erupted in a raucous hour-long demonstration for Franklin Roosevelt and his renomination. The series of events was far less spontaneous than it appeared. Perkins on the convention floor and Roosevelt loyalist Harry Hopkins, operating openly from headquarter suites in three hotels, were orchestrating events, and few Democrats were unaware of their activities. Still there was no doubt that delegates were enthusiastic about their action. Months of suspense and speculation were over. Politicians love the scent of victory! Celebrations spilled out of the hall and engulfed Chicago.

The following day, FDR informed the convention of his vice-presidential choice, Secretary of Agriculture Henry A. Wallace. At first delegates were surprised, then angry, and finally rebellious. Wallace was a man of ability and integrity, a committed New Dealer. But a growing segment of the Democratic party had lost its enthusiasm for the liberal priorities that marked the administration's policies of domestic reform and international involvement. Besides, delegates had well-founded doubts about Wallace's reputation as a "muddle-headed mystic" and an ineffective campaigner with no firm constituency. In the farm belt where the Wallaces were best known, the family had been traditional Republicans. A more conservative southerner or westerner with proven appeal on the campaign trail would at least preserve the tradition of balancing the ticket since delegates had already broken with one historical precedent. "A revolt of considerable proportions developed on the floor of the convention," the *New York Times* reported.[3]

Eleanor Roosevelt was spending the week at her cottage on the family's Hyde Park estate. Certain that her husband would be renominated but that he was determined to forgo a trip to Chicago, she had decided to leave the White House. The president did nothing to dissuade her. So during the days of frantic convention maneuvering, the two principals of the most extraordinary political partnership on the American scene followed events separated by almost two hundred miles.

The day after Perkins first spoke to FDR, she called the first lady, begging her to fly to the convention to pacify the delegates. Eleanor Roosevelt thought the idea was foolish. If the president asked her to go, she would, for an essential feature of their relationship was her willingness, however reluctant, to comply with his wishes, to serve his political needs. In light of the new uproar over Wallace, she would see what he wished her to do. She insisted, however, that if she were to go, Farley must invite her. She knew he was deeply upset over FDR's treatment of him in his personal quest for the nomination. Eleanor Roosevelt understood loyalty and knew how devotedly Farley had served her husband and the Democratic party. She could best apologize for behavior she did not condone and express her personal gratitude for past service by respecting his position as party chairman. Perhaps she could even persuade him to remain in that post.

When she called FDR for advice, he fenced in his habitual manner. "It might be nice for you to go, but I do not think it is in the least necessary," he told his wife.[4] Farley called later that morning, however, and she agreed to make the trip. She spent the rest of that day with close friends at the cottage, listening to nominating speeches and discussing the dramatic swings in delegate mood. It was three o'clock in the morning before the group finally went to bed. Still Eleanor Roosevelt rose before any of her guests, went for a brisk swim in the pool beside her cottage, packed a briefcase with correspondence to be attended to, and dressed for her flight. After a short plane hop to LaGuardia Airport, she met her son Franklin, Jr., and together they continued on to the convention.

At the hastily arranged press conference in Chicago, a reporter asked her how she had happened to come. "I came because a number of my friends asked me to come," she answered with unusual seriousness. Asked to identify those friends, she replied that she preferred to leave it to them to identify themselves. When another reporter wanted to know if Mr. Farley was one of those friends, she smiled, looked at him, and repeated her earlier reply. These reporters knew her well, and because they usually found her open and frank, they were puzzled by her evasive answers.

"Did the President wish you well?" "Did the President want you to come?" The questions continued. Still smiling, the first lady said she really did not remember if her husband had wished her well or not. "I suppose, of course," she continued, "that he was willing for me to come—or I would not have come." She explained that the trip was not her idea and that she had not volunteered to make it. As for how she felt about another four years in the White House, her serious manner finally dissolved and laughingly she told the group, "No one knows as yet whether there will be another four years, so I cannot say how I feel about it."[5]

The session with the reporters concluded, and the impressive motorcade made its way to the Stevens Hotel. Farley brought her up to date, including news that her son Elliott, attending as a delegate from Texas, was planning to second the vice-presidential nomination of Jesse Jones. Jones, head of the Reconstruction Finance Committee, was a conservative Democrat whose attachment to New Deal relief and reform programs lacked a good deal of enthusiasm. After arriving at the hotel, she quickly freshened up, attached a corsage of white orchids to the blue coat and dress in which she had traveled, and placed a call to the White House. She relayed Farley's assessments of delegates' resentments and nominees' strengths to her husband. Then she put Farley on the line, forcing FDR to speak to his alienated colleague. The president studiously avoided such confrontations unless cornered. Eleanor Roosevelt knew that well.

Nominating speeches for vice president were almost finished by the time the first lady and Jim Farley arrived at the hall. Party loyalists nominated Henry Wallace. Rebellious Democrats countered with Speaker of the House William Bankhead of Alabama, Jesse Jones, and assorted favorite sons. Observers thought the session was "uproarious" even by accepted standards of convention behavior. The gigantic hall reverberated with catcalls and boos when Wallace was placed in nomination. At every mention of his name, the jeering began again, growing in volume. Harry Hopkins was on the floor watching a situation rapidly moving out of control, and he became frantic over the likely prospect of a runaway convention. A reporter asked the governor of Oklahoma how he felt about the Wallace candidacy, and the governor replied that Wallace was his second choice. Who was his first choice? Anyone who could get the nomination, he shot back. Radio commentators talked of rebellion, but listeners understood the hostile roars that drowned out speakers on the rostrum and commentators alike.

The first lady unobtrusively took a seat at the end of the crowded platform and sent Franklin, Jr., to find Elliott. As deliberately as she and her husband tried to allow their children to run their own lives and follow their own political inclinations, she would not have her son publicly supporting a candidate in opposition to his father in the midst of this hostility and pandemonium. The mood on the floor was so nasty that even Frances Perkins regretted that she had played a role in what seemed likely to conclude in a variation of human sacrifice.

Eleanor Roosevelt sat calmly in the eye of this political hurricane. She was no stranger to public platforms. A day hardly passed without the first lady making brief remarks from the head table at a testimonial or fund-raising dinner or speaking formally at an official conference. In the few months prior to the Democratic convention, she had appeared before audiences ranging from the General Federation of Women's Clubs, where she discussed peace and world affairs, to the convention on Children in Democracy, where she outlined the problems of American youth. She addressed the annual banquet of the International Typographical Workers Union and talked to leaders of the American Jewish Congress. She began 1940, appropriately enough, with a speech at the School for Practical Platform Speaking. Furthermore, she held regularly scheduled press conferences and twice a year crisscrossed the country on lecture tours.

Still, an address to the hardened politicos and decision makers of the Democratic party in revolt against their president was not just another speech. Women, even presidents' wives, did not hold center stage at the nominating conventions of national parties. It was only twenty years earlier that American women had gained the right to vote. A handful of women like Frances Perkins had risen to positions of prominence. Politically interested and active women served both parties well but conventionally behind the scenes. The Women's Committee of the Democratic party provided a network of effective organizers and campaigners whose services were courted and respected by party leaders. The committee had provided Eleanor Roosevelt with some of her most important schooling in the mysteries and realities of partisan politics. But for all the women's efforts, the inner sanctums of party power remained male preserves. Eleanor Roosevelt had bemoaned that fact on a number of occasions, yet here she was on a political rescue mission of national significance.

Not since Julia Grant had one woman served as first lady through two full presidential terms. Not even Eleanor's Aunt Edith had supervised social functions at the White House and stood by Uncle Ted's side so long. The two branches of the Roosevelt clan—the Republicans of

Oyster Bay and the Democrats of Hyde Park—had a long tradition of political service. Now Eleanor Roosevelt, the former president's niece and the current chief executive's wife, not only stood on the threshold of extending that tenure in the executive mansion but was assigned the task of ensuring that outcome as well. If she failed, the Franklin Roosevelts might very well pack their belongings and return to New York.

As delegate opposition mounted, FDR grew so furious he decided to refuse the nomination altogether if Wallace did not fill the second spot on the ticket. In the White House with his secretaries and speech writers, he followed the riotous proceedings on the radio, grabbed a pad of paper, and scrawled a message. He would not compromise his progressive policies or his liberal running mate. It was up to the delegates. "By declining the honor of the nomination of the Presidency, I can restore that opportunity to the Convention. I so do."[6] His aides were astounded but had little doubt that he was serious.

The outcome of the convention, then, rested in the hands of the fifty-five-year-old first lady. Eleanor and Franklin Roosevelt had been married thirty-five years and had raised five children. The president had been confined to a wheelchair for almost two decades, but when he rose with the help of weighty leg braces, canes, and the strong arms of aides, he was still an imposing six-footer. Eleanor was also tall—over five feet ten inches—towering over all women and most men. Her soft brown hair bore more than a few hints of gray, and the once lithe figure had thickened. Because photographs were invariably unflattering and her protruding teeth and receding chin had become grist for cartoonists' mills, people who met her for the first time were always startled to find a gracious woman whose magnetic warmth lent her presence special qualities that overshadowed physical features.

Her behavior, not her appearance, transformed the position of first lady from its traditional post of social overseer and dutiful wife to outspoken public activist and publicist. Not that Eleanor Roosevelt shunned her duties as America's official hostess. The White House bustled with visitors at teas and receptions. The luncheon and dinner tables constantly overflowed with chattering and debating family members, secretaries and advisers, visiting dignitaries, and the assorted "waifs" the first lady often invited at her last scheduled stop on any given day. And Eleanor Roosevelt was certainly supportive—she would not have been at the Chicago convention hall otherwise. She was not especially pleased with her husband's choice for a running mate. But if he felt the strains and responsibilities of the coming term would be overwhelming, and he thought Wallace could help him best, then she would do her part to enable him to have the vice president of his choice. She would perform this service for her husband and do everything she could to command the attention and possibly influence the riotous audience around her.

At ten-thirty in the evening, Senator Alben Barkley of Kentucky, who was presiding over the convention, gaveled for some semblance of order and introduced the first lady. Quickly she approached the microphones without notes, for she had made it a practice to decide beforehand what themes were appropriate for an occasion and then to develop them extemporaneously as she spoke. She did not alter her practice now, even though no president's wife had ever addressed a national political convention. But then no president had ever done so, either, until her husband had personally accepted his first nomination to the ringing cheers of Democrats in 1932. Now she stood on the identical platform in the same hall where FDR had broken with tradition eight years earlier. The significance of the occasion was not lost on those assembled. They greeted her with warm, respectful applause and then extended the greatest honor that lies in the hands of delegates to an American political convention. They sat still, fell silent, and listened.

She greeted the "delegates, visitors, friends." Her first remarks were directed to Farley. With sincerity she praised his inestimable contributions to the party and added, "I want to give him here my thanks and devotion." Then she thanked everyone for the confidence they had expressed in her husband, especially during these most perilous times. The awesome responsibility of the presidency and the need for national unity were her themes. "You cannot treat [this nomination] as you would treat an ordinary nomination in an ordinary time. We people in the United States have got to realize today that we face now a grave and serious situation." The responsibilities of the president were so great, in fact, that he would undertake little active campaigning. Those gathered in this hall would have to assume those obligations, rising "above considerations which are narrow and partisan." Delegates must willingly unite around their president and their country in the face of worldwide upheavals.

But she also linked her themes of awesome responsibility and national unity to the liberal attitudes and programs she embraced. Whether or not these delegates were devoted to the New Deal policies of her husband's administration, she left no doubt where she stood. "This is the time when it is the United States that we fight for, the domestic policies that we have established as a party that we must believe in, that we must

8

carry forward, and in the world we have a position of great responsibility." The president, the party, and the country must act in unison. Demanding duties are "only carried by a united people who love their country, who will live for it to the fullest of their ability with the highest ideals, with a determination that their party shall be absolutely devoted to the good of the nation as a whole and to doing what this country can to bring the world to a safer and happier condition." She stepped back, acknowledged the applause, and walked from the platform.[7]

Balloting for vice president started. "Thanks to her the roll call began in a fairly dignified atmosphere," one newspaper informed its readers.[8] Wallace was nominated, but Bankhead received half as many votes. When the congressman graciously moved to make the nomination unanimous, as many loud nays echoed through the hall as ayes. Barkley, in time-honored fashion, announced the vote was unanimous. So much opposition persisted, however, that Wallace was persuaded to forgo an acceptance speech that might undo the calm the first lady had created. Delegates remained unhappy, but Eleanor Roosevelt had quelled a rebellion.

She did have a special gift for conciliation. Her words were not extraordinary nor especially eloquent. The high-pitched voice and the clipped consonants of her distinctly upper-crust, Eastern accent did not distinguish her as a great orator. Over two decades, however, she had developed the uncanny ability to convey ordinary, even mundane, messages with such sincerity and conviction that the simple, straightforward speeches took on a force of their own. She had also mastered the fine art of suggesting specific action without actually asking for it, especially if it might heighten tension. Her speech contained no word about Wallace or the vice presidency. Her audience realized "the potential dangers in the situation we were facing" and acted according to the wishes of its president with no explicit reference to the havoc FDR's wishes had caused.[9]

Immediately after the balloting concluded, Eleanor Roosevelt returned to the airport and boarded her plane. The president was on the phone, so she deplaned long enough to take the call. He "told me that he had listened to my speech and that I had done a very good job." That was his last direct reference, but she learned that on several occasions he told others that "her speech was just right."[10]

Political observers were more effusive. Helen Reid, publisher of the *New York Herald Tribune*, believed that the first lady had pulled off a political master stroke, that her speech was "the determining influence in the final vote for Secretary Wallace." Sen. George Norris, the veteran Progressive from Nebraska, was overwhelmed. All seemed lost, he wrote her, and "the battle for righteousness was about to be lost, [when] you came on the scene, and what you said in that short speech caused men of sense and honor to stop and think before they plunged." And he continued: "You turned a rout into a victory. You were the Sheridan of that convention. . . . That victory was finally realized is due, in my opinion, more to you than to any other one thing. That one act makes you heroic."[11]

Eleanor Roosevelt was no stranger to praise, but neither was she given to inflated notions of her own impact and importance. If any single feature marked her character, it revolved around her self-deprecating doubt about the value and effect of her activities. The letter from Norris touched her deeply. "I think I shall always be proud of it," she wrote a friend. "I must have done better than I realized. It is just something to be thankful for, one might so easily fail!"[12]

Praise from her daughter was especially welcome, for Eleanor was closer to Anna Boettiger than to any of her sons. Anna lived and worked with her husband in Seattle, where they edited a newspaper. Far from her family and the swirl of events, Anna clung to her radio. "I've listened to the Convention with such a mixture of emotions—and your speech practically finished me last night!" she wrote her mother. "By that I mean you did a wonderful job." But Anna also looked to the perilous future and what four more years in the White House would mean to her parents. For her father, she said, the immensity of the job was "really frightening to think of." But her mother had transformed the expectations of first lady to such an extent that pressures would bear heavily on her, too. "You have grown to be a part of that job in the eyes of most of the people—which puts such a terrific burden on both of you."[13] Indeed Eleanor Roosevelt had become a partner in the presidency, and most Americans admired the public stance of their first lady. Just that spring, the seniors at Fordham University had voted her the most popular woman in the world. The graduating class of the engineering school at Columbia University concurred. And George Gallup found that her popularity extended far beyond the college campuses of New York. As Anna realized, much was expected of her.

For some Americans, however, and especially for Republicans, her ubiquitous presence and outspoken positions were a public nuisance and credible campaign issues. Once the official presidential campaign began, large buttons announcing "We don't want Eleanor either" decorated many an anti-Roosevelt lapel.

At the White House, thoughts turned immediately to the fall campaign. Eleanor Roosevelt returned to her cottage at Hyde Park for a brief rest. The trip to Chicago and the role she had played were taxing even by her energetic standards: "I felt as though it had all been a dream with a somewhat nightmarish tinge." So she ate breakfast, went for a swim, filed her daily newspaper column, and resumed her other engagements "as though the past eighteen hours had not seemed the longest I had ever lived through."[14] She had invited thirty young students from the Hudson Shore Labor School to a picnic that afternoon and she had no intention of disappointing them. When the group arrived, she told them all about her latest adventure. They sang the rebellious labor ballad "Joe Hill" for her in return. That evening she drove the two and a half miles from her cottage to the "Big House" on the estate and ate dinner with her mother-in-law.

Her whirlwind trip was not a complete success. She had determined the Democratic party nominees and she had stated her commitment to the liberal direction she believed the candidates and their party should follow. She could not, however, salvage a political friendship. Jim Farley never forgave Franklin Roosevelt for what he considered shabby, disloyal treatment, and he joined the camp of inveterate Roosevelt haters. But Farley never tolerated the sight of a "We don't want Eleanor either" button in his presence. Rare was the person who met and worked with this remarkable woman and did not remain a loyal, admiring friend. And few were the Democratic politicians who did not recognize an astute and influential colleague when they saw her in action.

1

COMING OF AGE

For the Roosevelt clan who summered on Oyster Bay, 1884 began with devastating family tragedy. Theodore Roosevelt, the twenty-six-year-old scion of the family, was in Albany serving as a New York assemblyman when he received a telegram announcing that he had become the father of a fine healthy daughter. Hearty congratulations from his political colleagues had hardly begun when a second telegram arrived from his brother, Elliott. Not only was the new mother, Alice Lee Roosevelt, suddenly and mortally ill, but their own beloved mother was dying as well. Theodore traveled home as quickly as the railroad could negotiate dense mid-February fog, arriving in time to hold first his mother and then his wife in his arms before they died within hours of each other.

The family of Theodore Roosevelt, Sr., who had died in 1878, was boisterous and loving, which ensured that life would go on even in the face of incomprehensible grief. Young Theodore went off to the Dakotas to deal with his loss in geographic and emotional isolation. His older, unmarried sister Anna—"Bamie" or "Bye" to family members—took baby Alice into the family's Manhattan townhouse and raised her until Theodore's remarriage. Within weeks of the wrenching double funeral, brother Elliott and his beautiful wife, Anna, learned they would become parents in the fall.

On 11 October, their daughter, Anna Eleanor Roosevelt, was born.

The new parents had hoped for a son, but with memories of the perils of childbirth so fresh, they were relieved and grateful the delivery went smoothly for a first birth and that the mother and child were well. The ever-helpful Bamie notified the family. Elliott Roosevelt thought his new daughter "was a miracle from heaven." Theodore served as the ebullient godfather, and the insulated and prestigious elite of New York welcomed a new member.

The marriage of Elliott Roosevelt and Anna Hall the previous December had joined two of New York's privileged families in ways that resembled a European dynastic match, a practice common in the narrow rarified world of wealthy Knickerbocker society. The first Roosevelt had arrived in the New World from Holland when the small community at the mouth of the Hudson River was still called New Amsterdam. From obscure origins, succeeding generations slowly made fortunes in commerce, real estate, banking, and the manufacture of building materials. With economic success came social status. By the nineteenth century, two branches of the clan had developed. The Oyster Bay Roosevelts owned town houses on the most fashionable streets of Manhattan and spent their summers in sprawling mansions on the shores of Long Island. The Hyde Park branch lived on estates perched on the bluffs overlooking the Hudson River. Roosevelts served in appointed political offices; the rough and tumble of electioneering was considered beneath their dignity. The younger Oyster Bay Theodore, making his mark in the New York legislature, altered that pattern, and in 1901, he would add the ultimate political position to the social and economic fortunes identified with the family name.

The impeccable pedigree of the family made marriages with beautiful heiresses possible and desirable. Theodore, Sr., had wed the lovely southern belle Martha "Mittie" Bullock. The Civil War strained but did not rend the love shared by the huge, handsome, exuberant husband, who hired a Union army substitute, and his southern-born wife, who sent packages from New York to her brothers in the Confederate army. Both heaped demonstrative affection on Bamie, Theodore, Elliott, and their youngest child, Corinne. The younger Theodore's wedding to Boston Brahmin Alice Lee and Elliott's marriage to Anna Hall, whose ancestors were Livingstons and Ludlows, fit the pattern of good matches based on social status, mutual affection, and Victorian virtue.

Regardless of class standing, nineteenth-century Americans held firm notions about the proper roles and activities for men and women. Anna and Elliott Roosevelt expected to conform to the roles set out for husband and wife; their functions were distinct but complementary. Men occupied public space where they worked at the expanding occupations that powered the country's sometimes sputtering but ultimately booming economy. They succeeded or failed in their income-earning, family-supporting responsibilities according to their individual capacity for hard work and qualities of moral character. Wives, dependent upon their spouses' economic efforts, political decisions, and social standing, managed households that provided rest for work-weary husbands and reared children, instilling worthy pious values. Hard work in the marketplace and religious practices at home ideally ensured familial stability and happiness—collectively the glue that held an otherwise rapidly changing society together.

These social ideals, for all their trumpeting from pulpits, journals, and sentimental novels, prevailed more in rhetoric than in reality. Men and women up and down the social scale found shortcomings in its assumptions and strictures. Working-class men often found their earnings failed to support their families, and their children, occasionally even their wives, worked to supplement the family income. Daughters of the working class dusted the furniture and cooked the meals in Roosevelt mansions and even in the homes of less prosperous Americans. Middle-class women, who enjoyed economic security but sometimes chafed at the narrow range of domestic chores, scaled the walls of their "separate sphere" to engage in church activities, benevolent societies, even reform organizations, although they cloaked their activities in the rhetoric of nurture and love of home. Wealthy women were most able to supervise their commodious households bustling with children and servants. Juggling social schedules to accommodate streams of invitations and plans for reciprocating entertainment rounded out the routine of newly married former debutantes and aging dowagers alike.

Adherence to this pattern, however, could falter even among the wealthy. After the Civil War, Mittie Roosevelt retired to her sitting room, receiving callers with her usual graciousness but doing little else. Fourteen-year-old Bamie, on her way to becoming family ombudsman, took over the household duties abdicated by her mother. Father and children adored and admired Mittie just the same, but the Victorian ideal of womanhood was displaying another fissure.

Wealth also undermined the association of productive work with masculinity. By the 1870s, for example, Theodore, Sr., who had inherited a sizable fortune from his father, had retired from business altogether. But leisure did not lie heavily upon him. In a break with the cult

14

of motherhood, which decreed that mothers were responsible for all aspects of child care short of discipline, Roosevelt supervised the health and education of his children. He installed a gymnasium to encourage his older son to overcome his physical weakness and life-threatening asthma. Young Theodore responded with enthusiasm, determination, and success. Education was also home-centered. Early fundamentals in reading and arithmetic were taught by Mittie's unmarried sister, who made her home with the family. The elder Roosevelt conducted advanced lessons supplemented by rigorous grand tours abroad.

When Theodore, Sr., was not supervising family matters, he attended to civic and charitable affairs. He was one of the founders of several of New York City's famous cultural institutions, helped found the Orthopedic Hospital, and directed shelter homes for the city's newsboys and homeless young men. Wealthy people in a number of American cities discovered their social consciences and responded philanthropically during this time. Few did so, however, with the commitment and personal involvement of Theodore, Sr., who earned the sobriquet "Greatheart." Between his family and his charities, he found suitable and satisfying substitutes for a career in business.

Not all young men of means and leisure succeeded so well in giving their lives purpose and structure. The Roosevelt sons were cases in point and counterpoint. As boys, the younger and more robust Elliott often defended his more sickly, weak-eyed older brother against heckling youngsters. But Theodore responded more positively to his father's encouragement to develop his physical and intellectual potential. Exercise and sheer will power overcame ailments; reading and nature study were conducted so assiduously that pages were excitedly torn from their bindings after reading and piles of papers mixed distastefully with the odor of formaldehyde-preserved animal specimens. Life enthralled the young man, and he, in turn, made his presence felt with the same intensity.

Still, the results of family-centered self-education were haphazard. Theodore needed private tutoring to prepare for Harvard. Once admitted, however, his academic performance was commendable and his social attainments were outstanding. Membership in the prestigious Porcellian Club and the hard-won promise of marriage from Alice Lee were successes marred only by the death of his father. For Elliott, on the other hand, the scales that had once weighed so heavily in his favor became reversed. Although he was socially graceful and athletically proficient, his natural talents slowly gave way to emotional and physical disability. Having persuaded his father to send him to St. Paul's School in New

Hampshire, he found that the school presented a challenge he could not master. Debilitating headaches and fainting spells incapacitated him, and he wrote his father privately that he was taking his "anti-nervous medicine, and would like the receipt of more."[1] With or without medication, the sixteen-year-old was sent west for a prescribed dose of fresh air and hunting on the frontier. During that trip and future ones as well, his progress was uneven. His physical prowess and the masculine camaraderie he enjoyed mingled with sensitive introspection and generous doses of self-doubt. The ambiguities and instabilities in his character became especially noticeable when compared with the confidence and accomplishments of his older brother.

Although he could hunt buffalo with the energy of Theodore and move with greater grace and charm in society's drawing rooms, Elliott could not muster the drive or discipline to achieve self-defined goals. He bemoaned his lack of education but made no efforts to rectify the situation—how difficult to do so when one's older brother at twenty-two was already Phi Beta Kappa and the author of a highly praised naval history! Elliott was filled with self-recrimination. He admitted he was basically lazy and felt his shortcomings all the more acutely because Theodore was so confident, self-righteous, and successful at everything he set his hand to. And Elliott was sensitive and loving—he had nursed his dying father as tenderly as a woman according to his younger sister, Corinne—at a time when gentleness was not identified with manliness. The strenuous life identified "manly men" in the last quarter of the nineteenth century. Little wonder that Theodore Roosevelt wore his self-assurance so comfortably. He both invented and embodied the very attributes that defined masculinity.

When Elliott returned from a worldwide trip in 1881, he reentered the New York social scene with his usual ease and charm. In the drawing rooms and ballrooms of New York's wealthiest families, he met, courted, and won the hand of nineteen-year-old Anna Hall. One of the most beautiful of the loveliest bevy of debutantes Knickerbocker society had seen in years, she traced her family lineage to the prominent, landed Livingstons and Ludlows. There was one Irish immigrant in the otherwise unblemished genealogy. But even he had quickly amassed such a fortune that his son, Anna's father, was able to make a good match, build a palatial home for his wife and six children, and live as a leisured Hudson Valley gentleman like his neighbors. Unlike Theodore Roosevelt, Sr., however, who had mixed love with discipline throughout his household, Valentine Hall ruled his baronial estate like a prophet out of the Old Testament. The Bible and theological discourses on the Bible were his models of comportment and focus of interest. Education, especially for his four daughters, was minimal except for the meager lessons and religious instruction he thought were adequate for feminine, moral, and dependent adult women. Discipline was rigid; spontaneity and gaity were frowned upon. When he died unexpectedly and without a will, his widow, who had had little experience running the household or rearing the children, suddenly found herself mistress of the mansion and sole parent of six children. Anna, at seventeen, was the oldest. Two years later she married Elliott Roosevelt.

Several hundred invited guests witnessed the couple's exchange of vows at New York Calvary Church early in December at "one of the most brilliant social events of the season," according to the reporter from the *New York Herald.*[2] They composed Society, the older blue-blood families and the more recent millionaires whose money had gained them acceptance into the exclusive circle. They went to the same parties, belonged to the same clubs, attended the same operas, and lived in neighboring brownstones in Manhattan and estates that dotted the Hudson Valley for a hundred miles north of the city.

Anna Hall and Elliott Roosevelt, who had moved comfortably among them as long as they could remember, quickly became associated with the younger pleasure-seeking, handsome and beautiful "swells." The pace with which the young couple traveled the more frivolous social circuit would hardly have pleased the late Valentine Hall. Fashion arbiters of the day admired Anna Hall Roosevelt's aristocratic carriage, but that was hardly the reason her father had forced her to practice walking with her elbows supporting sticks held across her back. Anna delighted in fashions, dancing, and dining—all with a sense of frivolity and passion that hinted at overt revolt against her stern Victorian upbringing.

Elliott, although he made an effort to supplement the young couple's inherited income by working with the Ludlows, was attacking the less serious activities of the upper classes in ways that would not have gained the approval of the elder Theodore Roosevelt either. The polo games, the hunts, the horse shows, the exclusive clubs—all were not merely sampled with restraint but relished with insatiable appetite. He played games with an energy that bordered on recklessness. But no matter how frenzied his activity on the polo fields and in the grand ballrooms, the aura of gentility and gentleness always clung to him.

17

Theodore, who also partied with his young wife but in more serious circles, was the one who was already recognized as forceful, aggressive, and boisterous.

Ten months into this social fling, Anna Eleanor Roosevelt was born. Elliott's delighted entry into parenthood was not matched by the new mother's. Anna was more restrained. For her daughter to grow up and excel in activities that had come to mean so much to her, to make a striking debut and win the admiration of countless beaux, the child must be beautiful and sparkling. Apparently from birth, the younger Anna Eleanor was neither. She was plain and by her own later admission "entirely lacking in the spontaneous joy and mirth of youth."[3] When her mother called her "granny," as she sometimes did among groups of guests, she would explain to her friends that the title suited this child who looked and acted so solemn and old-fashioned. It was a stinging rebuke, and it caused resentment and scars that lasted a lifetime. "Granny" both created and described the awkwardness and unhappiness that clung to the child.

If Eleanor Roosevelt seemed to have been born sad, with a sense of impending doom, there was good reason. The silver glow that surrounded her parents' marriage was already showing signs of tarnish. Elliott could not and would not devote the energy to business affairs that he gave to male companions and liquor. His mood swings became pronounced and unpredictable. Eleanor was just past two when he stopped work altogether. Anna, in love and in despair, suggested a family trip to Europe. Only one day out of port, the ship collided with another vessel. For the child whose hands had to be pried loose from the rails in order to be dropped into her father's waiting arms in a lifeboat, the experience was terrifying. Water and sea travel were added high on the list of fears she was rapidly accumulating.

The trauma of separation followed on the heels of the disaster at sea. Because Elliott's deteriorating mental health had been the reason for the voyage in the first place, the young parents and one of Anna's sisters rebooked passage. The child balked with such vehemence at the idea of sailing on another ship that her baffled parents left her at Oyster Bay with a great-aunt and uncle. The relatives were doting caretakers, but six months seemed an eternity to a youngster, especially one who sensed a link between her unheroic behavior and the absence of, perhaps abandonment by, her parents.

When Anna and Elliott finally returned, Elliott tried to resume work. The family moved into a small house at Hempstead on Long Island while they built a summer home nearby. It was a happy time. The child celebrated her fourth birthday there in 1888. There was a lavish party with all the family gathered around, delicious treats, and exciting gifts. That evening Elliott Roosevelt reported that the enthralled child threw her grateful arms around his neck as he said good night and told him that she loved everybody and she knew everybody loved her.[4] That sense of affection, security, and contentment was short-lived. Elliott Roosevelt suffered a painful ankle break while, unsurprisingly, perfecting his somersaults for a society circus performance. Set improperly, the ankle had to be broken and set again. He eased the unbearable pain with increasing amounts of alcohol to which he added morphine and laudanum. His daughter later attributed her father's alcoholism to this accident, but he had been drinking heavily for years. The drug addiction, however, was new, and the pace of self-destruction and family tragedy quickened.

The birth of Elliott, Jr., in the fall of 1889 both delighted and unhinged the young father. He worked less, rode more recklessly with more falls and accidents, and partied and drank with greater intensity. In desperation, Anna suggested another family tour abroad. The trip began well. Elliott stayed sober while his wife encouraged and praised his efforts. Their young daughter swallowed her fears of the ocean steamer and once on land reveled in the constant company of her parents. Eventually Elliott discovered accessible supplies of liquor. The mood shifts became more extreme, and finally he entered an Austrian sanitarium. Again pregnant, Anna sent for the ever-dependable Bamie, who immediately sailed from New York to join her. Bamie also arrived with the unpleasant and embarrassing duty of informing Elliott, when the appropriate opportunity presented itself, that Theodore had received notice through lawyers that a former family servant, Katy Mann, was pregnant. The daughters of the working class not only cooked and cleaned for wages. Some also succumbed to the advances of their male employers. Katy Mann had named Elliott as the father-to-be and demanded payment for her silence.

Months passed before Bamie finally relayed the news to Elliott. He denied everything. He also left the sanitarium impulsively, moved his wife, sister, and children to Paris, and took a mistress. With his characteristic moral rectitude and self-assurance, Theodore sent instructions to Bamie: "If responsible then he must go where he can be cured; if irresponsible he is simply a selfish brutal and vicious criminal, and Anna ought not to stay with him an hour."[5]

Anna was more ambivalent. She feared Elliott in his more violent moods, but she adored him, too. Another son, Hall, was born in June, and she had begged for Elliott during her labor. Eleanor was sent to a convent outside Paris during her mother's confinement. Again physical separation from her family seemed like an instance of exile, this time compounded by social isolation among her young peers. They spoke a language she could barely understand and practiced a religion that was also foreign to her. In a poignant attempt to gain attention and recognition, she announced to the sisters that she had swallowed a small coin. Several days before, one of the young girls actually had swallowed one, causing much excitement and becoming momentarily the center of concern. The attempt of the six-year-old to duplicate the event dramatized her painful loneliness. To make matters worse, she refused to admit she was lying when confronted by the skeptical sisters. They sent for Anna, who was forced to take her back to their quarters in Paris. Eleanor was more confused than humiliated. Only Elliott ignored the family's embarrassment. He "was the only person who did not treat me as a criminal," she said later—at least when he was sober and not on one of his absentee sprees.

After the safe birth of their third child in June 1891, the father's erratic behavior worsened. Only Theodore was certain that Anna and Elliott should separate or even divorce, especially when an "expert in likenesses" reported that Katy Mann's newborn displayed unmistakable signs of Rooseveltian features. The payment of blackmail apparently silenced the new mother, for the scandal of adultery and paternity went unpublicized. Theodore initiated another scandal in its stead, filing suit to have Elliott, temporarily in a French sanitarium, declared insane and his assets placed in trust for his wife and children. The suit failed, but the family name was trumpeted in New York newspapers in ways Theodore had tried desperately to avoid.[6]

When Anna felt well enough to travel, the family returned to New York. Elliott arrived separately, escorted by his brother, who had made a special ocean crossing for that purpose. Upon returning, Theodore insisted that Elliott be exiled to southwestern Virginia where he could serve penance supervising the vast holdings of sister Corinne's husband, Douglas Robinson. There he acquitted himself well, overseeing the Robinson woodlands and coal mines and mingling easily with the townspeople of Abingdon. When sober, Elliott was warm and generous, and he quickly became a favorite with children. In the meantime, his daughter was heartbroken at yet another separation from her father.

Alone in New York, Anna Roosevelt tried to raise her children and reconstruct her life within the constraints of social convention and personal confusion. Her husband had humiliated her and abused her trust. But she missed his presence and loved him still, which only enhanced her sense of having been wronged. For Eleanor, the physical distance between her parents was paralleled by the emotional gulf between her mother and herself. Not that Anna did not try. In the typical fashion of the rich, she devoted a specific period of the day, usually after tea, reading to the children, and after the young boys were in bed for the night, she would spend an hour with her daughter. Because she was a religious woman, she wished to instill her own unquestioned faith in her children and carefully attended to prayers at bedtime. She even turned her attention to Eleanor's neglected education and organized a class for a small number of young girls under Frederick Roser, the tutor favored by New York's elite. The classes, which met in the home Anna had purchased on East Sixty-first Street, were long overdue. At the age of seven, young Eleanor could neither read nor write.

But Anna's valiant efforts to display maternal affection and practice parental duties came to a tragic halt. She entered the hospital for surgery, and Eleanor was sent to live with her godmother, Susie Parish. According to telegrams Elliott received from his mother-in-law, Anna's recovery was progressing satisfactorily. But suddenly she contracted diphtheria, and at the age of twenty-nine, the beautiful, frivolous, humiliated Anna Hall Roosevelt died. "Do not come" the last telegram to Elliott Roosevelt read. In fact, he arrived only after the funeral.

Eleanor Roosevelt was eight years old when her contrite, heartbroken father sat with her in Grandmother Hall's high-ceilinged, dismal library on the first floor of her Manhattan brownstone. He spoke to her in ways she never fully understood but always cherished. He explained how much he had loved her mother and said that now he had only the three children. He pointed out that her brothers were very young and said that "he and I must keep close together. Someday I would make a home for him again, we would travel together and do many things which he painted as interesting and pleasant, to be looked forward to in the future." She was not sure where her brothers would fit in that special far-off world, but she was certain "that he and I were very close and someday would have a life of our own together." The child's thoughts of her dead mother were singularly absent from this intimate recollection.[7]

The encounter had a fairy-tale quality of a Prince Charming vowing to rescue the beleaguered and faithful princess. But that rescue along with its undercurrent of romantic love lay only in the youngster's hopes.

The traditional fairy-tale ending crashed when her father died soon after and again years later when she discovered her own husband's infidelity. Thereafter the fairy tale would play itself out in other people's romances. She would become as closely involved as a third party could, vicariously enjoying their happiness. It was difficult to exult personally and openly when she herself was directly involved. The original Prince Charming had proved to be erratic and then he had disappeared forever; the one who courted her was always slightly suspect, perhaps undependable, too, in her insecure eyes. But other people's romances could be safely relished, even manipulated so that they would end as the prototype should have.

With her father's instructions and her own vows to be good, study hard, and grow up to be a fine young woman etched in her mind, Eleanor remained with Grandma Hall in the dark brownstone on Thirty-seventh Street. Elliott returned to West Virginia. His letters to his "dear little Nell" were cherished, even though the descriptions of the little Abingdon girls who shared his charmed company caused twinges of jealousy. He returned to New York only briefly in the spring of 1893 when Elliott, Jr., after surviving a bout of scarlet fever, succumbed to diphtheria. This time Eleanor was sent to Ludlow relatives in Newport and could console her father only by letter. "We must be happy and do God's will and we must cheer others who feel it too," the eight-year-old child wrote to him.[8]

The rehabilitative exile to Virginia was now without purpose or effect. Elliott drifted back to New York. Although physically closer to his surviving children, he communicated seldom and saw them even less. With a new mistress and uncounted bottles of whiskey at his side, in August 1894 he experienced one final outburst of delirium tremens, an overwhelming seizure, and fell unconscious. He died the following day. Anna Hall Roosevelt's sisters, Pussie and Maude, broke the news to the child who understood fully what had happened. But she had fantasized happy reunions with her father so often that the shattering reality of his death was less disruptive than her family feared. "I began the next day living in my dream world as usual . . . more closely, probably than I had when he was alive."[9]

As the family grieved, morally righteous Theodore had his way one last time. Gentle, caring, self-destructive Elliott must not be buried with his wife, whose marriage he had disgraced. Two years later, however, at Grandma Hall's request, his remains were transferred from the Roosevelt family plot and reinterred next to those of her daughter's. Elliott Roosevelt had possessed such tender, appealing qualities that even the mother of the woman to whom he had brought pain succumbed to the better side of his tormented character.

The ten-year-old orphan might later dwell on the polar qualities of her father and her uncle. She might even resent the role her uncle had played as a not-so-passive observer in her beloved father's downfall. Yet in the years to come, her own values and activities would succeed in bridging the gap in attitudes and behavior that had grown so vast and irreconcilable between the two brothers. When she turned her compassionate nature into social and political action, she would do so with the determination, discipline, and boundless energy that reconciled the best qualities of the two men. Her private life, however, would be another matter. Diffident, distracted Anna had not shown her daughter how to embrace one's children in love and tenderness. Loving but unreliable Elliott had undercut the trust and certainty upon which self-confidence and intimate personal relationships are constructed. On her fourth birthday she had assured her father that everyone loved her and that she loved everyone. But within six years her parents and her younger brother were dead. So many emotional earthquakes so early in life made it impossible for Eleanor Roosevelt ever to feel that secure and certain again.

After the death of Elliott Roosevelt, Eleanor and her brother Hall continued as the wards of their grandmother. She returned to the classes conducted by Frederick Roser, working hard at her studies and enjoying the company of her peers to the extent her feelings of awkwardness and her ill-dressed appearance permitted. At least classes were a respite from the lugubrious residence on Thirty-seventh Street. Her cousin Corinne, who lived nearby, dreaded visiting when her mother insisted that she go to play with Eleanor. Corinne remembered "the grim atmosphere of that house. There was no place to play games, unbroken gloom everywhere. We ate our suppers in silence."[10]

The depressing surroundings were hardly matched by the behavior of the Hall menage. Mrs. Hall had simply lost all control over her own brood of beautiful, flirtatious daughters and idle, drunken sons. Since she could not manage Aunt Pussie's countless tempestuous love affairs or Uncle Vallie's violent alcoholism, she compensated by exercising discipline over her two young charges. "No" became the common response to invitations from classmates and to most other requests for youthful diversions. A few exceptions were made when the Roosevelts of Oyster Bay asked the children to visit. But the family reunions were mixed occasions of pleasure and discomfort. On one visit to Sagamore Hill on Long Island, Uncle Theodore, who always insisted Eleanor was his favorite niece, tore her dress in his exuberant welcoming embrace and then proceeded to terrify her with a swimming lesson.

At a Christmas party at Aunt Corinne's, she danced awkwardly in her too-short dress with her distant cousin Franklin because Alice Roosevelt suggested he ask her—or dared him to! She always looked solemn and out of place among her buoyant Roosevelt relatives. But she also had a willful streak, a determination to confront uncomfortable situations and meet unpleasant challenges on her own terms. When her cousins saw the childish party clothes in which her grandmother had dressed her, they begged her to borrow a gown more appropriate for a fourteen-year-old, a long one like those that Alice wore. But "she was noble, martyred and refused," Cousin Corinne remembered.[11]

She scored one meager victory when she complained in tears about the fear she felt at the hands of a cruel governess hired by her grandmother. The woman had abused her verbally and physically, and Grandma Hall was appalled. The governess was immediately replaced. Still it was, as Aunt Corinne remembered, "the grimmest childhood one could imagine."[12]

Then came respite and rescue. She was sent abroad to a European finishing school, a different kind of exile from the ones she had experienced so frequently before. Separation from her family had always signaled crisis and increased her feelings of unworthiness and insecurity. "Looking back," she wrote years later, "I see that I was always afraid of something: of the dark, of displeasing people, of failure. Anything I accomplished had to be done across a barrier of fear."[13] For once she would succeed and please those around her as she basked in an atmosphere of warmth and admiration. In spite of their limited contacts, the Roosevelt family prevailed upon Mrs. Hall to provide more systematic education for Eleanor and suggested Allenswood outside of London. Headmistress Marie Souvestre had directed the school in France that Aunt Bamie had attended years earlier. Like Eleanor, her aunt had been the unattractive daughter of a renowned beauty. Still she was intelligent and wise, a source of comfort and strength to family and friends who confided in her, a source of counsel even to her brother when he became president. Her niece Alice, whom she had raised before Theodore remarried, remarked more than once that Bamie would have been president if she had been a man. Whatever special qualities she possessed Bamie attributed in large measure to the education and training she had received from Marie Souvestre.

By most standards Allenswood was unusual for a finishing school, given the educational levels upper-class Americans and Europeans considered appropriate for their daughters. While middle-class American women attended female academies and even colleges by the time Eleanor Roosevelt sailed for England, aristocratic families believed that a smattering of English literature and the French language supplemented with instruction in the social graces was adequate preparation for a privileged matron. By the age of eighteen young women of the Roosevelts' and Halls' background had presumedly mastered these essentials and were ready for formal introduction into society. The rigors of life and education at the new eastern colleges for women that were founded in the decades following the Civil War or at the coeducational public universities that reluctantly opened their doors to young women at the same time were believed unnecessary for the molding of a debutante and society matron.

Mademoiselle Souvestre was a remarkable woman who set high standards of instruction. With verve, she taught history and literature herself, introducing her students to unconventional and challenging ideas. Information was not to be digested uncritically. Opinions were encouraged, assumptions were challenged, critical judgment was demanded. The headmistress's own opinions and judgments were as unusual as her pedagogical methods. She was an atheist and pro-Boer at a time when she was teaching the daughters of the British Anglican elite. And she was an unswerving Dreyfusard who stated her views firmly and passionately when the case of the French captain was so controversial that polite society avoided discussing it. Her sexual preferences were practiced much more discreetly, but a violent quarrel with her female lover and cofounder of the French school Bamie had attended was probably the reason for that school's demise and Souvestre's move to England. There is no evidence that Eleanor was aware of the headmistress's personal affairs when she attended Allenswood. Rather it was the stimulating environment Souvestre created and the qualities of character and intellect she encouraged that slowly aroused new confidence and poise in her young student.[14]

Souvestre was not only a religious and political maverick but a perceptive observer as well. Upon greeting the awkward fifteen-year-old, she immediately sensed that Bamie Roosevelt's niece was an unhappy and sensitive girl who nevertheless had special potential. Eleanor was seated at Souvestre's table at dinner, and she became the focus of her teacher's interest and affection. Their exceptional relationship endured through the years at Allenswood, years Eleanor Roosevelt would always remember as the happiest of her life. At vacation time teacher and student traveled on the Continent. The younger woman viewed sites and learned lessons far different from those she had experienced when she had accompanied her parents years earlier. "Traveling with Mlle. Souvestre was a revelation. She did all the things that in a vague way you had always felt you wanted to do," she wrote in her memoirs. "As I think back over my trips with Mlle. Souvestre, I realize she taught me how to enjoy traveling. She liked to be comfortable, she enjoyed good food, but she always tried to go where you would see the people of the country you were visiting, not your own compatriots."[15] Learning how to look behind facades and encounter people for whom one sometimes had to search proved valuable lessons.

The intellectual excitement of literary discussions and European travel, however, was accompanied by academic limitations. In the years ahead Eleanor Roosevelt would work closely with women reformers and political activists. Absorbed with public policy issues and administration, these women brought investigative and analytic skills to their work, skills they had mastered in the rigorous social science disciplines in which they had been trained at colleges and universities. Eleanor Roosevelt would envy these women with their graduate and professional degrees, and she would understand the shortcomings of Marie Souvestre's teaching in the cloistered atmosphere of Allenswood.

But social acceptance by her peers and a doting surrogate parent more than compensated for the educational constraints of the school. The love and admiration Eleanor Roosevelt's classmates lavished upon her were no small achievements given her limited contacts with girls her own age and her privileged status as Souvestre's favorite. The girls at the school simply could not resist her warmth and generosity as well as the qualities of leadership she displayed in unaffected ways. Her younger cousin Corinne arrived at Allenswood during Eleanor's last year abroad and testified to the love and esteem accorded to her. When the girls were allowed on Saturdays to make small purchases in a nearby town, they invariably returned with gifts for Eleanor. Her room overflowed with flowers, books, and other tokens of gratitude and affection. For the young woman so starved for love and approval, these tangible expressions of acceptance and devotion were gratifying.

Gift giving was also part of the lavish and intense expression of same-sex affection that was so common among nineteenth-century middle- and upper-class women, especially during adolescence. They were often segregated in female academies, finishing schools, and colleges during a period in their life marked by budding sexuality. The female bonds they commonly formed often had physical and sensual overtones as well as emotional and romantic ones. Friendships formed during this period often endured throughout their lives even as they matured and followed conventional paths into marriage and heterosexual relationships. The women's correspondence, however, frequently retained its florid, sensual style, and physical embracing and kissing continued in a natural, unembarrassed, uncriticized manner. At Allenswood, Eleanor Roosevelt learned the strength and support women could offer each other whether through schoolgirl crushes and companionship or under the supervision of a compassionate elder. A time would come when she would ache for that kind of support, and it would serve her well when she found it again.

After three years, Marie Souvestre and her beloved student parted. Leave-taking was wrenching for both of them. The headmistress had salvaged an emotionally scarred young woman, but she knew that unhappiness still welled in the confident, poised friend who was returning home to family problems and demanding social whirls. "Elle n'est pas gai," Souvestre told Corinne, discerning an undertone of seriousness and sadness that would never completely disappear. The headmistress joined Aunt Bamie, Aunt Corinne, and her daughter who all "loved her. We admired her and we were sad about her."[16]

Upon returning home, Eleanor Roosevelt had reasons to be troubled. She was especially concerned about her brother, Hall, who had come increasingly under the influence of erratic Aunt Pussie. She wanted desperately to give him the love and attention she herself craved, the sense of family she felt they both needed. Renewed companionship and affection succeeded in weaning Hall from Pussie, and she shared the good news with Souvestre that she and Grandmother Hall had taken her brother up to Groton to enroll him in the prestigious college preparatory school.

But the orphans had problems that renewed sibling ties could not overcome. They were as storm-tossed as the orphans of fiction. They shuttled between the Halls' Tivoli estate in the Hudson Valley, where Uncle Vallie's erratic alcoholic outbursts presented a physical danger to everyone, and the Manhattan brownstone, where Aunt Pussie carried on as irresponsibly as ever. While Hall was at school, Eleanor went to live with her Parish cousins. At one point in the midst of the shuffling among family residences, she cried to her aunt Corinne in despair, "I have no real home."[17] For the time being, at least, she had her brother, but in the end, after a brilliant academic career and success in business, he would replay the scenario performed so pathetically by their father and uncles. Throughout her life, Eleanor Roosevelt would shoulder the burden of coping and caring for family members and their endless crises. When she returned to New York, that meant even walking the streets in the middle of the night searching for her drunken uncle and somehow getting him back home.

In 1903 a more immediate and unwelcome challenge was the official social season for which she felt ill prepared. The family concerns were "not good preparations for being a gay and joyous debutante."[18] Her feelings of unattractiveness and inadequacy resurfaced, cruelly reinforced by Aunt Pussie's caustic reminders that Hall women never failed to be the star attraction when they made their debuts. Actually Eleanor Roosevelt had returned to New York a very tall but graceful young woman, fashionably dressed by her mother's other sisters, aunts Tissie and Maude. Her lustrous brown hair was intricately arranged and mounted atop her head in the latest style. The large, protruding teeth that had become Uncle Ted's trademark were much less pronounced than they would be later when cartoons and photographs emphasized them. No one who met her failed to comment on her lovely blue eyes. She engaged in intelligent and sympathetic conversation to the delight of hostesses whose male guests often tired of gossipy fluff. But she did not see herself in that positive light. "I imagine that I was well dressed, but there was absolutely nothing about me to attract anybody's attention," she wrote years later. Surrounded by her beautiful aunts and the memory of her lovely mother, she was certain that "I was the first girl in my mother's family who was not a belle, and though I never acknowledged it to any of them at that time, I was deeply ashamed."[19]

Her formal debut at the Assembly Ball and her numerous invitations to dinner parties and dances afterward indicate that her entrance into Knickerbocker society was a well-negotiated rite of passage. Yet despite her social success, she still felt awkward and inadequate. Nothing could convince her "into thinking that I was a popular debutante!"[20] Marie Souvestre had instilled a measure of self-confidence, but the wells of insecurity continued to run deep.

Ironically Souvestre would not have applauded her former student's accomplishments during her first social season. "I hope that 'society' will stimulate you," she wrote her "dear little Totty," as she wished Eleanor well. She believed, however, that Eleanor also possessed qualities that transcended the "whirl of exciting social activities" that satisfied superficial women like her aunts and fellow debutantes. "I fear to hear you have been unable to defend yourself against all the temptations which surround you; evenings out, pleasure, flirtations," she wrote anxiously.[21]

Souvestre need not have worried that Eleanor Roosevelt would surrender completely to "the big season of social dissipation." As a debutante she was automatically enrolled in the Junior League, a newly organized group of young upper-class women who planned to add a dash of social responsibility to their debutante whirl. After all American Progressivism was coming into full flower. While Eleanor was abroad at Allenswood, a crazed anarchist had assassinated President McKinley. To the horror of mainstream Republicans who thought they had safely buried Uncle Ted in the obscurity of the vice presidency, he was now crowing with delight in the White House. He was also, according to his fashion, leading the country on its continuing quest for national greatness abroad while seeking to control the massive social and economic forces unleashed by unprecedented economic and technological development at home. Even rich young women felt compelled to address the dreadful conditions of working-class life in New York's slums. With good intentions, most of the girls studied the photographs Jacob Riis published in *How the Other Half Lives* and abhorred what they saw. But then they resumed their usual round of activities.

Eleanor Roosevelt took her role seriously. With her friend Jean Reid, the daughter of Mr. and Mrs. Whitelaw Reid, she taught classes at the Rivington Street Settlement House in the Lower East Side of Manhattan. Reid played piano while Roosevelt "entertained" the daughters of Jewish and Italian immigrants in calisthenics and fancy dancing. The instruction might seem frivolous and patronizing in light of the reality of conditions in the city's teeming ghettos, but the young girls actually enjoyed this reprise from their wretched tenements and crowded streets. And they adored their teacher, who treated them with genuine kindness and who taught her classes with total commitment and personal satisfaction.

The settlement house movement in America was barely a decade and a half old when Eleanor Roosevelt braved the hazards of public transportation to reach Rivington Street. Jane Addams established the prototype, Hull House, in Chicago in 1889. The movement spread rapidly, for the institutions filled the personal needs of their volunteer residents as well as the educational and welfare needs of the neighborhoods where they were springing up. Northern cities were transformed by economic growth and waves of immigration around the turn of the century at rates that caused severe social dislocation. Non-English-speaking peasants and petty tradesmen encountered an urban industrial setting for which they had little preparation or understanding. And the cities lacked the housing and public services to accommodate the newcomers. Sweatshops and heavy industries absorbed immigrants at work; overcrowded homes and tenements gave them shelter usually in neighborhoods where new arrivals found immigrants with similar backgrounds and created cultural oases in an otherwise alien society. The seasonal and cyclical nature of much unskilled labor quickly taught immigrant families that one income earned by a father was inadequate. Sons and daughters worked with mothers doing menial piecework at home. As the children reached employment age—twelve, thirteen, fourteen years old—they followed adults into stores and factories as unskilled wage earners.

The reaction of native-born Americans to this new urban industrial environment ranged from enlightened social concern to anxious fear of social upheaval and cultural doom. The concerned group included many recent college graduates seeking ways to use their knowledge to ameliorate the lives of immigrants and integrate them into their new country. The graduates were disproportionately females, who wanted careers commensurate with their educational background but could find few opportunities. Jane Addams provided one solution, a commodious residence in an immigrant ghetto that offered a nursery for working women, classes for adults, recreational facilities for youngsters, and incidentally, a home for the young settlement house workers who had severed familial ties in their quests for meaningful work after college. The settlements provided home and work for staff and lessons in adaptation for neighborhood residents, and they often served as agents for social change on behalf of their communities.

Like Hull House, the Rivington Street Settlement House was primarily residential. Some activities, however, like the class Eleanor Roosevelt taught, permitted "commuters" to encounter the world of the European newcomers on a part-time voluntary basis. Eleanor, at the same time, enrolled in the New York Consumers' League. If the settlement house brought her face to face with the city's worst living conditions, the league introduced her to the unsavory world of women's work. Accompanied by an older league member, she canvassed garment factories and department stores to investigate conditions. What she found was a revelation. "It had never occurred to me that the girls might get tired standing behind counters all day long," she admitted. "I did not know what sanitary requirements should be in the dress factories, either for air or for lavatory facilities." She learned quickly and well, but on a temporary voluntary basis. She escaped the hot city to spend the summer at Tivoli, but even her cursory introduction to the activities of socially conscious women had given her "a great deal of knowledge of some of the less agreeable sides of life."[22]

In her limited way, the young debutante had joined the legions of middle- and upper-class women who during the course of the nineteenth century and well into the twentieth addressed the problems of their communities as they discovered and defined them. Benevolent societies and reform organizations had engaged women in a host of ventures that sought to mitigate the social disruptions of the time.

Even before the Civil War, women in towns and cities dispensed charity to the poor, built institutions for the orphaned and needy, and campaigned against prostitution and its implied double standard. Members of female societies performed like a Red Cross during the Civil War, and afterward, women again turned their attention to the increased dislocations that followed in the wake of urban and industrial expansion. Under the auspices of the Young Women's Christian Association and similar organizations, female volunteers created homes for young women migrants to the city, who were homeless and searching for jobs. They raised funds to build refuges for unwed mothers and elderly women. They initiated employment bureaus for young arrivals and classes to teach job hunters occupational skills. In communities with little public support for social services, these women filled a void. In many cities, needs were so great and the female response so varied and complex that professionals were hired to supplement the efforts of the women's voluntary associations.

By the beginning of the twentieth century, one problem that was attracting particular attention was the working conditions of young female wage earners. In stores and factories, thousands of these new workers found employment at abysmally low wages and in unhealthy and unsafe surroundings. Women's clubs and associations first tried to provide respite for them with facilities for leisure-time activities, inexpensive meals, and dances. But as conditions in certain occupations became more onerous, a handful of New York women founded an organization to focus solely on the study of working conditions and the search for remedies. The New York Consumers' League was formed in 1890 and began its crusade with detailed investigations of women's employment in the city's department stores. Setting their own standards of adequate pay, maximum hours, and necessary safety features, league members then published white lists of establishments that met those guidelines. Shoppers were encouraged to boycott offenders. Like settlement houses, this was primarily a female endeavor: socially conscious women appealing to female consumers on behalf of working women. Successes were not overwhelming, but the league grew and was replicated in several other cities.

Eleanor Roosevelt's forays into this world of female reform appalled her family and most of her friends. Upper-class women were not altogether unfamiliar with organizations like the Consumers' League. Founders like Josephine Shaw Lowell and Maud Nathan were socially prominent matrons. But the arbiters of Knickerbocker society usually dispensed their charity from afar. Noblesse oblige was approved, but the women who practiced it should not come into daily contact with recipients or the social roots of their condition.

Eleanor Roosevelt was living with her cousin Susie Parish during the last summer and fall of 1903. The older woman was imbued with Victorian morals and elitist sensibilities, and she was appalled at Eleanor's earnest efforts. When her young charge kept a settlement house teaching assignment instead of attending a social engagement, Susie Parish found the choice incomprehensible. Eleanor's distant cousin Sara Delano Roosevelt disapproved too, but that was a more serious matter. For while Eleanor was overcoming her shyness and lack of confidence at the theater and on ballroom floors and awakening her social conscience with increasing determination, she was also spending more and more time with Sara's son, Franklin. She was nineteen years old, "a curious mixture of extreme innocence and unworldliness"[23] and much taken with the tall, slim, handsome young man who seemed equally taken with her.

2

MATRON AND MOTHER

"Featherduster" was the unflattering term the Oyster Bay Roosevelts used to describe their distant cousin Franklin from Hyde Park. He was certainly good-looking enough, a gregarious mixer at parties, and following the family educational tradition at Harvard. But somehow he was too tied to his willful mother, and he seemed to lack the goals and purpose that merited respect. The cousins were not altogether kind, but neither were they unfair in their judgment.

Franklin Delano Roosevelt was the only son of middle-aged James and his second wife, the formidable Sara Delano. Sara was half her husband's age when they married. "Mr. James," as his servants and Dutchess County neighbors called him, was the son of an eccentric, nonpracticing physician who had secluded himself along with botanical experiments on his Hudson Valley estate. His son was more worldly. After graduation from Union College and Harvard Law School, young James divided his time between the pleasures of English-style gentry life and the risks of mid-nineteenth-century American fortune building. His wealth was great enough that life in his Hyde Park manor, Springwood, would not be interrupted or threatened even if investments in coal mines and attempts at railroad mergers did not reap the anticipated financial rewards. Community service was also valued, and James Roosevelt served loyally on local charity boards, as town supervisor, and as warden of St. James

Church. Unlike his Oyster Bay relatives, he was a Democrat—except when the party took leave of its senses and nominated a wild man from Nebraska, William Jennings Bryan, in 1896. He voted for William McKinley in that election.

Death, not economic losses, disrupted the gentrified routine of the family. James had married Rebecca Howland in 1853. After a quarter century of devoted companionship and the shared joys of one son, James Roosevelt Roosevelt, always called "Rosy," Rebecca died. The widower was devastated and lonely. Like so many Roosevelts, he turned to distant cousin Bamie for consolation and then for her hand in marriage. With the help of the tactful and charming Mittie, mother and daughter deflected the courtship of the man who was twice Bamie's age. By chance it was at a dinner given by the Oyster Bay Roosevelts that James met Sara Delano, Cousin Sallie to the rest of the family.

Sara, like Bamie, was twenty-six when she was introduced to James Roosevelt. Tall, slender, regal in bearing, she was attracted to the older man. After a brief courtship, she accepted his marriage proposal. More important, her domineering father, Warren Delano, approved the match, for he ruled his family and estate with a patriarchal force that would have awed even Valentine Hall and Theodore Roosevelt, Sr. His wife, three sons, and five daughters were devoted and obedient to his every word and whim. On command, they had even joined him on a trade mission to China two decades earlier to recoup his first, lost fortune. Tea and especially opium refilled the family coffers, and all returned after years in the uncomfortable but exotic Orient to the huge secure estate, Algonac, overlooking the Hudson River.

In her mid-twenties, Sara Delano was by no means considered a young bride, but Hudson Valley society was still shocked at the disparity in the ages of the couple. Until James's later infirmities, however, there is little doubt that the two lived contentedly at Hyde Park, at their summer cottage on the island of Campobello, and on their frequent extended trips to Europe. Never was their son, Franklin, far from their side. The infant was born on 30 January 1882, and Sara had a difficult time during the delivery. Her physician probably advised against more children, and both father and mother heaped love and attention on their only offspring. With his father, the youngster rode, sailed, sledded, and learned to respect the bountiful treasures of nature. Even after the first of several heart attacks that curtailed his activities, James involved himself in all his son's interests and activities.

The intimacy between father and son, however, paled before the intensity of Sara's preoccupation with Franklin. While he had the nurses and governesses that were expected to cater to a child of his class, every detail of his daily routine was determined and closely supervised by Sara. She chose his playthings, selected his friends, read to him for hours on end. In an effort to perpetuate the dependency of childhood, she kept his hair in long curls until he was five, dressed him in skirts and then kilts until he was six, and supervised his baths until he was eight years old. When James became ill, she and Franklin established even closer bonds, entering into a great conspiracy to make life as pleasant and comfortable for the man they both cherished.

Under these conditions, Franklin Roosevelt's childhood was loving, secure, and smothering. He adored his mother, but even he periodically chafed at the constraints. His biographer, Geoffrey Ward, argues persuasively that he learned early and well how to use devious means to achieve his own purposes. Without seeming to challenge or offend his mother, he resorted to a combination of charm and mindless chatter in pursuit of his own goals. Sara had helped foster this duplicity herself by instilling self-assurance and belief in his ability to have whatever he wanted. At the same time, she taught her son to always consider the feelings of others, especially by denying unpleasantness. Franklin Roosevelt mastered these manipulative skills within his family circle; later they would drive colleagues to distraction and make him one of the consummate politicians of the twentieth century.[1]

After fourteen years of haphazard tutorial instruction at home and virtually none on long trips abroad, Sara and James finally enrolled their son at Groton, the prestigious school for the sons of the northeastern elite where Hall Roosevelt would also study five years later. The separation was wrenching for Sara; the boarding school experience was less than successful for her son. Adored and admired by family and assorted adults ranging from servants to European royalty, Franklin failed to impress his Groton peers. Some of the problems stemmed from his parents' reluctance to enter him two years earlier when other boys of his age group first enrolled. Those youngsters had already formed friendships and were veterans at coping with the spartan surroundings dictated by headmaster Endicott Peabody.

For the first time in his young life, Franklin Roosevelt was not the center of attention, but was actually an outsider. To make matters worse, Groton and its headmaster placed more emphasis on athletic prowess than academic achievement. Franklin was tall but slight. He had mastered riding and sailing, but he was dismally inadequate at baseball and football. His letters home were filled with news of scholastic, social, and athletic accomplishments, but reality was considerably different. A De-lano did not acknowledge unpleasantness and certainly did not cause parents concern.

Harvard College followed graduation from Groton and so did con-tinued disappointment. His grades were average; renown on the playing fields still eluded him. He directed his interest to the *Harvard Crimson*, the college newspaper, where all his energy and good-natured social at-tributes were needed to become president and editor. If his direction of the paper was uninspiring and his editorials lackluster, he had neverthe-less reached a position of some distinction. The same could not be said for his social conquests. Porcellian, the most prestigious of Harvard's clubs, which had made his father an honorary member and had actively sought Cousin Theodore, passed Franklin by. He was not raised to expect such snubs, and he reacted with anger and frustration. He also courted a lovely Boston belle who rejected his suit.

To complicate the happy charade he maintained with his family, Sara spent considerable time in Boston near her son. James Roosevelt died during Franklin's freshman year, and even after a decade of increas-ing invalidism, his death was a blow to mother and son. During those last years James had wanted for nothing in terms of Sara's doting solici-tude even as she lavished equal affection on their son. Now there was only Franklin as the sole object of the forty-six-year-old widow's loving dominance. She managed the Hyde Park estate capably but moved to Boston in the winters to escape the cold and be near her son. That arrangement was not unusual at the turn of the century for a widowed mother, especially for a mother like Sara. If Porcellian did not recognize a true gentleman, she certainly did and would live near him for good measure. Franklin's courtship of his cousin Eleanor was the supreme ex-ample of his ability to be a loving solicitous son and still maintain a measure of freedom away from Sara's constant gaze.

When he informed his mother that he and Eleanor were in love and planned to marry, Sara was visibly shocked, first by the announcement of which she had had no hint and then by the implications of that an-nouncement on her extraordinarily close relationship with her son. For more than a year before Franklin shared his happiness with his mother, the cousins had been seeing a great deal of each other; they corresponded with growing openness and exchanged professions of infatuation. Their paths had crossed on a few occasions when the two were growing up, usually at social gatherings hosted by one of the Oyster Bay cousins. In late 1902, soon after Eleanor's return from Allenswood, they met in Rosy Roosevelt's private box at a Madison Square Garden horse show. They saw each other at the usual round of social events attended by the rising generation of Knickerbockers. With separate invitations, both attended Theodore Roosevelt's annual White House open house on New Year's Day. Through the winter, spring, and summer of 1903, the handsome, outgoing young man and the shy, serious young woman spoke and wrote of their growing attraction to each other.

Although Eleanor later destroyed the letters Franklin wrote during their courtship, he kept hers. Along with his diary, their writings leave no doubt about the ardor of their feelings. The only misgivings were Eleanor's. She was always insecure and frightened that somehow this great happiness would prove elusive, that Franklin would lose interest and desert her, that she was unworthy of such happiness.

During their courtship, Eleanor Roosevelt's apprehensions were misplaced. Sara, not Franklin, would obstruct the straight path of romance and love. Sara did not object to her son's choice—Eleanor was one of the few Knickerbocker debutantes who met her impeccable social standards. But she recoiled from any infringement upon her special relationship with her son, so she fell back upon the one realistic objection to an immediate engagement announcement and setting of a wedding date. They were both so young, she insisted, and indeed nineteen-year-old Eleanor and twenty-one-year-old Franklin were. Before any of the Delanos knew what Franklin was telling his mother in the midst of their Thanksgiving celebration, Sara extracted a pledge that the couple would keep their engagement secret for one year to test their love and commitment. Sara had little doubt that much could happen to mutual affection in a year's time, given her own manipulative abilities.

But the couple and their love survived time, Sara, and the obstacles of Victorian conventions. Until an engagement was official, young men and women spent no time together unless they were properly chaperoned. Eleanor and Franklin saw each other as often as the activities of his final year at Harvard allowed. Franklin traveled to New York and called for lunch or tea with a Hall or Parish relative always present. Eleanor traveled by train to Cambridge for football weekends accompanied by a maid. Sara intended to spend another winter in Boston near her son whether or not Eleanor was present. She was deftly finessed by her son who proposed a Caribbean cruise instead in early spring—one last trip together. Like all separations, this one made Eleanor especially anxious, but she worried needlessly. Franklin enjoyed the vacation.

Franklin enjoyed everything but unpleasant personal confrontations.

After his return, he managed to substitute weekends in New York for maternal commands to visit Hyde Park. When he did go home, he insisted that Eleanor be invited. The couple succeeded in deceiving friends and family who attended the same dinners, balls, and sporting events they did. When their engagement was finally announced, everyone was surprised and almost everyone was delighted. Several cousins hinted that they thought Eleanor Roosevelt could have made a better match. While another misgiving may have been shared by other cousins, only Corinne actually voiced the unfortunate truth that someone who had endured as much trauma as Eleanor hardly deserved a mother-in-law like Cousin Sallie.

With great sensitivity and insight for one so young, Eleanor was aware of Sara's fears from the start. She did all she could to allay the concerns of the older woman, hoping in the process to gain what she had always craved, a true family. Once the engagement was official, the two women spent a great deal of time together, shopping, lunching, attending the theater. Eleanor was obsequious in her attention to her future mother-in-law. Sara seemed to grow more accepting, and the Delano clan welcomed Eleanor into the fold with genuine warmth. The Halls were equally pleased with Franklin. Even Uncle Vallie managed to remain sober in the young man's presence.

Plans for a March wedding progressed. Uncle Theodore offered the White House for the occasion, for a wedding as spectacular as his daughter Alice's had been, but Eleanor and the Halls agreed that the combined parlors of the connected town houses of Ludlow cousins in Manhattan would be more suitable. The president insisted on giving the bride away, an offer that thrilled Franklin. If Eleanor craved family stability and security, Franklin was no less anxious to become fully integrated into the Oyster Bay branch of the clan. Whether or not he was aware of the "featherduster" label, he certainly sensed he was not judged the Roosevelt of his generation most likely to succeed in comparison with Cousin Theodore's brood of four promising sons.

Franklin wanted desperately to model himself after his most illustrious cousin. He was marrying this president's "favorite niece" because he loved her, but moving into the older man's orbit certainly could not be disadvantageous to the first-year law student with political ambitions of his own. Two weeks before their wedding on 17 March—Uncle Theodore would be in New York that day for St. Patrick's Day events—the young couple joined the rest of the family in Washington. Theodore

Roosevelt, now elected in his own right, was inaugurated as president. Eleanor and Franklin were among those who listened to his inaugural address, lunched at the White House, and viewed the official parade. Eleanor was certain she would never witness such an event again. When her prediction proved wrong, her Oyster Bay relatives would be conspicuously absent—at the swearing in of Woodrow Wilson and at Franklin's own inauguration two decades after Wilson's.

At last the wedding date arrived. The gifts had all been acknowledged with the help of Eleanor's bridesmaids. Her trousseau was purchased under the approving eye of Cousin Susie Parish. Sara Roosevelt accompanied her to the photographer's studio for her wedding portrait. Surprisingly for a family that recorded all events with camera and pen, and never threw out a scrap, the formal portrait of Eleanor is the only surviving picture of the occasion. Several months earlier, Rosy Roosevelt's daughter, Helen, married Aunt Corinne's son, Teddy, also linking the Hyde Park and Oyster Bay branches. Franklin and Eleanor were members of the wedding party, and the photograph of all those principals is the closest clue to the late Victorian look of their own marriage.

Two hundred guests assembled in the combined drawing rooms on East Sixty-sixth Street for the occasion. Eleanor waited upstairs for her uncle; Franklin was closeted in a small room with his best man and his former headmaster, Endicott Peabody, who agreed to perform the ceremony. At half past three, with his usual exuberance, the president invaded the premises. He managed to slow his customary gallop long enough to escort his niece, whose wedding gown was covered with the Brussels lace Grandmother Hall and Anna Roosevelt had worn, to the altar. The day was the anniversary of Anna Hall Roosevelt's birth, and the guests who had known her thought, for once, that the stately young bride on the arm of the president of the United States truly resembled her mother. The Delanos were mere celebrants, but the fact that they were all present was a source of delight to Sara. It was a day for Roosevelts, especially the president. The young couple exchanged vows in the traditional Episcopalian service, "keeping the name in the family" according to the ebullient Theodore. Then all the guests followed him to the reception area, hanging onto every voluble word, basking in his expansive personality. Eleanor and Franklin became a half-forgotten opening act, although the bride claimed that she did not mind at all.

By five o'clock, "the lion of the afternoon had gone."[2] The newlyweds changed clothes and left under the traditional hail of rice. By train and coach they traveled to Springwood at Hyde Park where Sara insisted they stay for a week before returning to New York where Franklin was scheduled to take his final examinations to complete his first year at Columbia Law School. With these unorthodox preludes to honeymoon behind them, the young couple departed on the steamship *Oceanic* for an extended European tour. "With what qualms did I embark!" she remembered, but her fears of an ocean crossing and seasickness were unfounded.[3] She arrived in Liverpool without having embarrassed her husband, for whom water and ships were mainstays in his life.

For weeks the couple toured England and the Continent, entertained by hosts of family and well-placed friends, enjoying themselves on sightseeing jaunts, and merely shopping for bargains. London was their first stop and she "learned to like it better than I ever had before, because we poked into strange corners while [Franklin] looked for books and prints, with clothes thrown in."[4] They stopped at Allenswood, where she hoped to share the few pleasant memories of her youth with her new husband. But the brief "Bonheur" from Marie Souvestre she had received by telegram on her wedding day was the last message from her beloved teacher. Souvestre had died soon after, and walking through the familiar school without her friend at her side to share her newfound happiness was an unexpected reminder of life's limitless store of disappointments.

Sightseeing in Paris included expensive forays into the worlds of high fashion and rare books. Venice was the usual tourists' paradise, although for Eleanor, the breathtaking vistas were accompanied by bittersweet memories of earlier trips with her father and Souvestre. The newlyweds made the great sweep along the Dolomites to San Moritz and southern Germany before returning to London and home. Eleanor Roosevelt's anxieties and insecurities surfaced periodically. She was admittedly jealous of the charming woman they had met who accompanied Franklin mountain climbing when she declined the adventure. She "suffered tortures" when after-dinner etiquette called for a few hands of bridge. That she "felt like an animal in a trap, which could not get out and did not know how to act"[5] seemed a pitiful overreaction to a distaste for gambling in an English country home. And she quaked at the request to make a short public speech that was a mere verbal gesture.

In spite of her timidity, however, it had been an idyllic time, and she returned to New York assured she "was fitting pretty well into the pattern of a conventional, quiet young society matron."[6] She and Franklin also returned home knowing that Sara had been placated with long descriptive letters from them both and that she had spent her time furnishing their first rented home. Sara Roosevelt also sent her son his law books, which he studied on the Atlantic voyage home. He had failed two of the final examinations he took before his departure.

With Eleanor's encouragement he made up his work and successfully completed the final two years of study at Columbia Law School. In early spring 1907 he passed the bar examinations and joined the firm of Carter, Ledyard, and Milburn. At the same time, Eleanor seldom strayed from Sara's side, mastering the conventions of upper-class domesticity and leisure. She drove daily with her mother-in-law in Sara's carriage, dined with Sara, accompanied her to classes devoted to cultural uplift, and consulted her on the minute details of household management. And in early 1906 when a daughter, christened Anna Eleanor like her mother and grandmother, was born, the new mother deferred to Sara's decisions on hired nurses and child care. If the routine was stifling, the young wife and mother gave little evidence of discontent. Emotionally starved for love and acceptance, she dutifully accommodated herself to the wishes of those who could satisfy those needs and alleviate her feelings of inadequacy.

Sara Delano Roosevelt circumscribed Franklin's sphere of responsibilities as well as his wife's. She held the reins of management at Hyde Park and at Campobello in her capable hands. Together the young couple had an adequate if not lavish income from their respective inherited trust funds; the proceeds from Eleanor's principal exceeded Franklin's. The bulk of James Roosevelt's estate and her Delano inheritance remained in Sara's iron grip.

She was generous with her financial resources, however, when it suited her purposes. After the birth of her first grandson, James, at the end of 1907, Sara bought land on East Sixty-fifth Street. She hired the architect who designed side-by-side homes for herself and the young couple with drawing and dining rooms that could be opened and combined. The domestic design was not unfamiliar to Eleanor; she had lived with her cousin Susie and been married in just such shared spaces in the Parish and Ludlow homes. Still mother and son thoughtlessly excluded her from all consultations on the architecture and furnishings. Although she may have "left everything to my mother-in-law and my husband" to avoid possible disapproval and rejection, she was still disappointed and depressed at the results. She had let "their tastes and interests dominate me," and the sense of never having a home of her own persisted.[7] A new telephone and electric lighting did not erase the feeling that she was still somehow an outsider. To exacerbate her unhappiness, Franklin displayed little understanding of the reasons for or the depth of her resentment.

41

Eleanor's dissatisfaction with the living arrangements on Sixty-fifth Street were salved when Sara purchased a cottage on Campobello in 1909 for her son and daughter-in-law. They had spent several pleasant and leisurely summers on the quiet island off the coast of Maine but always in Sara's home. An elderly and obviously astute neighbor who was very fond of the young couple had died a year earlier. Her will specified that Sara could purchase her cottage for a paltry five thousand dollars if it were then given to Eleanor and Franklin. Sara complied, and now Eleanor Roosevelt had a home that was truly her own. Although Franklin spent a good deal of time in the city that first summer, she reveled in the freedom of arranging her own furniture and entertaining her own friends and her brother Hall, even substituting for Franklin on outings with little Anna and James. And there was the beautiful son born one day after their fourth wedding anniversary the previous March and named for her husband.

That summer and fall of 1909 was both a happy and a tragic time for the young mother and matron. The cottage represented the sort of independence she sought, and her management of the summer "migration" and efficient handling of household details demonstrated newly acquired abilities. She felt secure in her love for her husband and in his feelings for her. She even had her favorite nurse, Miss Spring, with her to care for the infant at Campobello. Unlike most of the nurses Sara had hired for her, she liked and trusted Miss Spring. Upon returning to New York, however, the baby's physical condition weakened. After a protracted bedside vigil, Eleanor watched helplessly as Franklin D. Roosevelt, Jr., died. Her carefully constructed sense of well-being and confidence proved fragile and vanished in the wake of her grief. Eleanor's self-reproach was punishing: "I felt he had been left too much to the nurse, and I knew little about him, and that in some way I must be to blame."[8] Submerged feelings of inadequacy as a mother and even as a woman surfaced and reinforced her despondency. Another son, Elliott, named for her father, was born ten months later, but only slowly did Eleanor Roosevelt come to terms with the death of yet another family member, not a parent or a sibling but her own child.

While Eleanor faced the joys and tragedies of her confined world, Franklin was mapping out his own future as he negotiated the labyrinth of municipal courts on behalf of his law firm. Cousin Theodore continued to provide the model he was determined to emulate. Public service was not foreign to nineteenth-century Roosevelts, but the political forays of Theodore, Sr., and Mr. James had been undertaken in a genteel tradition. They served their communities on a quasi-volunteer basis or they accepted appointment to positions of honor. Theodore had broken that pattern with an assault upon the political club of his New York district, slowly earning the trust and respect of local ward heelers. Even more unseemly, he sought public office and maneuvered for political power. On one occasion when he was governor of New York, he had traveled to Harvard and lectured to students, including his young cousin Franklin, on the virtues of public welfare. But it was social service filtered through and enhancing political power, not noblesse oblige, that he advocated and practiced. The new style appealed to Franklin, and he planned to follow the same route his illustrious relative had traveled to the New York Assembly, the Department of the Navy, the governor's mansion, and, he hoped, beyond.

When the district attorney of Dutchess County appeared at the law firm early in 1910 to evaluate the political fortunes of the Democratic party in that area, Franklin leaped at his invitation to run for the New York legislature. The "featherduster" demonstrated his determination to adhere to the party of his father and take a different path from that of the Republican Roosevelts, whose partisan allegiance was as unshakable as his own. He was also undaunted by the fact that a Democrat had not been elected to state office from the county in thirty-four years. And he ignored the reservations of his mother, who deplored the seamy world of electoral politics that ran so counter to her notions of propriety. Eleanor, on the other hand, encouraged his pursuit of public office from the position of wifely duty. "It never occurred to me," she wrote, "that I had any part to play. I felt I must acquiesce in whatever he might decide and be willing to go to Albany."[9]

After the votes were counted, they did go to Albany. Franklin had barnstormed his three-county Senate district in a red Maxwell automobile decorated with flags, talking to farmers and townspeople and any other group who would listen. Recovering from the birth of Elliott, Eleanor heard only his last speech. Her reaction to her husband's oratory was anything but complimentary. But victory indicated that it was his message and personality that swayed the voters, for "he spoke slowly, and every now and then there would be a long pause and I would be worried for fear he would never go on." Just two weeks after the successful campaign, the couple traveled to the state capital to rent a home. "My part was to make the necessary household plans and to do this as easily as possible if he should be elected."[10] So Eleanor Roosevelt supervised and completed the move with what was coming to be recognized and admired as her usual calm and competence.

She had good reason to be absorbed in family matters. "For ten years, I was just getting over having a baby or about to have one."[11] The devastating loss of Franklin, Jr., had been accompanied by much self-reproach. While she was certain she had allowed the nurses too much independence and should have nursed instead of permitting bottled formula, she was never comfortable or carefree with her children. The emotional distance that separated the mother and her youngsters was hardly surprising for a woman who had never experienced anything approaching a relaxed and loving childhood of her own and who deferred to her domineering mother-in-law where the children were concerned.

For all her personal shortcomings, however, there was much in the raising of the Roosevelt children that mirrored the standard infant and child rearing of Eleanor and Franklin's world. Years later she would lament her deficiencies, but nurses and governesses were expected and accepted members of the households of the elite whether they were ultimately hired by the mother or grandmother. A special and not too lengthy time of day reserved for parents and children was the usual practice. Some parents, however—even Knickerbocker parents—were more spontaneous and comfortable with their children than others. But at the beginning of the twentieth century, Victorian notions of children's place still prevailed. They were to be seen but not heard in middle-class families, and seldom seen or heard among the elite.

Although little had apparently changed in her conception of a proper wife and mother, the rented house in Albany represented an even greater milestone than their cottage at Campobello adjacent to Sara's. "For the first time I was going to live on my own: neither my mother-in-law nor Mrs. Paris [sic] was going to be within call," she remembered with satisfaction a quarter century later.[12] Calling upon her own reserves of strength and adaptability, she became the model politician's wife. Opening her home to the myriad types with whom politicians mingle, she entertained graciously, conversed intelligently, and with the possible exception of a constant visitor, reporter Louis Howe, made all guests feel the warmth and welcome she naturally radiated. She was not particularly well informed on political issues; she expressed her political interests through traditional duties of mother, matron, and hostess rather than expanding her own knowledge of public affairs. She had paid little attention to Uncle Theodore's inaugural speech just prior to her wedding and had been embarrassed on her honeymoon when English hosts asked her to explain American levels of government. She knew there were distinctions between the New York governorship and the American presidency, but the nuances of federalism eluded her. Even in Albany these gaps in her education persisted, although she sat in the gallery of the state senate chamber and listened to the politicians in her own drawing room.

Even for a woman sincerely committed to traditional feminine behavior, her political ignorance and naïveté were surprising. She was, after all, not only a politician's wife but an intelligent woman living in the midst of a vibrant, far-flung women's movement. All around her women were responding individually and collectively to the economic growth and social changes that marked the American landscape. Eleanor Roosevelt had once made her brief forays into the voluntary societies and settlement houses that tried to address complex social conditions, but she had relinquished her earlier activism. "I had lost a good deal of my crusading spirit," she wrote, "where the poor were concerned, because I had been told I had no right to go into the slums or into the hospitals, for fear of bringing diseases home to my children, so I had fallen into the easier way of sitting on boards and giving small sums to this or that charity and thinking the whole of my duty to my neighbor was done."[13] She would later retrace the steps from cautious benevolence to voluntary social service to political action.

She opted for the domestic virtues during the heyday of American Progressivism, that complex, ill-defined movement responding to the changes and challenges of urban, industrial society. At local, state, and ultimately national levels, businessmen and efficiency experts, professional men and educated women advanced reforms to promote honest, responsive government; to regulate and humanize the economy; to provide social services and ease community dislocation. Social welfare became the special preserve of a generation of female reformers. Settlement houses continued to offer dancing lessons to immigrant girls and athletic competitions for their brothers, but leaders like Jane Addams also had broader visions. Addams became a prominent figure on the national scene, defining issues, devising responsive policies, and articulating social philosophy that linked welfare with rights and justice. Addams's call for a humanized industrial state appealed to her fellow citizens. Whether her words called reformers to action or merely salved the troubled consciences of Americans who reacted with guilt to the less savory and exploitative aspects of industrial capitalism, she became the best-known woman of her time. At the zenith of her fame, however, there is no evidence that her words or works made any impression on Eleanor Roosevelt.

The young matron did not follow the progress of the New York Consumers' League either. The organization had broadened its scope and its staff since the days Eleanor had joined other volunteers studying labor conditions and encouraging consumer boycotts of offending employers. The indomitable Florence Kelley brought her European doctorate and work experience as a factory inspector in Illinois to the position of executive secretary of a network of leagues with headquarters in New York. Bright young women with college degrees worked as paid investigators and lobbyists as well, for the league leadership decided that the ultimate solutions to labor exploitation lay in the halls of legislatures, not in the pocketbooks of consumers.

Eleanor and Franklin Roosevelt had just moved to Albany when Frances Perkins, a staff member of the New York league, stood on a street corner in lower Manhattan one Saturday afternoon in March 1911 and watched the carnage of the Triangle Shirtwaist fire. One hundred forty-six immigrant girls suffocated, burned to death, or leaped to their doom as flames engulfed the top floors of their garment manufacturing loft. Perkins and Franklin's new colleague in the state senate, Alfred P. Smith, were appointed to a special commission to address the problems of industrial safety highlighted by the tragedy. While Eleanor Roosevelt was supervising the annual family pilgrimage between Albany, Hyde Park, New York, and Campobello, Perkins was testifying before legislative committees on behalf of laws to regulate the number of hours women worked and to impose safety standards in New York's factories.

While the social feminism of the women reformers flourished, the narrower political feminism of the suffragists captured the headlines and the support of tens of thousands of American women. The drive for the vote had waxed and waned since the astounding demand was first proclaimed in 1848. At the time of Franklin Roosevelt's election, however, new leadership and tactics invigorated the movement, and politicians found it difficult to hedge the issue especially if they were personally confronted and badgered by persistent suffragists. Franklin endorsed women's enfranchisement when he was pressed by feminist Inez Mulholland. Ever the dutiful wife, Eleanor Roosevelt "realized that if my husband was a suffragist I probably must be, too."[14] Actually she was not and argued passionately with her sometimes feminist aunt Pussie. Eleanor did not question male superiority, and she assumed that it extended into the voting booth. As late as 1919, on the eve of the ratification of the Nineteenth Amendment, she was still neutral on the issue. When the wife of a die-hard antisuffrage senator tried to enlist her support in combating the amendment, she was noncommittal. "I considered any stand at that time was outside my field of work." She was almost as indifferent to her husband's political fortunes. "I was too much taken with the family to give it much thought."[15]

The presidential election of 1912 indicated the firm boundaries that separated Eleanor's domestic world from the political and social maelstrom without. The campaign focused on the issues of Progressivism, including those that women reformers had made their own: government control over working conditions for women, abolition of child labor, establishment of juvenile courts, and more stringent standards of education. Concerns over the abuses of female and child labor were far removed from Eleanor's wifely duties and maternal vicissitudes. She could hardly ignore the fact, however, that her uncle Theodore stood in the middle of the political convulsions over who wore the true mantle of Progressivism and who should command its legions.

There was never any doubt in Franklin's mind about the best hope of Progressives. He championed the cause of Governor Woodrow Wilson of New Jersey. Working hard and enthusiastically on Wilson's behalf, he chaired the New York State Wilson Conference. Eleanor accompanied her husband to the national convention in Baltimore, but the June heat and the demonstrations all seemed so senseless to her, she made a hasty departure for Campobello. There she received a jubilant telegram from Franklin announcing: "Splendid triumph."

The exultant New York Democrat had his own reelection campaign to consider, but before he and his now-faithful adviser, newspaperman Louis Howe, had devised a strategy, Franklin became ill with typhoid fever. In the process of nursing her incapacitated husband, Eleanor also became ill. With her usual resilience, she was back on her feet before Franklin even though his case was less severe. In the meantime, the ubiquitous Howe, whose unkempt, gnomelike appearance offended Eleanor and whose constant cigarette smoke polluted her airy home to her great distress, singlehandedly and successfully managed Franklin's campaign.

In light of the complexities of the 1912 campaign, the couple was fortunate to have missed the heated election season. They were removed from the political dissension resulting from Uncle Theodore's challenge to mainstream Republicans. The Oyster Bay branch could tolerate Franklin's apostasy, but Cousin Alice was caught in an inextricable bind.

Her father opposed President Taft's bid for reelection and sealed both men's fates by splitting the Republican party. Alice's husband, Nicholas Longworth, represented Cincinnati in Congress, home territory of the Tafts. Alice may have been relieved at Wilson's victory, except that Longworth lost his seat in the debacle. In spite of the strains and cross-currents, other family members doted on the irrepressible Uncle Ted. Even Sara Roosevelt, who made patronizing appearances at Wilson rallies, spent election night at the headquarters of the Bull Moose party.

Franklin hoped for an appointment in the new Wilson administration, but no offer arrived by the time of the inauguration. Then the newly appointed secretary of the navy, Josephus Daniels, met the young New Yorker at the ceremony in Washington and invited him to serve as his assistant. Within two weeks, Franklin was confirmed and sworn into the office Theodore Roosevelt had held. His progress was on track, his timetable on schedule.

Eleanor Roosevelt dutifully and calmly supervised yet another move. For instructions on the responsibilities of an assistant secretary's wife, she consulted her knowledgeable and wise Aunt Bamie. The older woman had astounded the family by suddenly marrying a naval officer shortly after her fortieth birthday and making her home in Washington. The repository of all sorts of information, she advised her niece on the protocol of calling on the wives of government officials. She also counseled Eleanor on the less compulsory but more compassionate need to make life pleasant for wives of young naval officers. Since she had always taken a special interest in the families of New York assemblymen who felt lost in Albany, Eleanor understood her aunt's sentiments well. The young matron was very much her aunt's niece in terms of caring and kindness. Once her political instincts matured, she would even surpass her astute aunt in political savvy.

By her own account, acquiring a taste for public affairs seemed unlikely. "I could have learned much about politics and government, for I had plenty of opportunity to meet and talk with interesting men and women," she recalled a quarter century later. "As I look back upon it, however, I think my whole life centered in the family."[16] Assuming the role her aunt had played so long, Eleanor had already become confidante to various relatives and was especially involved in the education and then the marriage of her brother, Hall. So similar to her aunt in many ways, Eleanor gratefully accepted Aunt Bamie's offer to move into her home on N Street when she and Franklin first settled in Washington.

Eleanor undertook her new duties compulsively. "Nearly all the women at that time were the slaves of the Washington social system," and her descriptions of the calling ritual bear her out. "From ten to thirty calls were checked off my list day after day. Mondays the wives of the justices of the Supreme Court; Tuesdays the members of Congress . . . Wednesdays the Cabinet, and here was a problem to be met. If Mrs. Daniels invited me to be with her on that afternoon I could not be calling on the other members of the Cabinet."[17] Such dilemmas would have taxed the ingenuity if not the patience of State Department diplomats.

With the entertaining expected of the young couple at their home and the invitations they received in turn, their social schedule overwhelmed her. "I tried to do without a secretary," she wrote, "but found it took me such endless hours to arrange my calling list, and answer and send invitations, that I finally engaged one three mornings a week."[18] With these words—and only these words—Eleanor Roosevelt alluded to Lucy Mercer when she wrote her memoirs two decades after hiring the young woman, who would cast a long shadow over her life, as her part-time social secretary.

Young Lucy Mercer's lineage was more impressive than even the Roosevelts'. Descended from two well-connected Catholic families in Maryland, she traced her Mercer and Carroll roots to the colonial era. Her parents married young, had two daughters, squandered their respectable fortunes, and separated. She and her sister remained with her mother. When she arrived in Washington in 1913, she sought employment as a social secretary in order to support herself. She was lovely and charming as well as pedigreed, attributes that hostesses appreciated in the class-conscious capital. She often filled the need for an additional young woman at Washington dinner parties including ones given by the assistant secretary of the navy and his wife. Although Eleanor was adept at social amenities, she appreciated Lucy's help, especially when a second son to be named Franklin, Jr., was born in 1914 and John was born two years later.

In the meantime Franklin mastered his post at the Navy Department, concentrating on personnel and procurement. At a time when federal agencies were small and easily manageable and budget appropriations were correspondingly meager, the Navy Department was an exception. Together the astute secretary and his brash assistant succeeded in securing the funds to increase the size of the already impressive American fleet. Although Franklin was constantly enthralled with the trappings of office like seventeen-gun salutes and the use of the secretary's yacht, he also learned important lessons from the older man about the impact of federal funds on local communities and how best to secure those monies from congressmen looking out for the folks back home. Franklin's occasional annoyance at the slow-paced, deliberate style of his land-loving boss gave way to appreciation for Daniels's political skills and sophistication. Franklin Roosevelt absorbed these valuable lessons against the background of impending war.

Unlike Daniels and scattered members of the Wilson administration, the Roosevelts were pro-Ally from the time the guns began to roar on the European continent. But pro-Ally sentiment was one matter and prowar policies were another even in the wake of German naval attacks. The president called for neutrality, Uncle Theodore for action. As debate became more heated, the peace-loving secretary of state William Jennings Bryan resigned. The equally peace-loving secretary of the navy Josephus Daniels did not. Eleanor Roosevelt was confused and ambivalent; she was glad Bryan was no longer dissenting within the administration, but impressed with his adherence to principle and somewhat sympathetic to his pacifist stance. The peace movement initiated by American women under the guidance of Jane Addams lay outside her field of vision and interest.

The summer of 1916 was a difficult one for Eleanor. The annual trek to Campobello went without a hitch, although the last of the Roosevelt children was only three months old. But the reality of war was never far away, and Franklin was. Absorbed in preparedness plans and the upcoming presidential elections, he spent most of the summer in Washington. Eleanor was lonely and restless, but Franklin vetoed her plan to move the entourage to Hyde Park earlier than usual. The family was safest from a raging polio epidemic if they remained on the island, he argued. When the scare subsided and they could all sail directly to Washington, he promised to send the navy's yacht for them. Politically astute Daniels delayed the use of the official ship until primary elections had been held in Maine. "There I was entirely alone with my children, marooned on the island, and apparently I was going to be there for some time," Eleanor complained.[19] Franklin did not seem to chafe at the delay. He and Lucy Mercer spent much time together during that summer.

The reluctance with which Eleanor left for Campobello the following year indicated she may have had forebodings about the activities of her husband in her absence. But upon finally arriving back in the capital in September 1916, other ominous feelings engulfed her. "From a life centered entirely in my family I became conscious, on returning to the seat of government in Washington, that there was a sense of impending disaster hanging over all of us." For Democrats, the defeat of Wilson seemed imminent and was avoided by only the narrowest of electoral margins. Before the formality of Wilson's second inauguration, Germany declared the resumption of unrestricted submarine warfare. The nation whose newly reelected president had vowed to keep it out of war held its collective breath. Then in early April Wilson traveled to Capitol Hill and asked for a declaration of war. From that moment, Eleanor recalled, "the men in the government worked from morning until late into the night." And she added, "The women in Washington paid no more calls."[20]

Following the example set by Theodore in 1898, Roosevelt men rushed off to enlist. All four of Theodore's sons were soon in uniform, including Quentin, who along with Eleanor's brother, Hall, concealed his deficient eyesight and joined the barely existent air corps. All efforts by Uncle Ted himself to raise a division were rejected by Wilson and his military commanders. Although he also ached to see action, Franklin Roosevelt was persuaded that his services at the Navy Department would be of greater benefit to the war effort.

Eleanor's response to home-front programs to save and serve the war effort were fledgling and even embarrassing at first. To comply with government calls to conserve products at home, she efficiently rearranged a number of household practices and was selected as a model manager of a large household. But when asked by a newspaper reporter to explain how she conserved food, soap, and other domestic necessities, she replied, according to the interviewer, "Making ten servants help me do my saving has not only been possible but highly profitable." Then she described how her cook, her laundress, and other domestic help all aided the war effort under her watchful eye.

Franklin laughed uproariously when he saw his wife's remarks in print, and Eleanor vowed never to get caught again by any reporter when the published results would make her want "to crawl away for shame."[21] Still it was obvious to all Washingtonians that the rising young Roosevelts were a family of special social and political status.

Eleanor and Franklin did not question their place among the elite nor the values of the "restricted group of friends" with whom they associated. Theirs was still the narrow world of privilege and even pretension into which they had been born. The triple feathers worn by Eleanor's bridesmaids and the same design engraved on links for Franklin's ushers supposedly represented the Roosevelt family crest. There was no such thing. There was, however, a standard of living and behavior that was real indeed. When Eleanor mastered household management, that meant the hiring and supervision of governesses, cooks, and an assortment of other servants. For years she felt intimidated by the nurses, but she never considered doing without them, at least until she grew to have serious misgivings about the way she had raised her children and the need for hired help was long past. For all the later protestations that the couple should have forgone domestic servants altogether, when little Anna cried through a dinner party hosted by the young parents, Eleanor vowed "never again would I have a dinner on the nurse's day out."

When a cook walked out unexpectedly in the midst of preparations for another dinner party, Eleanor spent the rest of the day frantically canvassing employment agencies. For a few days afterward she tried to acquire some semblance of culinary skill. She never did. Her warmth as a hostess would become legendary along with the dreadful quality of the food she served, even when cooked by others. As first lady she learned to type but had a loyal, overworked secretary. She eventually learned to drive but always had a chauffeur at her disposal when she was first lady of New York and then the nation.

The war years modified many of the Victorian conventions that Eleanor Roosevelt had absorbed from Grandma Hall, Cousin Susie, and her mother-in-law. When her grandmother could not understand why Hall had not bought a substitute as gentlemen had done during the Civil War, Eleanor delivered a stern lecture on the duties of all American citizens in wartime regardless of class standing. She grew impatient with Cousin Susie's intolerance with war-induced inconveniences. And she disregarded Sara's half-teasing displeasure over her new efforts as a Red Cross canteen worker and a Navy Department volunteer distributing free wool for knitting.

Her entry into voluntary war work proved a liberating experience. Not since her venture into New York's Lower East Side had she tasted the challenges and satisfactions of public service. She displayed the enthusiasm, efficiency, and leadership qualities that Marie Souvestre had discovered and encouraged years before. She worked hard, and her efforts did not go unnoticed. Her coworkers thought she was a dynamo. The Red Cross wanted her to help establish and run similar canteens in England, but she had not cast aside conventional standards to the point that she would travel abroad alone no matter how important the assignment or exciting the prospect. Even without the trip to London, however, her activities were exceptional especially when compared to the voluntary efforts of Cousin Alice Roosevelt Longworth. She accompanied Eleanor to the train station one day to assist at the canteen, but no troop trains passed through. The more menial jobs the volunteers engaged in did not suit Alice. That was her first and last appearance at Union Station, according to journalist Joseph Alsop, cousin of Alice and Eleanor. Mrs. Longworth spent the war years nursing a mysterious case of "canteen elbow" that apparently prevented her from distributing coffee and postcards to the thousands of young men passing through the Washington railroad depot.

Alice found excitement and created entertainment in her own fashion. During the summer of 1917, Eleanor was again at Campobello, this time with the children and "the inevitable knitting which every woman undertook and which became a constant habit."[22] Alice discovered Franklin out riding on the outskirts of Washington with Lucy Mercer. After much teasing, she invited her cousin and his wife's social secretary to tea and to a number of dinners. Alice enjoyed playing hostess at gatherings where everyone enjoyed themselves. A half century later, she told a reporter that Franklin deserved a good time: "He was married to Eleanor."[23] There was little love lost between the two cousins. Alice had no patience with Eleanor's earnest behavior and the quiet competence that aroused admiration for reasons Alice could not understand.

Eleanor had no reason to suspect her cousin's complicity in her husband's romantic involvement. But she was not without ill-defined, uneasy suspicions. Her husband spent little time at the island that summer, although the demands of work at the Navy Department was certainly a credible excuse. Lucy Mercer assumed some of Eleanor's responsibilities at the Navy League for which Eleanor was adamant that she be paid. After returning to Washington and moving into a larger home, Eleanor increased her correspondence with Sara to the point of writing daily letters. The quantity of the communications was matched by the quality of a loving, almost fawning tone, so much like the letters she had written during the early years of her marriage. Like a nation beleaguered from abroad, Eleanor Roosevelt appeared to be cementing her alliances.

Before the next summer arrived, she had decided that she would spend most of it in the capital to help out at the canteen, because so many people planned to be away. She took the children to Hyde Park, helped get them settled, and returned to the capital to find that Franklin was to go abroad to inspect naval facilities. He sailed in July 1918 and did not return until the end of September, arriving on a stretcher with a severe case of pneumonia. While Eleanor nursed him and handled his correspondence, she discovered love letters from Lucy Mercer tucked away in a dresser. Her worst fears were confirmed; instantaneously her secure world crashed around her. Exactly one year earlier, she recalled with regard to her voluntary war work, "I was learning to have a certain confidence in myself and in my ability to meet emergencies and deal with them."[24] She dealt with this personal crisis by confronting Franklin with the evidence of his unfaithfulness and delivering an ultimatum: either he must never see Mercer again and they would remain married for the sake of the children or she would give him a divorce.

Aunt Corinne, who was close to Sara Roosevelt, later recounted the scenario that followed to her grandson, Joseph Alsop. Eleanor and Franklin both informed Sara of the circumstances that had led to Eleanor's decision. With more concern for social propriety and possible scandal than for her daughter-in-law's feelings, Sara threatened to cut Franklin off from all funds and title to the Hyde Park estate if he deserted his wife and five children. A thirty-six-year-old ambitious politician could not ignore the implications of limited income and the negative effect of divorce on his future prospects. But according to family insiders, he was willing to sacrifice everything for love anyway. In the end, Lucy Mercer's faith settled the family upheaval. She would not marry a divorced man whose wife was still alive. Catholic doctrine determined the outcome of the marital crisis quite apart from Sara's threats, Franklin's defiance, and Eleanor's pain.

How had their marriage come to this point? The upward trajectory of Franklin's career and the growing family circle masked differences in the personalities of Eleanor and Franklin that had been present from the start. But courtship and the early years of marriage were a private time when the couple explored similarities, when their differences took on the virtues of complementary qualities. As disparate as their childhoods had been, the experiences of both were highly unusual. One was sheltered and isolated in the adult-centered world of Hyde Park; the other was buffeted from house to house of one relative or another. Eleanor, who had always felt like an outsider, could sympathize with Franklin's feelings of rejection at Groton and Harvard. But these setbacks hardly dented self-confident, affable Franklin or fostered sensitivity toward the insecurities of others. He knew from the time he met Eleanor that she was shy and serious, but he believed that her love and sense of duty and purpose would steady his own course. He seemed less aware of what he could contribute to her psychological needs.

Eleanor did gain emotional strength in the apparent security of marriage and menage, and Franklin kept a firmer eye on his career than he might otherwise have done because of her quiet but effective prodding. But their differences were as likely to clash as they were to complement. Even their closest friends noted that Franklin remained the gregarious, charming "featherduster" while Eleanor seemed retiring and virtuous. William Phillips was an assistant secretary of state and, along with his wife, a member of a close circle of Roosevelt friends who saw one another on frequent and less formal social occasions than was usual in Washington. "I knew him then as a brilliant, lovable, and somewhat happy-go-lucky friend, an able Assistant Secretary of the Navy, but I doubt if it ever occurred to us that he had the making of a great President," Phillips wrote years later. "His wife, Eleanor, whom we all admired, was a quiet member of the little group. She seemed to be a little remote, or it may have been that Franklin claimed the attention, leaving her somewhat in the background."[25]

Eleanor Roosevelt could be more than remote. She could carry self-effacement and the need to avoid confrontation to the point of distraction for everyone involved. When angry and hurt she would retreat into her "Griselda moods," seeking refuge in silence and self-inflicted martyrdom. These occasions were not rare. She crawled into her passive, but angry shell when the young couple moved into the brownstone Sara built for them. When her brother, Hall, fell short of her expectations, she retreated emotionally from him as well, temporarily at least. On one occasion she and Franklin attended one of Washington's more dazzling affairs. She left early and alone, a habit she had cultivated since she had little patience for small talk and endless whirls around the dance floor. When she arrived home without a key, she was forced to sit peevishly and furiously on the stoop until Franklin, who had had a marvelous time, finally arrived at three in the morning. She greeted him with aggrieved but silent suffering.

These passive, depressive moods were punishing, intended to inflict hurt on those subjected to her evasion but especially devastating to herself, feeding her own pain and self-pity. She would lose touch with the causes of her hurt and agree with Franklin that she was the "silly goose," when in fact he displayed incredible insensitivity to the fragility of her emotions and the depth of her needs. She was not a beautiful woman or lighthearted companion, but she was attractive, gracious, and much admired in the circle in which they moved. She had been more than patient with her domineering mother-in-law, but rarely did Franklin shelter her from the older woman's imperious demands. She did not enjoy or partake in the social frivolities and the excursions that Franklin reveled in, but she played the prescribed supportive role of a rising politician's wife with compliance and increasing effectiveness.

One wifely role was not performed with pleasure and finally was not performed at all. Eleanor Roosevelt came to her marriage bed with all the sexual inhibitions and distaste of passionless Victorianism at high tide. She admitted to her daughter years afterward that physical intimacy repelled her. After the birth of their sixth child, Eleanor moved to a separate bedroom. She had done her duty and had little understanding or concern for her husband's sexual needs. Nor was this an issue to be discussed, not just because of her own reticence toward sexuality but because serious, intimate discussion was as foreign to Franklin as it was to her. The couple had rarely talked seriously about any critical matters, let alone about the gulf that had slowly grown between them and about their increasing inability to meet each other's needs and expectations.

The Lucy Mercer affair not only altered their relationship irrevocably; it also changed each of them individually. Aunt Corinne's family believed that the Franklin Roosevelt who eventually dominated the American political scene emerged in the aftermath of his renunciation of Lucy Mercer. Her grandson, Joseph Alsop, believed that FDR's disappointment in this great and genuine love affair helped banish the "featherduster" features of his personality, that he emerged tougher, more mature and profound even before his valiant battle with polio. The family sensed that he now brought new strength, resolve, and judgment to political goals he had previously only dabbled in.

The emergence of a new Eleanor Roosevelt was a more arduous undertaking over a longer period of time. The process was fraught with difficulty because she would have to construct an entirely new person with abilities and strength of character she hardly knew she possessed. She had built one identity patterned on an ideal of womanhood that glorified duty and sacrifice to home and family only to discover the formula failed to bring her the love and security she hungered for. No longer would she place her faith in dependence on others, including her husband, or in deference to conventional values. Somehow her shattered self-assurance, the undermined concept of what it meant to be a woman, would have to be re-created to serve as the springboard for autonomy, defined and achieved on her own terms.

Eleanor (*right*) with her father, Elliott Roosevelt, and brothers Elliott and Hall (ca. 1892).
Franklin D. Roosevelt Library

Eleanor at age sixteen in 1900.
Franklin D. Roosevelt Library

Eleanor with Franklin's mother, Sara Delano Roosevelt, at Campobello Island, New Brunswick (ca. 1904). *Franklin D. Roosevelt Library*

Wedding portrait of Eleanor, March 1905. *UPI/Bettmann Newsphotos*

The Roosevelt family in Washington, D.C., 1919. The children (*left to right*) are Anna, Franklin, Jr., James, John, and Elliott. *Franklin D. Roosevelt Library*

Reporters surround Eleanor Roosevelt at one of her first White House press conferences in March 1933. *Historical Pictures Service, Chicago*

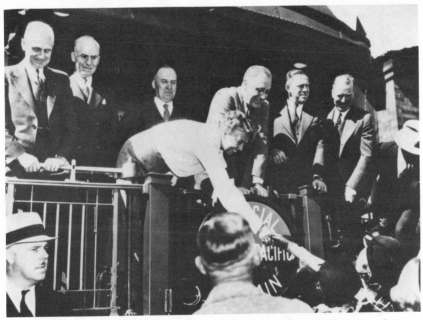

Eleanor and Franklin visit Freemont, Nebraska, in September 1935. *UPI/Bettmann Newsphotos*

Eleanor Roosevelt in front of the plane that flew her to Guadalcanal, 15 September 1943. With her are (*left to right*) Adm. William F. Halsey, American Red Cross Supervisor Marie Coletta Ryan, and Adm. William Harmon. *Franklin D. Roosevelt Library*

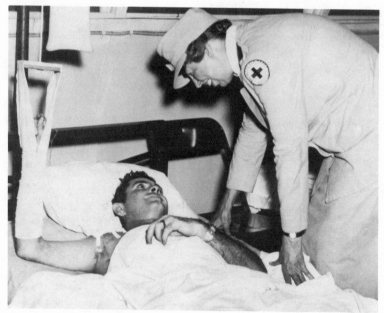

Eleanor Roosevelt on a visit to a military hospital during her 1943 tour of the South Pacific. *Franklin D. Roosevelt Library*

The Roosevelts and their grandchildren, 20 January 1945, following the President's inauguration. *UPI/Bettmann Newsphotos*

Eleanor Roosevelt with her daughter Anna Boettiger at the burial of F.D.R. at Hyde Park, 15 April 1945. *UPI/Bettmann Newsphotos*

Eleanor Roosevelt converses with Soviet Foreign Minister and chief United Nations delegate Viacheslav M. Molotov on 23 October 1946. In the background is Andrei A. Gromyko, Soviet delegate to the U.N. Security Council. *UPI/Bettmann Newsphotos*

Eleanor Roosevelt displays a poster proclaiming the United Nations' Universal Declaration of Human Rights, November 1949. *Franklin D. Roosevelt Library*

Eleanor Roosevelt is buried at Hyde Park, 10 November 1962. Among her mourners are (*center to right*) President John F. Kennedy, Vice President Lyndon B. Johnson, and former presidents Harry S. Truman and Dwight D. Eisenhower. *New York Times*

3

POLITICAL APPRENTICE

As 1919 ended, Eleanor Roosevelt confided in her diary that she had never "felt so strangely as in the past year." More specifically, she admitted, "all my self-confidence is gone and I am on edge though I never was better physically."[1] Sixteen months had elapsed between the discovery of Lucy Mercer's letters and the diary entry. The outward mien of a dutiful wife and concerned parent masked the tortured uncertainties of a betrayed woman whose hard-won, seemingly secure world had collapsed around her. The symptoms of depression were palpable even if she had no clinical label for her anguish.

It was a year in which her personal crisis served as metaphor for national convulsions, and vice versa. A woman at war with herself and her smug world of Victorian conventions resembled the nation encountering convulsions in its own struggle to rediscover and redefine social and political values.

At first, on the surface, all seemed well for the Roosevelts as well as for the country. Their domestic routine continued without interruption, and the family rejoiced with the nation when the Armistice was signed. Eleanor continued her volunteer activities. Earlier she had directed the canteen that tried to make circumstances pleasant for the young man sent off to war; now she spent her time at St. Elizabeth's Hospital, comforting the casualties upon their return.

The wounded and the shell-shocked were not the only Americans who were bedridden during the winter of 1918. The worst pandemic in modern times swept the world, and in the United States alone, half a million Americans died of influenza and its complications. Eleanor escaped the virus, but she nursed the rest of the family and the servants, too, who were all less fortunate.

With spring, a different sort of disease infected the political landscape. Public trust fell temporarily by the wayside. Almost a year passed before Americans were reassured that foreign and home-grown Bolsheviks were few in number and constituted no threat to the body politic. In the meantime, economic warfare erupted. Industrial workers and coal miners—and even Boston policemen—demanded increased wages to cope with rampant inflation as well as the right to organize into unions. Employers responded with intransigence, creating a reservoir of distrust and frustration. When race riots broke out in major cities during the summer, the violence added to the longing for national unity and purpose that had seemed so palpable just a year earlier when Americans had marched off to war.

The Roosevelts were not passive observers of these disturbing events. In June, the home of Bolshevik-hunting attorney general, A. Mitchell Palmer, was bombed. Palmer lived directly across the street from Eleanor and Franklin Roosevelt, who returned home from a social engagement that evening to find their street under siege. Only James was at home. For years afterward he regaled the family with descriptions of his mother calmly explaining and reassuring him that nothing was wrong—it was only a bomb!

Industrial violence was more distant, but Eleanor Roosevelt attended a tea that fall for American delegates to the International Congress of Working Women. Many of the women were union members; they and their supporters voiced ideas that sounded unorthodox and radical to Eleanor. Still they engaged her increasing interest in public issues, and she invited several of the women to lunch. On R Street they were served by her newly engaged staff of servants, the first blacks she had ever employed. Although black household help was common in Washington, she had bowed to Sara's and Cousin Susie's certainties that only white servants could be trusted. Dissatisfaction with domestic help persuaded her to hire "darkies." They served her well, but inbred prejudices did not dissipate rapidly simply because the meals were well cooked and served. And the race riots that scarred Washington and other cities that summer aroused anxieties over Franklin's safety while she and the children were safely ensconced with Aunt Maude at Fairhaven, yet another mansion on the Hudson. Race relations would eventually join labor relations on her agenda of public causes, but not in 1919.

That year still had to be emotionally surmounted. Eleanor and Franklin made studied efforts at reconciliation. They began with an ocean trip to Europe, their first since their honeymoon. Assigned to oversee the decommissioning and demobilization of naval units, Franklin traveled in an official capacity. He insisted that Eleanor accompany him, and she made arrangements for sailing. Together they toured sites of trenched battlefields and with friends, Eleanor visited service hospitals. Ever disciplined she never flinched, but the sights of the wounded unnerved her. Scarred land, scarred men, and black-clad mourning women cried out for assurance that desolated Europe would never experience such human and material destruction again.

The trip also coincided with the Paris Peace Conference, but Eleanor and Franklin were marginal observers. The Wilsons and their entourage sailed home on the same ship that carried the Roosevelts back to New York, and on board they had their first look at the covenant creating a League of Nations. They agreed that the document represented a noble experiment, the best hope against a repetition of the horrors they had just viewed. Upon landing, however, the Roosevelts quickly sensed the palpable antagonism toward the treaty and its covenant. Franklin went on the political offensive; Eleanor returned to the mundane chores of restaffing her household, monitoring her older children's mediocre academic performances, and trying to be a more relaxed and companionable parent to her younger boys.

Closer links with her children took on special urgency and poignancy as the older generation who had been her substitute parents passed from the scene. While they were aboard the ship to Europe, news had arrived that Theodore Roosevelt had died. Eleanor's diary does not reveal a great sense of loss. It had been Aunt Bamie and Aunt Corinne who had maintained close ties with her beloved father during his self-destructive years and with herself as well, but still an essential tie was severed. Then in August Grandma Hall succumbed to the vagaries of age. Years later, Eleanor Roosevelt would use her grandmother as a model of self-sacrificing, indulgent motherhood, one who invested everything in her children without regard for her personal interests or for the need to raise self-sufficient, responsible adults. Her aunts and uncles, she felt, "might have been well in their youth if they had not been able to count on her devotion and her presence whenever they needed her."[2] At the time of Grandma Hall's death, however, her feelings were not so critical and were less a reflection of her own misgivings over her relationships with her own children. "It is only of late years," she wrote in her diary, "that I have realized what it meant for her to take Hall, Ellie and me into her home as she did." And she added, "Pussie and Maude were wonderful about it too."[3] Within months the erratic, irrepressible Pussie was also dead, burned in a tragic fire. Eleanor accompanied the remains to Tivoli for burial.

More than funerals marked the passing of her old world. During summer and fall of 1919 she fired the opening salvos in her efforts to redefine her relationship with Sara, the values her mother-in-law represented, and the overbearing ways in which she tried to impose them. Harsh words passed between the two women on more than one occasion. Although Eleanor apologized profusely when tempers cooled, her former obsequiousness gradually disappeared. In the meantime the family occupied Sara's town house when they returned to New York from Washington because theirs was still rented.

Social disruptions and a rancorous debate over the peace treaty did not bode well for the Democrats. Franklin Roosevelt did not wait for a national referendum on issues or personalities. He resigned his post, joined a New York law firm, and directed the New York office of a Maryland surety bonding house. But politics was never far from his mind, and he kept abreast of affairs among state Democrats, even testing the possibilities of a race for the Senate.

In June 1920 Franklin Roosevelt traveled to the Democratic National Convention as Eleanor packed up the household for the summer pilgrimage to Campobello. She was on the island when an unexpected telegram arrived from Josephus Daniels announcing that Franklin had been nominated for the vice presidency. In the days before FDR himself would dramatically alter the practice, candidates were officially informed by visiting party dignitaries when nominated for national office. Eleanor immediately packed up the menage for Hyde Park and the occasion. While Sara beamed proudly at her son and glared disdainfully at the newspaper reporters trampling her immaculate lawn, the notification ceremony took place.

The campaign meant long tours through the country for Franklin, who reveled in the public contacts and attention. He insisted Eleanor accompany him on the last major campaign swing. Dutifully she became the only woman among the traveling politicians and newspapermen. The schedule was grueling, and Franklin's verbosity both blossomed and bored. "It is becoming almost impossible to stop F[ranklin] now when he begins to speak," she wrote Sara. His campaign managers tried to curb his oratorical relish, "but when nothing succeeds I yank his coat tails!"[4] Although she believed her contribution to the campaign was negligible, she learned much about political problems and processes, and more essential, she made an enduring and endearing friend. Eleanor Roosevelt made peace with Louis Howe. The ex-reporter was determined to make FDR president some day and had followed him to Washington from Albany in 1913 to serve as Franklin's secretary at the Navy Department.

Beneath Howe's slouching, rumpled, chain-smoking exterior lay a shrewd and sensitive man. For a decade, Eleanor had barely tolerated his presence. On the train, however, he sensed her loneliness and unhappiness. He sought her out, explained their strategies, listened seriously to her ideas. She responded with gratitude and eventually with love. Howe also explained the vagaries of public moods and shared with her the disappointments of political defeat. The Cox-Roosevelt ticket had campaigned on a platform pledged to progressive reform and ratification of the Versailles Peace Treaty. The Democrats were trounced.

Howe had become one of the first of several new friends outside the immediate family circle who helped rebuild the confidence that underlay the emergence of the new Eleanor Roosevelt. She had begun to chart her own course even before Franklin's national campaign. Although living with Sara, she had broken loose from the conventional routine and activities that bounded her mother-in-law's world. She sought more active roles than those offered by honorific service on the boards of philanthropic societies. She joined the League of Women Voters.

The league was the reconstituted National American Woman Suffrage Association (NAWSA). When the long struggle for female suffrage finally seemed won, the incomparable president of the suffrage organization, Carrie Chapman Catt, called on the organization to change direction, to educate newly enfranchised women, to study issues at all levels of government, to meet in convention and take positions on policy, and to devise strategies for securing policy implementation. The stance was nonpartisan; the tactics were primarily educational. But the organization had strong links to the social welfare advocates of the early twentieth century. Members brought concerns about child labor, protection for working women, efficient government, and since the Armistice, an ardent commitment to peace to the new association.

At the height of the suffrage movement, NAWSA engaged two million women in its campaigns, but significant numbers deserted the ranks after the ratification of the Nineteenth Amendment. Many women who had held leadership positions, however, continued to pursue their varied interests within the structure of the League of Women Voters. Two New Yorkers, Elizabeth Read and Esther Lape, were especially effective in initiating Eleanor Roosevelt into the female sphere of political awareness and action.

Elizabeth Read was a quiet and scholarly lawyer who had been an ardent suffragist. Her friend Lape taught at both Swarthmore and Barnard colleges. She was a gifted publicist who easily shifted her expertise from the suffrage movement to the league. The two women shared love and living arrangements, introducing Eleanor Roosevelt to the distinctive world of female support and devotion that formed the foundation for many single women's professional achievements. Read and Lape were among the generation of women who renounced marriage and domesticity in order to translate their education into social activism and public careers. By remaining single and seeking work in cities apart from their families, they altered patterns of long standing in which unmarried daughters and spinster aunts found productive labor and living space within the family fold. Their predecessors, like Jane Addams, who spoke directly to the issue of women's need to renounce the "family claim," had solved the problem of surrogate homes and kin within settlement houses in which they resided and often worked.

By the 1910s and 1920s, living arrangements like that of Read and Lape became more prevalent, modeled on the "Boston marriages" of the late nineteenth century. Female couples made comfortable homes for each other, creating and sustaining the emotional and sometimes sexual relationships needed by adults as a foil for demanding careers. Eleanor Roosevelt learned to appreciate this private and efficacious arrangement, describing it decades later when Read died and left Lape a virtual widow: "Between Esther and [Elizabeth] there was a deep relationship, built over 30 years & she was unselfishly devoted to Esther. Each had interests & friends of their own but Elizabeth always subordinated anything to Esther's interests tho' she had the stronger character & tho' less brilliant, she had better judgment & in some ways a better mind than Esther's. Their lives were in all but the physical relationship, like the best of marriage & I think Elizabeth built it. . . . I can see why Esther is lost without her."[5]

If women like Read and Lape also had, in fact, "the physical relationship," Eleanor Roosevelt would undoubtedly have chosen to look away, deny, or even repress the possibility. She could not and would not

62

accept the reality of lesbianism. Esther Lape once sent her a novel by André Gide, a story with an undisguised homosexual theme. Lape told Joseph Lash, the future first lady's devoted friend and biographer, that what she had considered a sensitive tale had repelled her friend. "She read it in terms of a forbidden subject," Lape recalled.[6] Years later, Eleanor's roommate at Allenswood almost half a century before sent her a fictionalized account of Marie Souvestre's love affair with her female partner in their French boarding school. The novel was written by a former student and later teacher at Allenswood with whom Eleanor Roosevelt had corresponded briefly. She thanked her old friend for sending the book, but she left no record of having contacted its author nor of how she reacted to the thinly veiled tale of homosexual love. Eleanor Roosevelt ignored few achievements by acquaintances, remained silent on few subjects, and reacted with intolerance to few aspects of human behavior. In this instance, however, her responses spoke volumes.

However circumscribed her understanding of her friends' private intimacies, she absorbed their lessons on public issues with eager enthusiasm. Read and Lape were her guides as she reluctantly accepted a position on the legislative committee of the New York League of Women Voters. She learned to address problems and critique legislative remedies, and she was soon serving on policy-making committees. Tactfully and effectively, she kept debates on track. Read and Lape were impressed. Eleanor returned their admiration and soon was spending pleasant evenings at their apartment near Washington Square discussing politics, reading classics aloud, and relishing informal social interchange.

By early winter 1921 Eleanor was selected to represent Dutchess County at a convention of the state league where social welfare, political reform, and legislative strategies dominated discussion. She played a significant role in drafting proposed laws for whose passage the league planned to lobby. In April she traveled to Cleveland for the organization's second national convention. It was a dramatic assembly at which sessions focused on the many issues that had already engaged the league: wage-and-hours regulations for women workers, child welfare, efficient government, the civic responsibility of women. With their eloquent pleas for an end to war, Carrie Chapman Catt and Cleveland lawyer Florence Allen galvanized the delegates. Catt's oration was a clarion call "to put war out of the world"; Allen introduced a motion on behalf of her peace plan to amend international law in order to criminalize war.

Few delegates had actually seen the ravages of war-torn Europe as Eleanor Roosevelt had, but the peace issue immediately struck receptive chords among the women. Their response was so strong that the local and later national league president, Belle Sherwin, encouraged the formation of a separate organization devoted solely to issues of war and peace and support for the League of Nations and the World Court. She feared that pacifist sentiment would subsume all other league efforts. Membership in the League of Women Voters and invigorated pacifist groups overlapped greatly, but the league remained multifaceted in its thrust. Eleanor did not formally enroll in the various antiwar organizations, but her commitment never wavered as the peace movement engaged an astounding degree of female support. It became to an even greater extent than the League of Women Voters the true inheritor of the prewar women's movement.[7]

Although she wrote reports and even made speeches for league groups after returning from Cleveland, Eleanor Roosevelt's attention turned to preparations for the summer at Campobello. Franklin planned to spend his first full summer since entering political life on the island, and Louis Howe was invited to join the family.

The summer began with the sunny pleasures of sailing, picnicking, and mapping political strategies. In August that secure and secluded interlude collapsed. After an outing and a swim, Franklin returned to the cottage cold, wet, and tired. He went to his room for a short rest but awakened complaining of aches. He had a fever and then felt severe pain and creeping paralysis. Three weeks elapsed before a definitive diagnosis of polio was made. Anxiety alternated with terror as Eleanor and Franklin both met the crisis with their individual kinds of courage. The patient managed to remain cheerful and optimistic in spite of growing pain and immobility. Eleanor nursed him with devotion and compassion that temporarily obliterated the hurt and resentment that had marked her feelings for the previous three years. Doctors and friends marveled at her zeal which was matched only by her competence as nurse, secretary, and family stabilizer. In spite of moments of anxiety and despair, Franklin's display of high spirits reassured the frightened and confused children. The outward behavior of both forced Sara, newly arrived from her annual sojourn in Europe, to follow their sterling example.

Upon the advice of doctors, Franklin was moved from the isolated island to Presbyterian Hospital in New York. It was a complex maneuver accompanied by purposeful distraction of the curious. Island residents carried a makeshift stretcher laden with the heavy patient two miles to the wharf. A motorboat continued the journey to the mainland where a private railroad car waited to complete the trip. The stretcher could not be carried on board but had to be hoisted in—and later out—through a window. Finally an ambulance drove the patient and his wife to the hospital. The expectation that treatment would result in recovery made the macabre trip tolerable. Instead almost two months later, Franklin Roosevelt was discharged with pain and paralysis virtually unchanged. Like his physical condition, transportation difficulties and public deception would become permanent features of his daily existence.

Eleanor Roosevelt later described the months that followed as the most trying winter of her life as she walked an emotional tightrope strung between her incapacitated husband, disoriented children, and manipulative mother-in-law. Only Louis Howe was close at hand to bolster her resolve and deflect some of Sara's fury when the plans she announced for her son's future were rebuffed. Howe moved into the family town house on Sixty-fifth Street when Franklin was discharged from the hospital. There he became part of Eleanor's familial problems as well as partner in masterminding Franklin's personal and political solutions.

In assigning limited living space, Eleanor gave her daughter Anna's bedroom to Louis. At fifteen, Anna reacted like any sensitive adolescent to an encroachment on her privacy and territory even though her mother was sleeping, without complaint, on a cot in one of her brothers' rooms. And the clash was exacerbated by Sara's maneuvering, as she fed Anna's resentment toward both her mother and Louis Howe.

The older woman had long used her grandchildren as a wedge for maintaining her position in the household. She spoiled them with gifts and blatantly overrode their parents' attempts at discipline. She referred to them as "my children," explaining on more than one occasion that their mother had only borne them. Now she used Anna in the battle over the direction of Franklin's future. She was determined that Franklin return to Hyde Park to lead the life of a leisured country squire, a comfortable, protected invalid much like his own father had been. His wife and his trusted aide were just as determined that the patient maintain his business and political contacts at the same time he strove to regain use of his legs. Franklin had his own moments of doubt and depression, but for the most part he was a full-fledged member of the determined triumvirate. But Sara did not concede defeat without fanning the flames of Anna's anger, encouraging her granddaughter to blame Eleanor and Louis for her resentment. The emotional alienation of Anna added to the other pressures and problems of the winter of 1922 that finally destroyed Eleanor's studied "serenity and composure." One evening while reading to the younger boys, she was suddenly overcome by a hysterical, uncontrollable torrent of tears, the "only time I remember in my entire life having gone to pieces in this particular manner."[8]

Mother and daughter eventually reconciled, building a close and loving bond. Mother-in-law and daughter-in-law pulled at the ties that had once bound them until they snapped. Eleanor had begun to chart a new course when she discovered Franklin's infidelity. The trial they both endured during his illness completed the process. Sara as well as Franklin would have to deal with a forty-year-old woman who was discovering new sources of strength and independence, regaining her balance and sense of purpose. She resolved to stand on her own two feet in regard to the lives of her husband and children as well as her own. Sara's place in this configuration was best described two decades later. After her mother-in-law's funeral, it was to Anna that Eleanor Roosevelt wrote, "I kept being appalled at myself because I couldn't feel any real grief or sense of loss and that seemed terrible after 36 years of fairly close association."[9] It was not the lack of feeling and grief that was terrible but rather the relationship between the two women.

Louis Howe's presence was a major factor in outmaneuvering Sara and in directing the courses both Eleanor and Franklin traveled during the years following the polio attack. Franklin was certain he would walk again and was determined to seek any remedy and follow any regimen that offered hope. Alternating between hospitals for therapy and brace fittings and warmer climates where sun and water seemed to salve his affliction, his absence from the public arena cast a pall over his political future. Eleanor filled the void, partially at Louis's insistence that she act as stand-in to maintain the visibility of the Roosevelt name, partially because she also understood the importance of independent activities to her own well-being. Besides, she had already proven herself as a capable worker during her stint with the League of Women Voters. She needed no introduction to the world of political issues, and welcomed expanding areas in which to exercise her growing store of impressive competence and energy.

Her activities extended in two directions—voluntary reform societies and clubs on the one hand, partisan politics on the other. Both spheres added to her circle of colleagues and devoted friends and to the reputation of the Democratic Roosevelts.

Among the organizations committed to social change was the Women's Trade Union League. Founded by upper- and middle-class reformers in 1903, the group was unique among Progressive Era women's groups in its explicit desire to build bridges of common purpose and equality between founding well-to-do activists and working-class women. The league not only pledged to assist female workers in unionizing but also insisted they be league members and hold leadership positions. For a decade, leagues in New York, Chicago, and Boston played crucial roles supporting bitter strikes involving thousands of women especially in the garment industry.

Hard-won victories, however, were often partial and temporary. New trade unions of working women seldom endured; improved working conditions reverted to earlier, exploitative patterns. And league members discovered that cross-class ties were difficult to build and maintain, for the habits of patronizing benevolence were not easily changed. Even more difficult to overcome was the neglect, even hostility, encountered at the hands of the male-dominated labor movement, which pledged support that never materialized. As historian Nancy Shrom Dye has shown, by 1913 the thrust of the league, especially its New York branch, moved from union organizing by women to support for legislation that was designed to improve and regulate the conditions of female labor.[10]

Although the New York Women's Trade Union League that Eleanor Roosevelt joined in 1922 was no longer the visionary, militant group of earlier years, its leaders were still committed to an ideal of industrial democracy and safety. Possibly women workers would find progress in trade unions, probably through legislation. Activists like socially prominent Mary Dreier and former cap-maker Rose Schneiderman had much to teach their novice member. Eleanor Roosevelt had met them briefly in 1919 on their way to Europe and now she became their avid student. League reports indicate that some of her activities lay within the earlier tradition of the lady bountiful—raising money for a clubhouse and hosting the annual Christmas party. But she also embraced the league's stance on legal remedies for unregulated working hours and abysmally low wages as well as its advocacy of the right of women to organize into trade unions. On a cold, cloudy December day in 1926, she joined three hundred striking paper-box makers on a protest march through the streets of Manhattan's Lower West Side.

Although the voluntary nonpartisan women's organizations were essential outlets for her continued concern for social welfare and justice, Eleanor Roosevelt was also substituting for an incapacitated Democratic politician whose social agenda was far less defined than his political ambitions. In early 1922, she was invited to speak on behalf of the newly organized women's division of the New York Democratic party. Her immediate reaction was to decline, but Franklin and Louis Howe persuaded her otherwise. In her first official appearance on behalf of the party, her appeal for funds was a great success. Partisan allegiance had begun.

At the same luncheon that launched her political career, she met Marion Dickerman and Nancy Cook. The women were intimate companions who shared a Greenwich Village apartment. Like Eleanor's friends Esther Lape and Elizabeth Read, Dickerman and Cook were college-educated women, veterans of the suffrage movement, proponents of child and women's labor laws, and advocates of peace; both had served as nurse orderlies overseas during the war. They had taught school and had tested their newly won political opportunities when Dickerman ran for the New York legislature and Cook managed her campaign. The ensuing defeat did not dim their enthusiasm for partisan politics. They found a ready convert and eager coworker in Eleanor Roosevelt.

Her new friends taught her the importance of local organization, lessons they had acquired during suffrage battles. First in New York counties and then at state headquarters, Eleanor concentrated on building a network of women's groups formed at the grass-roots level. The scope of her activities and her sphere of new friends expanded. She formed close ties with Caroline O'Day, with whom she toured the state, meeting local party leaders. With Elinor Morgenthau, wife of the Roosevelts' Dutchess County neighbor, Henry, she cochaired the finance committee, raising funds to give the women a base of independent action. She edited a newspaper to keep women abreast of issues, and, at Howe's insistence and with his coaching, she overcame her timidity to speak before public forums. By 1924, the sight and sound of Eleanor Roosevelt delivering a partisan message from a New York podium had become commonplace.

The constant activity succeeded in keeping the family name in the public domain, but even Howe was amazed at the recognition and acclaim it brought Eleanor Roosevelt in her own right. He marveled at the distance she had traveled since the days political rituals were disdained and he, himself, barely tolerated. In early 1924 state Democrats met in Syracuse to endorse a candidate for president at the upcoming national party convention. Eleanor Roosevelt and Henry Morgenthau led their county delegates in favor of the nomination of Governor Al Smith for president. Franklin remained at Hyde Park, where Howe wired him: "Al nominated with great enthusiasm. Morgenthau and your Missus led the Dutchess County delegation with the banner three times around the hall."[11] Twelve years earlier she had left a national convention in disgust over the circus atmosphere.

Moreover, five years before, she had hardly acknowledged women's right to vote. Now, at the Syracuse convention, she was leading the battle against party bosses on behalf of the right of women to join the men in selecting all delegates and alternates to the national conclave; furthermore she insisted half those chosen should be women. Her demands were met, the "only inharmonious note of the gathering so far," according to the *New York Times*.[12] The newspaper also printed much of a compelling speech she made to the female delegates on page one, above the fold! In her remarks she appraised the impact of suffrage and party leaders' reaction to the women's vote. Some women fall quickly into line and can be counted on just like men, she reported, while others are apathetic and can easily be discounted. The two major parties court only the smaller group of women who are informed and independent. Finally, she said, there is a "still smaller group [that] is working actively in the parties, trying to realize its hope and belief in the influence of women." It will be an uphill fight, she concluded, to earn the right and respect of men within the party, to work with them rather than for them, especially when women cause controversy. Her evaluation was as firmly grounded in personal experience as in political realities.

Campaigning for the presidential nomination, Al Smith invited Franklin Roosevelt to deliver his nominating speech when Democrats invaded New York's Madison Square Garden for their convention. Eleanor received an invitation, too. She accepted a request from party managers to chair a women's subcommittee to conduct hearings and suggest planks to the official platform committee.

While William McAdoo and Alfred Smith battled each other for delegates at the convention, Democratic wets and drys fought over the merits of Prohibition, and party stalwarts debated the stance they should adopt toward an invigorated Ku Klux Klan. Simultaneously Eleanor Roosevelt held hearings to determine the resolutions her advisory group would present. The planks that emerged underscored the issues that engaged the reform-minded women of the 1920s. Her subcommittee called for vigorous enforcement of Prohibition and for ratification of the Child Labor Amendment, although neither proposal had the support of Smith. The women's planks also demanded increased appropriations to the Children's and Women's bureaus of the Department of Labor as well as expanded services under the Shepard-Towner Act. That landmark legislation designed to aid mothers and infants was the first federal health and welfare program in the nation's history. It had been passed after intense lobbying by women's reform organizations, which continued to monitor its precarious existence, funding, and implementation.

The suggested planks of the women's subcommittee moved beyond social welfare reforms and advised that the party affirm its support for the right of workers to organize unions and to bargain collectively in good faith with their employers. Only during the war had the federal government made such a commitment and then primarily to ensure undisrupted production levels. Finally the women agreed on a plank that highlighted the timidity of Klan opponents who demurred in challenging overt bigotry. In the document they prepared, the members of the subcommittee clearly spelled out their opposition "to the attempts of organizations or individuals to create prejudice against groups of citizens because of race, color or religion as detrimental to American institutions and national progress."

The progressive thrust of the women's proposals was ignored behind the closed doors of the official platform committee. Eleanor Roosevelt had learned much about partisan politics in four short years, but with her inability to gain entrance into the inner sanctums of decision making and power at the national level, she personalized the warnings she had expressed earlier to her colleagues on the state level. She "was to see for the first time where women stood when it came to a national convention," she later wrote. "They stood outside the door of all important meetings and waited."[13]

The rebuff to Eleanor Roosevelt did not obscure the brief but memorable reentrance of her husband into the political arena. In his first public appearance since his illness, FDR dragged his steel-encased legs to the podium with the help of a cane and the strong arm of his son James. Once steadied, he delivered his "happy warrior" nominating speech on Al Smith's behalf. The delegates on the floor and the guests in the galleries responded with affection and enthusiasm for the speaker if not for his candidate. In the end the convention deadlocked after 102 ballots. In the stifling August heat of Madison Square, Democrats turned to John W. Davis, a Wall Street lawyer whose political positions were scarcely distinguishable from those of his Republican opponent. Franklin Roosevelt took no part in the campaign that followed, returning once more to the obscurity that cloaked his desperate attempt to walk again. He had four more lean years to go.

Unlike some disappointed Democrats such as her friend Caroline O'Day, Eleanor did not desert the ticket for Progressive party candidate Robert La Follette. Instead she threw her energy and convictions behind Smith's reelection campaign for governor of New York. At the state convention, the platform committee listened more attentively and incorporated as planks her call for ratification of the Child Labor Amendment and regulations for working women. She seconded Smith's nomination and worked at party headquarters on his behalf. "And so," she wrote later, "ended the early phases of the education of Eleanor Roosevelt, both in life and politics."[14]

At the time, however, no break in the flurry of her reform and political activity was obvious except for a decidedly more partisan stance. Prior to the national convention, Eleanor had joined the New York Women's City Club. A number of these organizations had formed in American cities at the height of the prewar women's movement. Members were upper-class society leaders and middle-class professional women who identified, publicized, and devised public policy responses to civic and social problems. Purposefully nonpartisan, Eleanor, who eventually chaired its legislative committee, encountered political divisiveness over her committee's proposals to address social issues and to reorganize state government offices and election procedures. In the process she formed ties with the most prominent, capable, and socially conscious women in New York on projects that paralleled many of the undertakings of the League of Women Voters. In committee work, debates, and speeches, her skills were further enhanced along with a reputation for patience and fairness toward those with whom she did not agree.

The 1927 legislative agenda of the Women's City Club bore the decidedly Democratic party stamp of its committee chair. She had inherited a varied program that included regulation of child marriages, testing for venereal disease prior to the issuance of marriage licenses, compulsory education in American history and civics, and effective monitoring of motion pictures. Although Eleanor Roosevelt was not opposed to legislative proposals that carried heavy moral and patriotic overtones, her attention centered on reforms to alternate gubernatorial and presidential elections in the state, a stringent maximum-work-week bill for women workers, maintenance of the fourteen-year-old minimum age law for working boys, and compulsory school attendance.

Within a year the thrust of her committee endorsements was modified. Historian Elisabeth Perry suggests that Eleanor, who may have encountered open opposition from Republican members of the bipartisan Women's City Club, was acknowledging that the direction of political and social changes to which she was drawn did not always coincide with the educational, nonpartisan stance of women's organizations like the WCC and the League of Women Voters. "On the whole, the Democratic Party seems to have been more concerned with the welfare and interests of the people at large," she wrote in a league bulletin.[15] In the aftermath of their suffrage victory, politically active women traveled two distinct paths, one inside the partisan arena, the other issue-oriented and politically nonaligned. During the mid-1920s, Eleanor moved comfortably in both camps.

At the conclusion of one WCC meeting, she was introduced briefly to Mary "Molly" Dewson, who was serving as civic secretary for the club. She had been superintendent of parole for girls in Massachusetts and had also done considerable research and lobbying on behalf of state minimum wage legislation for the Consumers' League. Within a short period of time, the two women formed a firm friendship and working relationship that eventually had great impact on the roles of Democratic women in New York and later in the federal government.

While Eleanor Roosevelt's circle of activist friends grew immeasurably in a few short years, the focus of her intense personal relationships contracted. By 1925, Nancy Cook and Marion Dickerman stood at the center of her emotional universe. They above all others gave her the love, comfort, and understanding she sought. On brief excursions with Franklin to Florida during winters, Eleanor missed her friends and expressed her longing for their company with intensity. "I would be having such a good time if you two & my little boys were along & as it is I've just tried hard to forget how much I am missing you," she wrote Marion.[16]

Franklin liked his wife's new companions and appreciated the role they had come to play in her life. They were bright, politically sophisticated women with well-defined social concerns. He enjoyed their company and took their ideas seriously. On one outing on the Hyde Park grounds, he offered his wife, Dickerman, and Cook a lifetime lease of land by the Val-Kill Brook. The three women accepted his proposal to build a cottage of their own in which they could live together and could use as they wished, especially when the big house—Sara's house—was closed for the winter.

Franklin himself supervised much of the design and construction of the cottage. By April 1926 the women were comfortably settled in their private retreat. Cook, who had taught crafts and was especially skilled in handiwork, built the furniture for the cottage. The results were so successful that a full-scale business venture followed. With capital from the three women and Caroline O'Day, a small-scale factory with Cook in charge hired young local men to create handmade replicas of fine wood pieces. Their first commission came from Franklin, who ordered furniture for his planned venture in Warm Springs, Georgia.

Marion Dickerman taught classes and served as vice-principal at Todhunter School in Manhattan. The private school for girls embraced the latest methods advanced by the advocates of progressive education. At her invitation, Eleanor began to teach at the school several days a week. Her classes in civics and American history were popular with the girls, whose enthusiasm for their teacher was exceeded by hers for them. She adored teaching, an activity that invoked the memory of her beloved headmistress among the other pleasures it brought. With her own funds, she made it possible for Marion to purchase the school.

During this time, while spending his winters sailing and fishing the waters around Key West, Franklin happened upon a run-down spa in Georgia. Convinced that he felt motion in his legs as he maneuvered in the waters there, he was determined to buy the land, the pools, and the dilapidated inn. For an authentic American aristocrat, his personal wealth was not impressive. Sara held the inherited purse strings, as she had reminded him at the time of the Lucy Mercer affair. His earnings were modest after he returned to law practice—his partners thought little of his abilities as a lawyer whether or not he could walk. He had invested in a number of speculative ventures like many fellow Americans during the 1920s and had not reaped untoward rewards. It was a mark of his desperate search for a cure and his disregard for money management that he did not hesitate to part with his limited capital to purchase properties at Warm Springs.

In addition to the financial uncertainties, Eleanor Roosevelt had serious misgivings about her husband's plans for a therapeutic center in Georgia. His political fortunes might be compromised, too. "Georgia is somewhat distant for you to keep in touch with what is really a big undertaking," she wrote to him.[17] Personal distaste also underlay her lack of enthusiasm. She simply did not like Warm Springs any more than she had enjoyed the trips to Florida. Once Franklin held resolutely to his decision, she found all sorts of excuses to spend as little time at the resort as possible.

Distance added another dimension to the complex marital arrangement Eleanor and Franklin were fashioning. With her husband absent from home for long periods of time, she had to play father as well as mother, especially to the younger boys. She took them to Groton each fall, traveled to parent-oriented gatherings, and met with teachers and counselors. Although she had always shunned athletic activities, she finally mastered swimming. She learned to drive, and although her frequent automobile mishaps caused both family laughter and concern, she took the boys on motor tours and camping trips. Her women friends usually came along as guides and companions. Although Franklin had rarely mediated between his wife and his mother, his absence exacerbated their growing conflicts. Daughter Anna married now at the age of twenty, mostly to escape the tension between the two women. Eleanor handled all the engagement and wedding arrangements as well as her personal misgivings about Anna's decision alone.

Somehow, however, in the wake of the emotional and geographic separations, Eleanor and Franklin slowly built a creative and productive political marriage. Common vision and interests forged a bond of shared work that compensated for lost intimacy and trust. Admiration grew and affection endured, although Eleanor expressed her feelings of solicitude more openly in writing than in action. Letters from Anna indicate her father used her as a conduit to convince Eleanor to join him in Warm Springs. Eleanor resisted. James recalled that his father often held out his arms to his wife; she kept her distance. At Hyde Park there was no pretense. If appearances had to be maintained, she entertained at the "big house" and slept overnight. But Val-Kill was her home, where Nan and Marion filled the need for the emotional support and understanding she failed to get or refused to accept from Franklin.

The cottage was the tangible symbol of the redefined independent Eleanor Roosevelt. It represented full emancipation from Sara and nineteenth-century upper-class standards. It represented the emotional distance she willfully created from Franklin in the aftermath of discovered infidelity. It represented the world of female competence, intimacy, and encouragement so necessary to fill the void left by the renunciation of social certainties and marital love. At Val-Kill Eleanor Roosevelt joined her initial with those of Nancy Cook and Marion Dickerman in a coat of arms more meaningful than any emblems to which the Roosevelts lay claim. Although she still sought the sage advice of Louis Howe and her husband on political matters and maintained ties to Franklin on her own terms, the cottage was where she lived and learned and loved. The cottage was the home she had never known before.

These women with whom she lived and others with whom she worked were the emotional mainstay of her recovery and redefinition. Eleanor Roosevelt needed love; she craved affection. She was also compelled to love in return, and her new friends gloried in the intensity of the attention and affection she showered on them. They also learned quickly that intimacy and caring were not necessarily doled out in equal proportions. Marion Dickerman described the pecking order of the 1920s to Joseph Lash, who would stand at the center of Eleanor Roosevelt's "world of love" a decade later: "Esther and Elizabeth were closer to Eleanor than Rose [Schneiderman of the WTUL] but not as close as Nan and I were, particularly Nan, whom Eleanor loved. . . . Eleanor loved me but not with the devotion that she had for Nan. I was not jealous." Lash could identify with the complex dynamic Dickerman described. He too would relinquish center stage and admitted more frankly than Marion when his turn came, "I was jealous."[18]

The political challenges of 1928 highlighted the shared interests and divergent paths of the Roosevelts. Both remained fervent supporters of Al Smith for the presidency, seeing him as the best hope for advancing the progressive tradition. Smith, in turn, courted them both assiduously. Eleanor had become a valued ally, publicizing his virtues and traveling to Albany with her coterie of experts to lobby a recalcitrant legislature on behalf of the governor's bills. Her testimony advocating government restructuring and legislation to limit working women's hours to forty-eight hours a week was well informed and delivered in straightforward terms. When invited to contribute an article to the *North American Review* explaining "Why Democrats Back Smith," she was delighted to comply. But the picture she drew of Smith as a "practical idealist" was not very convincing. She could not help betraying some of her misgivings over the governor's refusal to endorse the Child Labor Amendment at the same time he opposed Prohibition. It was she who was truly the practical idealist, a woman with firm political convictions who also realized an ally might very well deviate from some of them. Smith shared most of her positions and was far preferable to a more conservative Democratic candidate, let alone a Republican.

Franklin Roosevelt's role was more passive and reflected Smith's cynical calculations. A symbol of the rural patrician, Roosevelt could soften the harsher urban, parochial image that clung to Smith, the ambitious son of Irish immigrants. Franklin delivered a second stirring nominating speech at the party's national convention in Houston while Eleanor remained behind at Hyde Park. Their delight in Smith's first-ballot victory was quickly tempered, however, by the candidate's appointment of John J. Raskob as chair of the Democratic National Committee. Catholic, wet, and an executive with Du Pont, Raskob seemed to reinforce all Smith's political weaknesses, adding the onus of "big business" besides.

In spite of her disappointment over Smith's choice of advisers, Eleanor Roosevelt accepted an invitation to codirect the Women's Division of the national office. In July she moved into party headquarters. She organized committees to court special female constituencies: college students, working women, business and professional women, independents. While personally answering hundreds of letters each week with the help of secretaries, she oversaw the activities of publicity committees and speakers' bureaus. One new secretarial recruit was Malvina Thompson, who became her personal secretary during the campaign. "Tommy" remained an indefatigable worker and devoted friend for the rest of her life. Another newcomer, Grace Tully, chafed at the rigors of Eleanor's schedule. After the election, she joined Franklin's camp with undisguised delight.

The pace at headquarters was staggering. "I worked till 4:30 a.m. on account of the radio speech this morning," Eleanor wrote Franklin at Warm Springs. "Tonight I go to speak at Beacon & spend the night with Elinor & Henry [Morgenthau] & return to New York tomorrow but go to Hyde Park with Miss Thompson Sat. night!" Work was also discouraging. Smith's popularity in New York was not easily exported beyond state lines. His anti-Prohibition stance rankled; his Catholicism frightened; his radio voice irritated. "If I needed anything to show me what prejudice can do to the intelligence of human beings," she wrote twenty years later, "that campaign was the best lesson I could have had."[19]

Smith knew his chances were nil without a victory in his home state. He and his advisers turned to FDR, certain that the still-popular upstater could win the governor's race and carry the top of the ticket with him. Franklin was both reluctant to renounce his therapy and buoyed by the opportunity to reenter the political fray. He fenced with the pleading callers from Albany. Eleanor's role in his final decision is problematic, but in the end he allowed his name to be placed in nomination. The seven years of self-imposed exile were over. Significantly, Eleanor remained at national headquarters. Franklin crisscrossed the state with his own staff and advisers. When a reporter asked her to assess her husband's chances on the eve of the election, she replied with unusual abruptness. "I don't know the state situation. I haven't been active with the state. I feel sure the Governor [Smith] is going to win, though."[20] Only on the last statewide campaign swing did she join her husband's campaign train.

In spite of Smith's predictable defeat, her own political reputation soared. But with Franklin's victory, she had to decide what direction, if any, she would follow. Her activities as stand-in had yielded unexpected personal dividends, but the wife of an elected official was expected to play far less public and partisan roles. Prior to FDR's election, she notified the state Democrats that she could no longer serve in official capacities. Once the votes were counted, she resigned from the League of Women Voters and the Women's Trade Union League. She reordered her priorities. She would fulfill the social responsibilities of New York's first family; she would oversee the boys' progress at Groton and Harvard; she would continue to support Nancy Cook's factory at Val-Kill and the annual show and sale of crafted products; she would continue to teach three days each week at Todhunter School.

The ways in which she reordered her activities, like the delight with which Grace Tully had moved from the employ of one Roosevelt to another, dramatized the distinct paths Eleanor and Franklin traveled. Separate entourages surrounded each. When the new governor took up residence in Albany, Marguerite "Missy" LeHand moved into the rambling red brick mansion along with the rest of the family. LeHand, a bright, handsome, outgoing woman, worked for the Democratic National Committee in 1920. When that disastrous campaign was over, FDR hired her as his personal secretary. After her boss's polio attack and his purchase of the Warm Springs properties, she became the house-keeper-hostess-secretary there as Eleanor, who disliked the spa, found reasons to stay away. Similar division of duties continued in Albany. Eleanor Roosevelt took the train to Manhattan every Sunday evening to meet her classes at the Todhunter School and did not return until Wednesday afternoon. If an official function was scheduled in her absence, Missy served as hostess in addition to her other duties. Grace Tully followed her example; she was dedicated and hard-working to the point of self-denial. Franklin's fishing buddies and growing circle of intellectual advisers added to his clique.

The new first lady's camp included Cook and Dickerman, with whom she still lived at the cottage, as well as working with them when time permitted. Tommy Schneider stayed on as her secretary after the 1928 campaign. As the first lady of New York, she was assigned a chauffeur, an affable, good-looking state trooper, Earl Miller, who accepted his assignment with the hoots of his fellow troopers ringing in his ears. Driving the governor's wife on her various trips was not a highly prized duty. Like so many others who entered her charmed circle, however, he soon became a devoted admirer and solicitous friend. He taught Eleanor Roosevelt to ride horses and to shoot the unloaded revolver the Secret Service insisted she carry; he accompanied her on enough social engagements to cause raised eyebrows. At one point Eleanor even introduced him to Missy LeHand when gossip about the close relationship between the governor and his secretary also surfaced. Tongues continued to wag until Miller married. FDR made a point of attending the wedding ceremony and posing for pictures with the new bride and groom. Several wives entered and departed Miller's complicated romantic life, but his friendship with Eleanor Roosevelt and her affection for him kept him a member of her circle.

To outsiders the two camps presented a united front. Secretaries joined children and grandchildren at the dinner table like members of the family. Eleanor often shopped for Missy's clothes and attended LeHand family occasions. Marion and Nan retained their personal fondness and political enthusiasm for the governor and later president. But the individuals themselves knew where their loyalties lay and drew clear and steadfast lines in terms of devoted service. Only Louis Howe remained sincerely loyal to both and retained their trust in equal measure.

Although she guarded her own sphere of friends and activities, Eleanor Roosevelt was hardly uninterested in the political affairs of New York or her husband's potential impact on them. She encouraged Franklin's efforts to put his own stamp on his appointments, to circumvent Smith's intention to play puppeteer in the new administration. Discharging Smith's close aide Robert Moses was accomplished with dispatch. He was one of the few public officials whom FDR truly loathed. Dealing with Smith's loyal adviser and confidante Belle Moskowitz was a more delicate matter, but Eleanor's insistence sealed Moskowitz's fate. She knew capable women who would serve Franklin's needs without divided loyalties. Molly Dewson suggested that Consumers' League activist Frances Perkins be appointed labor commissioner, and Eleanor arranged the meeting with Franklin where Dewson made her case. It marked the opening salvo in a campaign conducted by the two friends to enlist women into positions of responsibility in government. Although Eleanor Roosevelt always understated the impact she had on this process, she had quickly realized the leverage one gained from easy access to the seat of power, and she cleared the path for colleagues who had issues to discuss and candidates to promote.

Her avowed renunciation of political and voluntary reform activity was short-lived. Effectively and anonymously, she directed publication of the party newspaper and wrote the editorials. With Franklin's encouragement she attended party functions across the state, walking the thin line between innocuous speech making and policy advocacy. She accompanied Franklin on inspections of state facilities and conducted the fact-finding on her own, following her husband's explicit, hardheaded instructions. And she also undertook investigations on her own, mastering techniques of examination and reporting.

Women's magazines discovered she made good copy. Interviewers sought her out as the "ideal type of modern wife." The unconventional complexities of her personal relationships did not deter her from answering such questions as "What is a wife's job today?" or sharing "ten rules for success in marriage." Interviewers even printed her replies with her characteristic exclamation points. "Marriage! If only more of us would see that it is a partnership in which neither can succeed without the other and that the success of both depends upon the success of each!" An ideal wife must develop her own interests not only so that she would be a good companion to her husband but also so that she would not smother her children. As for newlyweds, they should live apart and free from parental advice. In the end, a successful relationship rested on character, self-control, honest self-assessment, the ability to "meet things squarely, to put yourself through any real difficult situation without self-pity and without weakening in the main purpose of your life."[21]

The readers of *Pictorial Review* could hardly grasp the revelations behind the "rules": the reconstituted terms of her own marriage, the veiled rebuff to her mother-in-law, and especially the sheer willpower and determination with which she had fought despair to a draw over the past decade. She suggested that the spirit of courtship be kept alive: not love, romance, and intimacy but rather "that thoughtfulness which existed before marriage." The partnership she advocated was precariously balanced in her own life. On the eve of the gubernatorial election in 1930, she snapped at a reporter who asked about her feelings as the candidate's wife: "In this particular case, at any event, the candidate's wife will go on pursuing the even tenor of her ways. Politics does not excite me. It never did. I take things as they come. If my husband is reelected, I shall be pleased. And if he isn't—well, the world is full of interesting things to do."[22]

Denials aside, politics did excite her, and she was not indifferent to FDR's political fate. She had completed her apprenticeship and was a full-fledged master of the trade. A late convert to progressive reform, she eagerly embraced the social welfare proposals of her female friends and coworkers. Within the issue-oriented nonpartisan women's organizations, she learned how to collect information, publicize facts, and lobby those who wielded political power. But unlike many female activists in the postsuffrage era, she joined her programs and her skills to intense partisanship. She was an ardent Democrat, and within the party, she learned the promise and frustrations of American political realities. The New York legislature taught tolerance for compromise and gradualism; Al Smith taught the necessity and strains of uneasy alliances.

Franklin Roosevelt was reelected with a quarter-million-vote margin. A lackluster opponent, a Prohibition party candidate who appealed to Republican drys, and the growing ramifications of economic collapse all contributed to the impressive victory. So did the Women's Division of the state Democratic party with Eleanor behind the scenes orchestrating meetings, speeches, and publicity with her efficient, effective network of erstwhile teachers.

Her political expertise did not go unnoticed outside the hard-working sanctum of the Women's Division. The *New Yorker* considered her worthy of a "Profile." Subtitled "Noblesse Oblige," the article outlined her political heritage as a Roosevelt and her wide range of activities over the previous decade. The author contrasted her prominence as a "woman leader" with that of Belle Moskowitz, a hard-boiled woman thought of as a capable politician "without reference to sex." Written by a feminist and member of the National Women's party, the comparison was not meant to be entirely complimentary to New York's first lady. But the writer gave Eleanor Roosevelt credit as an extremely able executive and a shrewd tactician who "has a better grasp of the intricacies of state business [than Smith's former adviser, the renowned reformer Lillian Wald] and she has a decided flair for putting things aptly."[23]

Former muckraker and fervent antisuffragist Ida Tarbell visited the executive mansion in Albany to interview New York's first lady soon after the second term began. She found nothing to criticize, drew no comparisons. Tarbell marveled at the grace with which Eleanor Roosevelt grafted "acquired 'rights' on fine feminine traditions" in a deft, quiet, efficient blending of the old and the new. Her hostess taught school, was an expert on children's literature, performed all the social duties of a governor's wife, and responded to pleas and requests from "multitudes of people of New York State [who] regard Mrs. Roosevelt as their particular friend at court." So much activity, Tarbell gushed, and "all free from hustle and hurry."[24] The interviewer was not inaccurate, just incomplete. Only Eleanor Roosevelt's closest friends knew how carefully and painfully the aura of serenity and competence had been constructed. But not even they detected the emotional storm clouds gathering on the horizon.

Franklin Roosevelt's impressive victory propelled him into the front ranks of Democratic presidential candidates. "This prospect did not interest me particularly but it did interest his political supporters,"[25] she later wrote. Despite this disclaimer, it did interest her, but in terrifying ways. Her interview with Tarbell indicated how successfully she had negotiated and outmaneuvered the visibility of the executive mansion and the conventional duties of a governor's wife. Surely the glare of national publicity and the traditional role played by first ladies in Washington could not be so easily finessed. If her husband achieved his ultimate goals, what would happen to hers? How could she preserve the autonomy she had so painfully and carefully established? How could she advance a social agenda to which she was committed and utilize the political skills she had acquired? Never had a potential first lady appeared on the national scene with comparable experience and an independent political base. Would the social conventions she had so deliberately cast aside triumph after all?

4

THE FIRST LADY AND
THE GREAT DEPRESSION

By the time Franklin Roosevelt considered a second term as governor of New York, signs of the impending economic turmoil were clear. In March 1930, the Little Church Around the Corner in mid-Manhattan had opened a soup kitchen. Two thousand hungry men waited patiently in a single line that stretched five blocks from the door of the church on Twenty-ninth Street up Fifth Avenue. Because more fortunate New Yorkers strolling the elegant street were offended by the sight, police condensed the human chain to three abreast so that the men would occupy only Twenty-ninth Street. When the well-intentioned church ran out of food, hundreds of the unfed quietly dispersed.

By summer 1930, Roosevelt had toured the state and already confirmed that the depression was not confined to a few of the larger cities but extended to all of the smaller cities and the villages and rural districts as well. He had no specific remedies but announced to the legislative session that convened after his inauguration that a government representing modern society has an obligation to prevent the starvation and the dire want of any of its fellow men and women who try but cannot maintain themselves. His wife shared that philosophy.

FDR sought the Democratic nomination for president as well as another stint in Albany. His aides, who fanned out across the country to assess his strength and develop convention strategy, discovered that economic distress was hardly confined to New York. By late 1931, the gross national product had already fallen by 25 percent in two years. The average rate of unemployment, which was 3.2 percent in 1929, soared to 16.3. Farm prices, which had remained weak throughout the 1920s, continued to skid while distress and unrest among farm families rose. Middle-class Americans were more likely to feel the growing economic disaster as their savings evaporated in failed banks. From mid-1929 to July 1930, 640 banks closed their doors, and during the next twelve months another 1,553 failed. However dramatic the statistical measures of collapse, the worst was yet to come.

For an ambitious politician the 1932 Democratic presidential nomination was worth fighting for, and FDR's campaign advisers weighed the impact of depression on his political fortunes. They also displayed genuine interest in the Women's Division of the party. The party chairman, James A. Farley, accepted the view of state politicians that Eleanor Roosevelt was an influential figure in her own right. As the wife of an avowed candidate, however, her activities had to be carefully orchestrated far from the limelight. Molly Dewson served as her surrogate, as capable an organizer and campaigner as any party or candidate would want. Dewson looked like a dour New England schoolteacher, but she was a shrewd, determined political activist whose appearance masked Irish spirit and humor. She and Farley got along famously as she moved into party headquarters.

Eleanor Roosevelt was purposefully relegated to less visible activities. She spoke in out-of-the-way spots around New York where she was invited by those who felt she understood their hopes and needs and so, therefore she had a duty to speak to them. As the time for the convention drew closer, she traveled more widely, especially through the South. Her speeches were inspirational and nonpolitical, like the articles she was invited to contribute to magazines—"Building Character," "Ideal Education," "Good Citizenship." But occasionally the groups she faced wanted specific details about her husband's political plans and policies, and especially the perennial flaps over Tammany Hall corruption in New York City. She answered questions and diffused misgivings with consummate skill, even though she herself did not always agree with her husband's stands. He waffled on the United States's joining the World Court and he opposed Prohibition, but she put the best possible face forward despite personal disagreement.

The road to the Chicago convention during the summer of 1932 was tortuous for Franklin Roosevelt and his supporters. As the depression extended its relentless grip over the American economy, favorite sons from a dozen states leaped at the chance for a nomination that would lead to almost certain victory. The new speaker of the House of Representatives, John Nance Garner of Texas, had won the important California primary. And Al Smith with undisguised bitterness believed he had earned and deserved another reach for the gold ring. Deft Roosevelt managers had pledges of a majority of delegates, but two-thirds were needed for the nomination. A first-ballot victory was out of the question; even the final outcome was uncertain.

As the convention approached Eleanor Roosevelt became withdrawn and uninterested. When the actual balloting began, she paid more attention to the comfort of the newsmen gathered in the garage of the executive mansion in Albany than to the news of three deadlocked votes in the Chicago auditorium. A full day passed before William Gibbs McAdoo, Al Smith's nemesis in 1924, released the California delegation and assured Roosevelt's nomination. The extended family assembled in Albany embraced and celebrated. Eleanor Roosevelt scrambled eggs in the midst of the euphoria. Only a reporter for Associated Press, Lorena Hickok, sensed that her official hostess and future first lady was disquieted by the events swirling around her.

Eleanor Roosevelt dreaded the inevitable spotlight that would shine on the president's family. She was convinced that all their actions would become part of the public domain while her own activities would be necessarily curtailed. Years after her fears had proved unfounded and she had revolutionized the role of first lady, she still recalled: "I knew what traditionally should lie before me; I had watched Mrs. Theodore Roosevelt and had seen what it meant to be the wife of a president, and I cannot say that I was pleased with the prospect. By earning my own money, I had recently enjoyed a certain amount of financial independence and had been able to do things in which I was personally interested. The turmoil in my heart and mind was rather great that night, and the next few months were not to make any clearer what the road ahead would be."[1]

She had good reason to fear that her hard-won autonomy would be compromised. Even closer at hand than the example of Aunt Edith was the present first lady, Lou Henry Hoover. As a young woman at the turn of the century, Hoover had majored in geology at Stanford University and translated classic works in the field from Latin. She had matched her husband's more renowned organizational skills when, after bicycling around China in the midst of the 1912 revolution, she formed a committee to assist stranded Americans returning home. But the social demands and traditions of Washington had stilled the earlier effervescence. Eleanor Roosevelt had little reason to believe she would escape Lou Hoover's fate. In a moment of incredible loss of control, she wrote to Nan and Marion, who were monitoring FDR's progress at the convention in Chicago. She would not become first lady! She would not oversee foolish White House social events! She would run away with Earl Miller—even though he was about to be married. The horrified women shared the letter with Louis Howe. He tore the paper to bits, pledged the two women to secrecy, and prayerfully wagered that this woman he knew so well would recover her self-discipline.

Gradually Eleanor Roosevelt confessed her anxieties to Lorena Hickok. The AP reporter was assigned to the campaign train to cover the candidate and his family. She was a mini-mountain of a woman, five feet eight inches tall, almost two hundred pounds, plainly dressed, professionally successful. She had escaped an abusive father at the age of fourteen, one year after her mother's death. On her own she managed to alternate school and menial jobs, saving enough money to register at a nearby university. The pattern persisted as college classes were first abandoned for newspaper work and then resumed. For many years she shared the life and love of a devoted friend in Minneapolis, but when her companion walked out abruptly, a devastated Hickok made her way alone to New York. Talent and drive earned her a respected position with the wire service. Journalistic competence and a harsh exterior masked the keen sensitivity that allowed her, alone of all those who celebrated FDR's achievement, to sense the quiet despair of the candidate's wife.

When the official campaign began, the two women shared much time and railroad car space. Interviews gave way to informal conversations that evolved into soul-searching, intimate confessionals. Hick, as she came to be called, became the new emotional core of Eleanor Roosevelt's world, to whom she poured out her apprehensions over what lay ahead. As she articulated her anxieties, some of the reluctance and fear evaporated and was replaced with a renewed sense of purpose and possibility. Behind the scenes she continued to plan and direct the activities of the Women's Division. They wrote and printed millions of copies of bright-colored "rainbow flyers," as they were called, which were distributed through committeewomen in every state and county. The brochures succinctly introduced the candidate and described his program. The latter was a challenge. Franklin Roosevelt was a canny politician bent on gaining the presidency. His speeches were tailored to particular audiences, and consistency was a frequent casualty. Even committed backers wondered at times if FDR had a program at all. Pledges of a new deal for the American people seemed strangely at odds with calls for government austerity. But the hard-working Women's Division never wavered.

Democratic women proved such effective campaigners that Republicans were forced to follow suit. Lou Hoover was even persuaded to make campaign appearances. Alice Roosevelt Longworth needed no coaxing to campaign vigorously against Cousin Franklin. Theodore Roosevelt's widow cut short a trip abroad to address a huge Republican rally at Madison Square Garden. The Oyster Bay clan never wavered in their political loyalties even though Eleanor was one of their own.

In spite of her day-to-day involvement with the campaign, the ambivalence with which Eleanor Roosevelt watched her husband gain the presidency persisted. With a curious mixture of partisan gratification and personal uncertainty, she admitted to Hickok, "For him, of course, I'm glad—sincerely." Then she added, "I couldn't really have wanted it to go the other way. I am a Democrat, too. Being a Democrat, I believe this change is for the better."

"And now—I shall have to work out my own salvation."[2]

At first she sought a solution as a traditional helpmate, as subordinate member of a husband-wife partnership. She offered Franklin her assistance with the voluminous mail she knew would flood the White House. He declined, explaining that Missy LeHand would find her presence an encroachment on Missy's responsibilities. Eleanor admitted she had known it would have been an unsuitable arrangement, "but it was a last effort to keep in close touch and to feel that I had a real job to do."[3] This "last effort" was a tentative interlude when the new first lady was still certain that the White House would become a prison. Her offer also seems to have been a thinly disguised plea for renewed intimacy between husband and wife: a decade of political activism—much of it behind the scenes—surely had convinced Eleanor that there were many ways to keep abreast of public affairs and "in close touch" other than handling mail. The offer and the rebuff served to highlight the emotional complexities of their marriage.

Lorena Hickok supported Eleanor Roosevelt in the search for real jobs and the discovery that the White House need not be the inhibiting place she feared. Gradually she replaced Cook and Dickerman at the center of Eleanor's emotional universe. The two earlier friends remained close, but their attachment to FDR and their stake in a Democratic victory prevented Eleanor from sharing her anxieties with them. Hickok now filled the need for someone to whom she could bare her soul, which had become such effective therapy for her sense of self-worth over the last decade. "I never talked to anyone," she confessed to her new confidante. "Perhaps that was why it all ate into my soul, & I look upon so many emotions more seriously than the younger generation. In other words, I was a morbid idiot for many years! Only in the last ten years or so have I made friends to whom I have talked."[4]

By the time of the presidential inauguration, she had regained her poise. As the nation was mandated to conquer its fears, she conquered hers. Hick had assured her she could once again fashion a life of public achievement to compensate for private hurts. The day before the official ceremony, Eleanor took Hick to a cemetery where she had sat in disillusioned despair in the aftermath of the Lucy Mercer affair. As they both stared at the Saint-Gaudens statue that Henry Adams had commissioned to memorialize his deceased wife, she confessed to her friend, "In the old days when we lived here, I was much younger and not so very wise. Sometimes I'd be very unhappy and sorry for myself. When I was feeling that way, if I could manage, I'd come here alone, and sit and look at that woman. And I'd always come away somehow feeling better."[5] On this historic occasion the statue and her new friend had the same comforting effect.

Simultaneously, an entire nation was seeking comfort and assurance. The winter of Eleanor Roosevelt's discontent was mirrored by an American economy limping toward paralysis. All the standards of measure signaled disaster as the interregnum dragged on. Initial efforts of industrial leaders to maintain wage levels had collapsed. Manufacturing and mining production levels followed suit, increasing the numbers of jobless and reducing the pay scales of those who hung on to their jobs. No one knew the exact scope of unemployment, but a few argued that, at best, a quarter of the labor force was out of work. Tent cities, "Hoovervilles," dotted the urban landscape. The more mobile rode the rails as an army of hoboes populated the railroad embankments of the nation. American farmers had no problems maintaining production. They harvested bumper crops and watched price levels plummet. Across the Great Plains, debtor farmers planted their seed, prayed they would not be dispossessed before it was time to harvest, and nursed resentment bordering on rebellion. And the country's banking system was in shambles along with private charities and local relief agencies.

As a female journalist, Lorena Hickok was acutely aware of the price depression was exacting. She was particularly sensitive to the precarious professional circumstances of her colleagues. "People were losing their jobs on every hand, and unless the women reporters could find something new to write about, the chances were that some of them would hold their jobs a very short time," she told her friend.[6] Hickok suggested that Eleanor hold press conferences for the women, Louis Howe approved the idea, and Eleanor Roosevelt met thirty-five "press girls" for the first time just two days after the inauguration.

The press conferences proved mutually beneficial. By limiting the session to female reporters, the wire services and Washington bureaus of leading newspapers had little choice but to hire, retain, and even promote women at a time when so many female professionals in nontraditional occupations were losing ground. The handful of women who were now assured secure, even enhanced positions were grateful for the windfall. They became devoted admirers and protective guardians as well.

Dorothea Lewis, who covered Eleanor Roosevelt's activities for a chain of Wisconsin newspapers, was certified to attend the press conferences. She remembered that after the Roosevelts called on the Hoovers, the soon-to-be first lady told a number of assembled women journalists that she had heard her husband and the president discussing a possible bank holiday. With the nation's banking system on the verge of total collapse, FDR had told Hoover to close all the banks himself or he would do so after his inauguration. It was a sensational scoop with broad implications that were immediately apparent to the reporters. "The New York Stock Exchange would close. The country would go off the gold standard. There would be a worldwide panic," the women cautioned Mrs. Roosevelt. "If you promise not to tell anyone else about this, we will promise not to write it," Lewis recalled the exchange of pledges. When reporters thought that Eleanor Roosevelt was overstepping an ill-defined line, "a vigilant newspaper woman [was] sure to interrupt and say, 'this is off the record, isn't it?'"[7] Just as photographers had an unwritten agreement to mask the new president's physical disability, female reporters shielded the first lady's occasional enthusiasms and naïveté.

The press sessions were not planned to deal with substantive issues. "You are the interpreters to the women of the country as to what goes on politically in the legislative national life, and also what the social and personal life is at the White House," she told the first assembly of reporters.[8] The latter took precedence at first. Plans to curtail official entertaining were revealed. An impromptu lecture on the value of summertime leisure and a description of Franklin, Jr.'s trip to Europe after his Groton graduation were standard fare. Although reporters felt that she seemed unsure of herself and said little of consequence, more serious matters quickly intruded.

In July 1932, thousands of unemployed war veterans had descended on the nation's capital demanding that the bonuses promised them in 1945 be paid immediately. The army had been called out to rout them from their camping grounds. A second bonus march of veterans gathered in Washington shortly after FDR took office. Public reaction ranged from anger over assumed Communist backing to fear that the violence that had accompanied the army's attack on the first march would be repeated. The new administration provided camp sites for the protesters, but anxieties over potential radicalism were not quelled. One afternoon Louis Howe suggested to Eleanor Roosevelt that she drive him to the camp. Upon arrival he remained glued to his front seat in the car. He prodded her to get out, she recounted, and walk "to where I saw a line-up of men waiting for food. They looked at me curiously and one of them asked my name and what I wanted." When she answered, the veterans invited her to join them. "I did not spend as much time as an hour there; then I got into the car and drove away. Everyone waved and I called, 'Good luck,' and they answered, 'Good-by and good luck to you.' "

At her next news conference, she announced, "It was as comfortable as a camp can be, remarkably clean and orderly, grand-looking boys, a fine spirit. There was no kind of disturbance, nothing but the most courteous behavior."[10] One reporter noted that the casual manner in which the first lady described the camp was obviously intended to defuse apprehensions over the protest and create sympathy for their demands. The reporter was right; the first lady had discovered the impact of the personal appearance on the tone of subsequent publicity and also on public policy. The *Washington Times* correspondent noted after an early press conference that "Mrs. Roosevelt realized her value in publicizing these projects, whose aim was to employ the unemployed, feed the hungry, and pull the country out of the Great Depression."[11] The first lady was on her way to becoming an effective agent for mobilizing support for the New Deal.

The press forums also provided a stage on which Eleanor Roosevelt introduced women officeholders who helped direct the New Deal programs she supported. As historian Susan Ware has demonstrated, during the first Roosevelt term, more women were engaged in administrative positions than had ever worked in Washington before. These women, many of whom had cemented ties with Eleanor and Franklin Roosevelt during the previous decade, formed a political and social network rooted in shared educational attainments and social reform endeavors. They now reached the pinnacle of their careers with significant support from the first lady. Although she minimized her role in these appointments, she admitted that occasionally appointments would be discussed, and she might "go to my husband and say that I was very weary of reminding him to remind the members of his cabinet and his advisers that women were in existence. . . . As a result I was sometimes asked for suggestions and then would mention two or three names."[12] The names invariably came from Molly Dewson, who took over as head of the Women's Division of the Democratic party after the election, making increased participation of women in elective and appointed office her personal crusade.

The women who served in the administration brought to their posts a commitment to the broad-based relief and reform that marked the New Deal generally. Within that framework Eleanor Roosevelt added special concerns for women, whose problems were usually slighted by policy planners and program administrators. With the White House as her bully pulpit, she adopted a watchdog stance and publicized projects that ignored women or discriminated against them. Her efforts brought mixed results.

The first women introduced to the "press girls" were Rose Schneiderman, who had been appointed to the Labor Advisory Board of the National Recovery Administration (NRA), and Nellie Tayloe Ross, first woman to be appointed director of the mint. Eleanor Roosevelt stressed the importance of the "women's voice" in the code-writing process undertaken by firms in every industry as mandated by the National Industrial Recovery Act (NIRA). In addition to setting prices and production and distribution standards to stabilize economic conditions, this early piece of New Deal legislation also called for codes to establish labor guidelines.

For the first time minimum wage and maximum hour regulations for men and women as well as their right to organize into unions and bargain collectively became official public policy. By summer 1933, however, it became clear that numerous codes contained wage differentials that were detrimental to women workers. The leaders of women's organizations including the League of Women Voters, the Women's Trade Union League, and the Consumers' League protested. Both the first lady and Secretary of Labor Frances Perkins assured them the discriminatory features would not survive public hearings and administrative approval. But in the haste to stabilize production and wage levels, the codes never received careful examination and the protests over wage differentials went unheard. In the end, over one-fourth of all codes contained provisions for lower pay scales for women than for men, and since those codes covered industries in which large numbers of women were employed, significant numbers of women in industry were affected. To achieve standards that would regulate working conditions, specific discriminatory policies were tolerated. Eleanor Roosevelt, like other women in the administration, acquiesced in the name of expediency.

The Consumer Advisory Board (CAB) of the NRA engaged the largest contingent of women in that agency. An afterthought of Frances Perkins, the agency was intended to counter the weight of industry and labor. Perkins harked back to the early days of the Consumers' League and the notion that women as consumers could serve as engines of social change. Along with Molly Dewson and Eleanor Roosevelt, Perkins pushed for appointment of capable women to the agency. The first lady used her press conference as a vehicle to introduce chairman Mary Harriman Rumsey and offered the White House as a dramatic setting for a CAB-sponsored conference. In spite of the publicity, however, the board had little influence on NRA industrial codes. It had no effective mandate to protect consumers, concentrating instead on a "Buy Now" campaign to stimulate the economy through increased demand. "We have got to get the buying power up sufficiently to bring up the whole economic system,"[13] Eleanor Roosevelt announced in Rumsey's presence. Poorly conceived and empowered from the start, the CAB proved the weakest link in the convoluted structure of the NRA. Female officials contributed little to the process of writing and approving industrial codes.

The shortcomings of the Consumers' Advisory Board were not surprising. National Recovery Administration policy was built on the concept of voluntary business-government planning and cooperation fostered by Secretary of Commerce Herbert Hoover during the 1920s. Many progressives from the turn of the century were drawn to the dream of productive efficiency and prosperity promised by cooperative industrial planning. In the early New Deal, the NRA enhanced that expectation with the addition of government sanction. Female progressives had hewed closer to their earlier commitment to social welfare during the most conservative, inhospitable twenties. Trade associations and the efficiencies of standardized production and distribution held little appeal for female reformers more concerned with the underside of capitalism's productive processes. In 1935, they deplored the Supreme Court ruling that relegated the NIRA to the dustbin, but the demand for new approaches to the recalcitrant depression renewed attention to their call for social welfare and justice rather than economic planning.

While the first section of the NIRA had dealt with conditions of industry and labor, the second centered on relief for those workers who had no jobs at all. Under the direction of Interior Secretary Harold Ickes, the Public Works Administration (PWA) created by the legislation supervised carefully planned and constructed buildings, roads, and bridges. Even though there were 2 million unemployed women in the early 1930s, PWA projects were not designed for them. Eleanor Roosevelt's mail dramatized the plight of jobless women in a way that statistics did not. She responded with determination to publicize their problems. With the encouragement of Ellen Woodward, Mississippi-born assistant to Harry Hopkins of the Federal Emergency Relief Administration (FERA), the first lady hosted a conference at the White House designed to gain support for programs that could aid unemployed women.

The FERA was established in May 1933 to distribute federal monies directly to states and localities for work projects. By the time of the November conference, Hopkins reported only fifty thousand women had received any kind of assistance. Woodward explained to the assembled government officials, social workers, and leaders of women's organizations that finding appropriate work projects for women without construction skills was difficult. As the first lady presided, invited participants gave Woodward numerous suggestions. They formed the basis for women's work relief projects that Woodward later initiated and supervised as she moved from the FERA to the Civil Works Administration and finally to the Works Progress Administration (WPA).

The massive WPA programs begun in 1935 put large numbers of women to work during its productive but controversial life span. In December 1938, over 400,000 women obtained aid in projects ranging from sewing rooms—the perennial port of last call for women—to adult education, book repairing and cataloging, and recreational programs. With the best of intentions, however, Woodward's unflagging efforts and Eleanor Roosevelt's constant support failed to dent the disparities between men and women in qualification requirements or project assignment and especially in compensation. But much more was accomplished than would have otherwise been the case, and years later Woodward wrote Eleanor Roosevelt, "*you* deserve the major credit."[14]

To qualify for work relief, a woman had to certify she was independent or the head of a household. Single women who could not meet these standards had no place to turn. Eleanor Roosevelt personally tried to replicate the Civilian Conservation Corps (CCC) programs for women. The CCC enlisted young men from depressed cities and sent them to camps throughout the country where they engaged in reclamation, reforestation, and other conservation efforts while earning money to send home to their families on relief. The concept of simultaneously salvaging natural resources and human beings was immensely popular with regard to men. The first lady found that the idea was not easily transferable to women. All her efforts and support for Hilda Smith of the FERA and later the WPA resulted in the founding of only eighty-six camps for sixty-four hundred women at the same time that hundreds of thousands of men were working in CCC camps. And the women received fifty cents each week, whereas men earned as much as 50 dollars a month.

Despite drawbacks, relief programs marked a changed course in American public policy, one that Eleanor Roosevelt welcomed enthusiastically. Working and jobless women would have to wait until economic distress generally was adequately addressed. "Imperceptibly we have come to recognize that government has a responsibility to defend the weak," she told reporters early in 1935, echoing the words of her husband while he was still governor of New York. "I also think that in spite of criticism, the administration of relief has been a great achievement." At the same press conference, she looked ahead. She wanted to see a program of economic security launched "which will include old age pensions, a permanent ban on child labor, better unemployment insurance, better health care for the country as a whole, better care for mothers and children generally."[15] She was reviewing the items on the unfinished agenda of the social reformers with whom she had worked for over a decade.

The first lady was also describing proposals being hammered out by the President's Advisory Council on Economic Security at the very time she spoke. With the exception of a full-scale medical assistance plan, all the priorities she favored found their way into the Social Security Act of 1935. Proponents of welfare legislation were disappointed with many of the final provisions, but they recognized that the act marked a watershed in American social policy. The groups excluded from coverage in the new programs and the meager benefits financed by regressive taxes could all be corrected in time. Eleanor Roosevelt was accustomed to savoring victories in gradual doses. She also knew that the act, whatever its short-comings, had not suddenly appeared out of FDR's bag of magic tricks and was far from complete.

Eleanor herself was well aware that years of research, publicity, and lobbying by activists in women's organizations helped lay the educational groundwork for the landmark law that institutionalized the role of the federal government in buttressing the vagaries of urban-industrial society. In April 1937 she attended a dinner celebrating the twenty-fifth anniversary of the establishment of the Children's Bureau in the Department of Labor. When Julia Lathrop, a Hull House alumna, had been named to head the first federal welfare agency in 1912, she became the highest ranking woman in the federal government. The bureau itself had been established after intensive lobbying by reformers like Lathrop, Jane Addams, and Florence Kelley to address the startling health problems and working conditions of women and children. A quarter century later, the current agency head, Katherine Lenroot, and her boss, Frances Perkins, had reason to look back on years of effort and accomplishment.

Eleanor Roosevelt was specific about the foundation upon which her husband's administration lay the first bricks of the American welfare state. Speaking at the commemorative dinner, she noted that the record of the first Roosevelt term had its roots in the past. "The last four years are the outgrowth of years of thinking and working by individuals and groups throughout the country," she wrote in her column the next day. Specifically she credited two generations of female activists. "Our increased sense of social responsibility, if it exists, is due in large part to many of the people who either attended the dinner last night, or who have finished their work in this world but were nevertheless remembered by those present last night."[16]

Significantly she also spoke of work still to be done—better health care and improved educational opportunities—for the original goals of social feminists were nearing completion. In 1938, Congress enacted the Fair Labor Standards Act. NRA codes that had guaranteed certain labor standards vanished when the NIRA was ruled unconstitutional. The new act set wage and hour guidelines and prohibited child labor as well—an elusive objective that finally survived the Supreme Court. The legislation's road through Congress had been a tortuous one, but even with its drawbacks, female reformers hailed a victory.

The first lady worked as effectively and sympathetically with the capable women who served the New Deal as she worked with and in front of the "press girls." Yet there was one important issue that created a gulf between the social reformers and the professional journalists that even she could not and would not bridge. Issues of legal equality for women, definitions of womanhood, and strategies for achieving political and economic equity divided the two groups. The passage of the Fair Labor Standards Act highlighted this schism, but it also held out the possibility of healing it.

Protective legislation for working women had galvanized women reformers from the beginning of the twentieth century. Their determination to have women's hours, wages, and types of employment regulated by law was unshakable. Eleanor Roosevelt had honed her skills as a lobbyist and witness by working on behalf of hours legislation in New York. The appeal of these laws was both expedient and ideological. Attempts by states to establish work guidelines for men and women, or in some cases for specific classes of workers like miners or bakers, had been struck down repeatedly by the courts. Only legislation that focused on the most vulnerable workers, women and children, sometimes stood the test of judicial scrutiny. In the well-known Brandeis brief of 1909, compiled to support an Oregon maximum hour law for women, the legislation was defended on the basis of female social roles as mothers and their physical vulnerability as women.

Once the Supreme Court upheld the Oregon hours bill, the reformers rigidly adhered to this rationale. They sincerely believed that the biological differences between women and men underlay different social expectations. As the mothers of the next generation, the young single women who composed the majority of the female work force should not share identical workplace conditions and experiences with men. The reformers' arguments brought slow but tangible legislative results. Through the 1920s, maximum hour laws spread among states, minimum wage lobbying became more extensive, night work was widely prohibited, and employment in seemingly dangerous occupations was outlawed. After 1923 a threat to these apparent advances came from an unexpected quarter.

In the aftermath of the suffrage victory, militant feminists of the National Woman's party (NWP) realized that the right to vote did not automatically guarantee legal equality. The small group of women proposed a constitutional amendment to achieve that goal. Reformers immediately understood that a blanket guarantee of equality between the sexes would destroy the gender-based protective legislation for which they had worked and continued to work so hard. Their opposition to the proposed Equal Rights Amendment (ERA) was implacable, and Eleanor Roosevelt stood firmly with the reformers.

The membership of the NWP was small but composed of accomplished professional women. Several of the "press girls" like Ruby Black of United Press, May Craig of the *Portland Evening Express*, and Winifred Mallon of the *New York Times* were members. At an early press conference, a question about the proposed ERA brought a negative response from the first lady. "I think that the National Woman's Party ignores the fact that there is a fundamental difference between men and women," she told the reporters. "I don't mean by that women can't make as great a contribution, nor if they do the same work they not be paid the same wages. The mere fact that women basically are responsible for the future physical condition of the race means for many restrictions," she insisted,[17] trying to justify protective and restrictive legislation.

In *It's Up to the Women*, which Eleanor wrote late in 1933, she restated her position, in the process exposing its many underlying contradictions. On the one hand, she extolled the special qualities and responsibilities women brought to their families and communities especially during the perilous conditions brought on by the depression. She encouraged women to become involved in local politics and to strive for the appointed and elected positions attained by the competent women in her husband's administration. But she also reaffirmed her belief that "women are different from men, their physical functions are different, and the future of the race depends upon their ability to produce healthy children." Extolling the virtues and primacy of motherhood, she harked back to traditional ideals of feminine goals and behavior strangely at odds with her own growing influence and the life-style of the coterie of activist women around her.

The movement for a constitutional amendment challenged her to reconcile her belief in women's "specialness" with the principle of legal equity and she could not do so. Protection was necessary for women workers because they were different, but constraints, she insisted, were not synonymous with inferiority. In certain instances, women excelled. When a dramatist insisted women could never be great writers because they lacked the knowledge and experience of men, Eleanor Roosevelt drew on her own experience to reply that "as a rule women know not only what men know, but much that men will never know. For how many men really know the heart and soul of a woman?"[18] The personally revealing remark underscored her belief in the unique qualities of women. She refused to distinguish between her applause for the achievements of strong, capable women as individuals and her insistence that women as a class needed special treatment.

When she introduced Mary Anderson of the Women's Bureau or Rose Schneiderman of the Labor Advisory Board to the "press girls" to discuss issues of particular concern to working women, the threat of the proposed amendment to protective labor laws stood like an invisible wall between the feminist reporters and the liberal government officials. The passage of the Fair Labor Standards Act should have ended the dispute over the ERA threat to protective legislation since it established work standards for men and women alike. NWP members asked that controls over the hazards of the workplace be extended to men. They argued that special treatment for women was no longer mandated or expedient, that there was no longer reason to oppose the ERA. The reformers would not budge.

Although the first lady gradually modified her opposition to the ERA, arguing that growing numbers of women in trade unions would eventually control their destinies through collective action rather than imposed legislation, her colleagues could still count on her support when growing numbers of professional women jumped on the ERA bandwagon. She was fully informed, for example, of plans by Molly Dewson and Mary Anderson to scuttle attempts by the feminists to write equality planks into international treaties. She also played a more active role than she admitted in manipulating the appointment of Mary Winslow of the Women's Trade Union League to an inter-American commission for women, replacing a member of the National Woman's party who served in that position. When she then introduced Winslow to her press conference, rare rancor surfaced. Winifred Mallon of the *New York Times* wrote two long, scathing features castigating the clique of social feminists and the first lady herself for their devious plotting.

Mallon's articles represented a rare break in the affection and admiration the reporters felt for Eleanor Roosevelt. At a 1935 press conference Ruby Black asked her for a definition of feminism, and she responded without reference to the ERA. But Black could not help admiring the first lady's independence and concern for so many other issues that involved fair treatment for women. In the official publication of the NWP, Black concluded that Roosevelt "talks like a social worker and acts like a feminist." As the ultimate mark of esteem, Black wrote the first published biography of Eleanor Roosevelt, a flattering account of a unique American woman.[19]

On the occasion of the first lady's fiftieth birthday, she observed the event by taking the newspaper women with her on a tour of the depressed areas of West Virginia. After a day of train travel and countless stops at remote towns and hollows, one of the reporters, Marie Manning, was exhausted. Her praise, however, was effusive. Eleanor Roosevelt's "light-brown hair is untouched with grey and her eyes are as young as her daughter's," she wrote. "Her expression changes momentarily, which accounts for the fact that none of her photographs does her justice. The quality which draws people to her is her great adaptability. When she talks to miners' wives, she is a housewife; when she talks to ambassadors, it is usually in their own language. And when she is with the press, she never forgets the ominous shadows of the 'deadline,' and has helped us accordingly."[20]

Eleanor Roosevelt at fifty had a broader perspective on adaptability and change than even her fondest admirers could imagine. She had survived a devastating childhood and a disappointing marriage, although both had left enduring scars. Her children were grown and embarking on a series of stormy marriages and precarious business ventures that tested the mettle of the most patient of parents in or out of public view. She had emerged as a force in her own right in spite of and (although she rarely acknowledged it) because of her husband's political fortunes. Privately she extended love to friends and craved affection and intimacy in return with a passion that bordered on obsession. Publicly she conveyed an image of contentment and tranquillity: "I'm not so sure that it isn't the better part of wisdom to make up your mind to live as happily & as fully as you can. Seize on everything that comes your way which makes life more interesting, or agreeable. Meet whatever circumstances arise in what some critics call a haphazard or opportunistic manner, but in what you, yourself, may consider is the only way to face an ever-changing life in an ever-changing world—with a smile and a retention of a sense of values."[21]

The reporters who covered the White House and accompanied her marveled at her indefatigable pace. Her schedule was unlike anything veterans of the Washington social and political scene had ever encountered. Press conferences usually began with an announcement of her planned engagements for the one or two weeks that followed. On 30 April 1934, for example, she announced she would meet Hilda Smith, who was working on camps for unemployed women, at eleven that morning. The following noon she would receive a May basket in conjunction with Child Health Day and then entertain wives of senators at a picnic lunch. Ambassador to Mexico and the president's former mentor Josephus Daniels with his wife would spend two days at the White House, after which the first lady would travel to Philadelphia to speak at the national conventions of the YWCA and of the Jewish women of Hadassah. Then she would spend the weekend at the Women's Federal Prison in Alderson, West Virginia. After a few days in New York she would return to Washington to attend a conference on Negro education hosted by the Commerce Department. The days in New York would not be a respite. She would meet with her friend and colleague Caroline O'Day, who was running for Congress and for whom she would eventually campaign, another role without precedent for a first lady. And in addition, "I will speak at a luncheon for the League for Political Education. I will go into the Roosevelt House to have a photo taken with one of Uncle Ted's grandchildren."[22]

Her travels took her all over the country and beneath it as well. When the *New Yorker* published a cartoon in which two coal miners poked their heads above ground, one exclaiming to the other, "My gosh! Here comes Mrs. Roosevelt," the magazine's limited number of subscribers chuckled in recognition. The image, however, has become a lasting comment on her peripatetic activities and appearances. Considerably more American women read the *Woman's Home Companion,* for which she wrote a monthly column, and in 1934 she began weekly radio broadcasts with sponsors vying to become identified with it. When her program was briefly sponsored by a mattress company, she wrote her daughter, "I'm getting lots of protests on my radio [program] from manufacturers of other beds and bedding!"[23]

During this same period—what she called "The Peaceful Years: 1934–1936" in her memoirs—she also undertook lecture tours. She credited FDR's support for this venture. "I did not need to go on lecture trips or to inspect projects in different parts of the country, but my husband knew that I would not be satisfied to be merely an official hostess. . . . For my sake he was glad when he found that for a few weeks in spring and fall I could and did go on paid lecture trips."[24] In fact, Eleanor craved respite from the White House and from Franklin, too. When pressed on the subject, daughter Anna admitted that her father probably welcomed his wife's absences as well.[25] To a nation of Roosevelt watchers, a competent and caring first lady acted as the eyes and ears of an immobilized president. For the husband and wife, the travels alleviated the strains of their relationship while promoting their shared political concerns. The letters exchanged during their separations conveyed care and affection that was often absent when they were together, firmly ensconced among their respective circles of friends and aides. Only Louis Howe continued to bridge the gap between them. With his death in 1936 that essential human link between Eleanor and Franklin was severed.

Shortly before Howe's death, Eleanor Roosevelt began yet another project, a daily syndicated column. Six times each week "My Day" appeared in growing numbers of American newspapers. As in everything she wrote and every speech she delivered, the words were her own. She was rarely at a loss for something to share with her growing audience of readers. Only the circumstances under which she dictated to Tommy tested the ingenuity of her friend and secretary. "There have been days when my typewriter was perched on a rock; sometimes on my lap in a fast moving automobile," Tommy recalled. "We have used the bed in a hotel room when no table was available and my position was a little awkward; on a destroyer lurching from side to side and on trains with the typewriter sliding under my eyes when keeping my eyes on its movements was a bit disconcerting." And Tommy attested to the fact that "Mrs. Roosevelt has written every word of [the columns] as well as everything else which appears over her name."[26]

The columns became so much a part of her daily pattern that they did not even merit comment when she wrote to Anna from Erie, Pennsylvania, in 1937: "While I wait to go to my lecture I'll start this! I did two lectures Monday for pay, last night I went to Newark for the Women's Trade Union League (a labor of love and a long one!) & this day Tommy & I journeyed from 9 a. m. to 6:25 p. m. & now we've had a bath and dressed, eaten something & at 8 the gentlemen [sic] calls for us[,] at 10:30 back to the train, a rush across New York tomorrow between 9 and 9:30 & the train to Washington."[27] And she also dictated two columns and dispatched them in time to meet her deadline.

In Washington there were the official duties that swelled the frenetic schedule she maintained daily, weekly, year after year. By the end of the decade, she enumerated 4,729 people who had come for lunch or dinner during 1939, 9,211 who had come to tea, 323 who were guests at the White House, and 14,056 who were officially received at teas or receptions and served refreshments. Among these imposing numbers were the king and queen of England. They were official guests at the White House and then accompanied the first family to Hyde Park, where Eleanor served them hot dogs to the delight of many Americans and the consternation of others—including her mother-in-law.

Little wonder that a few hours of rest were worthy of a newspaper

column. "Yesterday I enjoyed that rare thing for me, an evening of leisure," she wrote in late 1936. "I dined on a little table in front of my
fireplace, read all the things my brief case contained that I had been
waiting for days to read, did some knitting that required a little bit of
attention and could not be done automatically . . . and enjoyed the
company of a friend."[28] Undoubtedly she chatted with Lorena Hickok,
who lived at the White House during much of the late 1930s. She had
resigned her post with Associated Press after the Roosevelts entered the
official mansion because she feared her intimate friendship with the first
lady compromised her objectivity. For two years she scoured the country
on behalf of federal relief agencies, evaluating relief needs for Harry Hopkins and writing moving accounts of the costs the depression was exacting from the American people. Her reports to Hopkins found their way
to Eleanor and also to Franklin. Half a century later they remain moving
social documents and testimony of Hickok's skills as a journalist.

Once that assignment ended, Eleanor helped Hick find employment
promoting the New York World's Fair and then working with the Wom-
en's Division of the Democratic party. As the years passed the emotional
intensity of the women's relationship diminished at least for Eleanor,
who moved on to expanding interests and new friendships. But she never
ceased to be concerned with Hick's well-being. Others in her complex
circle of loving intimates always resented Hickok even more than they
resented each other as they vied for the first lady's attention and love.
Eleanor, however, seemed to realize more than the others what Lorena
Hickok had sacrificed in renouncing the occupation in which she excelled and finding little professionally to compensate for her gift of love.

The private jealousies paled in comparison to the public storm that
raged around Eleanor Roosevelt. Some Americans were offended by the
unconventional nature and scope of her activities, complaining that "because I make speeches, I am more in the press, I'm not dignified, I do
something that isn't the proper thing to do." She answered simply that
she was sorry she offended these critics but that she was determined to
follow her inclinations. "Everyone must live their own life in their own
way and not according to anybody else's ideas."[29]

On the other hand, criticism came from readers who found "My
Day" banal. "Why don't you make your daily column a constant appeal
to individuals and organizations to do their part—instead of filling it up
with inane chatter about your family affairs—words, words, words, which
are of very little interest to anyone and only once in a blue moon of any
value whatsoever,"[30] wrote a woman who was undoubtedly astonished to

find her letter printed verbatim in a column shortly after the first lady had received it. There seemed to be no way to satisfy the expectations of those who wanted a traditional hostess and helpmate and others who wanted an effective agent of social change.

The fact that her activities also earned income made her vulnerable to charges that she commercialized her honorific position. When her earnings became a campaign issue, she responded frankly that she "made a great deal. Now it has not all gone into charity. It has gone into wages to a certain extent. It has gone into many charitable things." And furthermore, "I pay income tax on everything."[31] Her earnings were important to her, for they made it possible to adopt an independent stance and give financial support to projects about which she cared deeply.

Few New Deal initiatives caught her imagination and sustained her interest as much as the Subsistence Homesteads program, especially the resettlement community of Arthurdale. Eleanor Roosevelt was deeply moved when she visited the depressed mining community of Scott's Run, West Virginia. Neither militant Communists nor benevolent Quakers who worked among the mining families had brought respite from chronic unemployment. To the first lady, the emotionally and economically depressed people of the West Virginian hollow were ideal candidates for relocation to Arthurdale, the first planned community under the new Subsistence Homesteads program. She translated her concern into pressure, pushing bureaucratic buttons that she hoped would expedite the project.

She envisioned human rehabilitation within a model environment complete with modern health care, progressive schools, and most important, productive industry. The latter was the centerpiece of the experiment, patterned in large measure on the type of small-scale manufacturing she had encouraged and helped finance at Val-Kill. Like her husband, and a good many other Americans, Eleanor Roosevelt harbored an anti-urban bias. Related to the distaste for urban sprawl was a desire to counteract the concentration of industries in cities. The real value of Arthurdale, she believed, "lies in the suggestion which it is making to the industry of the country that decentralization and moving out of large cities . . . [makes it] possible for great numbers of people to have more in their lives than they would otherwise have."[32]

From the purchase of land to relocating miners' families, from finding a suitable industry to housing the new residents, Arthurdale was the center of political controversy. Conservative critics complained that it was a communist ploy to ruin Scott's Run by removing supposedly rent-paying miners. Potential factories raised visions of competitive threats to related industries around the country. Prefabricated houses upgraded to withstand harsh winters were condemned as luxury cottages furnished by an extravagant government. Congress rebelled over appropriations, and Eleanor Roosevelt clashed with cost-conscious Interior Secretary Harold Ickes, whose department administered the program. When resettlement communities were placed under the auspices of the Department of Agriculture, Assistant Secretary Rex Tugwell proved a more sympathetic colleague, but in the end he believed that marginal farmers, not employed miners, were the prime candidates for relocation.

But the first lady remained undaunted and enlisted the aid of Bernard Baruch, wealthy financier and adviser to presidents including FDR, who made a hefty contribution. She herself donated substantially to the Quakers' American Friends Service Committee, which worked actively on social services in both Scott's Run and Arthurdale. She financed the experimental progressive school and paid teachers' salaries singlehandedly. But a firm economic base was never established and political support remained elusive. Before its final dismantling, she admitted that Arthurdale was not secure. But real people, not the unpredictable results of public policy, mattered. "It is not a solved problem of life if you have got, as one family has, 12 children. It isn't easy to make ends meet. But still, as I looked at the graduating group in Arthurdale high school, as I looked at all the other people, they were well fed and they looked healthy. And looking back at Scott's Run, I couldn't help feeling that the contrast was very great."[33] She had learned the limits of social planning and her own ability to affect it, but her ideals remained firm and her faith was only slightly shaken.

The first lady visited the community often during the 1930s, and the families adored her. She returned their affection and admiration. The ballrooms of high society always bored her, but at square dances in the community hall, she joined the festivities with delight. An emotionally remote mother when she was young, she sat with Arthurdale mothers and listened with sympathy and understanding to their concerns, gently bouncing young children unselfconsciously on her knee. On one trip a man handed her a photograph of his two-year-old daughter who had been born at Arthurdale. Her middle name was Eleanor, he told her. For many American parents during the depression, naming a child Eleanor was the equivalent of bestowing a saint's name.

On behalf of distressed Americans who wrote her to ask for a job, a way to save their home, or just some cast-off clothing, she took personal action. Pleas for employment or complaints about relief administrators were forwarded to the appropriate agencies with a cover letter signed by the first lady herself. Officials were seldom shaken loose from their accepted procedures even by Eleanor Roosevelt, but her correspondents believed that she truly cared and a note by return mail confirmed their confidence in her. "You have saved my life. I would have killed myself if I would have lost my house," a grateful woman wrote the first lady after she advised the woman to consult the local office of the Federal Home Loan Agency.[34]

Requests for used clothes combined heart-rending pleas, wounded pride, and specific orders. "Among your friends do you know of one who is discarding a spring coat for a new one. If so could you beg the old one for me. I wear a size 40 to 42," wrote a woman from Kansas to "My Dear Friend." A similar request came from Florida. "I am greatly in need of a Coat. . . . I wear size 36 or 38. . . . I assure you I am worthy of any help you render," the writer assured her, begging for anonymity. "I haven't had a new coat in 16 years so please don't think me unworthy," a mother from Iowa wrote. "I do not wish my children to feel ashamed. Regardless of what you do please do not put my name and letter up for people to laugh at," she concluded.[35]

There was no storeroom with coats at the White House, so often the first lady simply sat down and wrote a personal check. Friends teased her that she was a soft touch for any sad tale that crossed her desk. She was. But it was difficult to read the mail conscientiously as she did and remain immune to the hurt pride and tangible deprivation. One day she found Tommy making out a check in response to an especially moving plea.

Although she believed in the basic goodness and honesty of people, she was not so naive as to think that her position and reputation guarded her from fraud and deceit. "Occasionally those of us who deal with many people have things happen which shake our faith in human beings," she confided to her readers. A woman who wrote to her for a relief job lied about her qualifications and then wrote to a friend explaining how the friend should cover her story when the welfare agency came to investigate. The letters were mixed up, and Eleanor Roosevelt received the instructions meant for the friend. She printed the letter in her column, aware that softhearted liberals must not ignore open invitations to cheating and that criticisms of government investigators who "were a little too hardboiled" for her taste were sometimes justified.[36]

For the most part, however, her support for New Deal relief programs and the officials who administered them was unstinting. As a columnist she described herself as a "painter of pictures and a reporter of unimportant events," not a writer who interpreted and influenced public opinion. Self-effacement came naturally to Eleanor Roosevelt, but her assessment was simply not accurate. When she visited a WPA sewing room in Knoxville and reported that most of the women thought their skills had been improved through training, highly criticized relief projects for women received a boost. Everything at the Bonneville Dam on the Columbia River filled her with admiration from the engineering marvel itself to the runway constructed for fish to the flowers planted around workers' homes. "When people tell me," she explained to her readers, "as they often do, that shovel-leaning is the general characteristic of those who work on W. P. A., I accumulate more and more pictures in my mind which I can paint for them."[37] The pictures she sketched for the readers of "My Day" were also impassioned endorsements for federally funded relief and construction projects. Unless all readers were already among the converted, she did indeed affect public response to New Deal policies.

During the 1936 reelection campaign, her columns were as effective as any Democratic party literature. In simple, clear—and mawkish— ways, she translated experiences along the campaign trail into glowing praise for FDR's presidency and its achievements. She described her encounter with a waiter in a Detroit restaurant who told her, "I'm for Mr. R. He saved my home and my family." What a responsibility for a president to know the impact of his policies on "the lives and hopes of so many people," she concluded. And she recounted the story of a three-year-old girl who prayed that "the president be fat" because, the child explained, "then he won't be hungry the way we were before he helped Daddy get a job."[38]

The first lady also lent credence to Republican attacks on FDR and his New Deal. A vote for Alf Landon would not only send Roosevelt packing, according to GOP faithful, but would also remove his busybody wife from the national scene. Political cartoonists discovered a windfall in her unattractive appearance. Lack of beauty was equated with renunciation of conservative verities, with a woman who did not know her place and posed as a do-gooder. But for all the bluster, Eleanor Roosevelt could not be turned into a political liability. Wherever crowds gathered to see their president and listened to his appeals for support, people called for a glimpse of their first lady, too.

The 1936 campaign concluded with a resounding victory for FDR.

It also marked a turning point in the voting patterns of significant sectors of the American electorate. A tenuous but enduring coalition that had been building for several years finally emerged and made Democrats the majority party for decades thereafter. Tensions would surface among conflicting elements, and parts of the coalition would fall away. But one group held tenaciously to the partisan revolution wrought by Franklin Roosevelt. As historian Nancy Weiss has demonstrated, black Americans in the North bid "farewell to the party of Lincoln" during the 1930s, not because the administration supported civil rights for the racial minority but because New Deal policies—although discriminatory in their application—prevented the unraveling of the economic fabric of black lives. If there was any perception in black communities, however, that this federal government did care about racial justice, that notion stemmed from the ideals and actions of Eleanor Roosevelt.[39]

Overcoming her inbred prejudices and stereotypes was an arduous and incomplete process. In 1937, one of her daily columns retold a tactless joke in tasteless dialect because many Americans "do not appreciate what we owe the colored race for its good humor and its quaint ways of saying and doing things."[40] But the pleas and complaints she received by mail and during on-site visits to black communities convinced her that Negro problems not only mirrored other Americans' need for relief and reform but also extended beyond those needs. Pervasive racism compounded economic distress and political liabilities. She addressed these issues with her usual fervor. Letters pleading for aid or complaining about prejudicial treatment at the hands of local relief officials were forwarded to the appropriate agencies. Unfortunately, the letters often made their way back to the local agencies in spite of the first lady's good intentions and her correspondents' pleas for anonymity.

She addressed the call from black leaders for more voice in administrative posts by pressing for the appointment of black educator Mary McLeod Bethune to the National Youth Administration. Efforts to place other capable blacks were less successful. Even as close a colleague as Frances Perkins refused to name a black to one of the bureaus in the Department of Labor, claiming social and personnel difficulties would undermine efficiency. When otherwise liberal government officials backed away from integrating their staffs, they were reflecting prevalent American attitudes toward racial minorities.

Eleanor Roosevelt was not intimidated. Tours of black schools, churches, and relief projects were constant items on her busy schedule. She spoke at conventions of black organizations, appeared at interracial gatherings, and invited black leaders to White House receptions. Not only prominent blacks saw the executive mansion firsthand. In May 1936, she inspected the National Training School for Girls, the District of Columbia reformatory for black girls. She was appalled at the conditions and described the visit in great detail at her next press conference. She also invited the inmates to a garden party at the White House. "I feel if these girls are ever to be rehabilitated and, as far as possible, returned into community living prepared to meet the difficulties of life, they need much more than they are getting. Therefore, it seems to me, as every young person enjoys an occasional good time, these youngsters should have an occasional good time."[41]

Washington was aghast, but the party went off without a hitch. The League of Women Voters provided transportation, and uniformed staff served ice cream and lemonade on the rear grounds. The girls, however, did not tour the public rooms on the first floor. That would have caused an uproar that exceeded the limits of public controversy. Their gracious hostess not only understood those limits but also had no illusions that a two-hour outing was the solution to delinquency or the means of rehabilitation. Education and training was essential as well as "wiping out the causes which bring the necessity for these institutions," she believed. She never thought that a garden party would resolve poverty or erase racial disharmony. Blacks needed a climate in which they could avail themselves of the opportunity to succeed on their merits.

Her stress on individual opportunities for blacks precluded an assault on social arrangements like racial segregation. Although Eleanor Roosevelt personally protested the forced separation of the races at a public assembly by deliberately moving her chair to the middle of the aisle that separated blacks from whites when she attended a conference in Atlanta, she did not attack Jim Crow laws in the South or more subtle forms of discrimination elsewhere. Her gradualist approach to social welfare and justice applied to racial policies. Opportunities for advancement could best be promoted within existing structures: blacks must respect the limits of the possible and not overextend their reach; patience was the ultimate virtue and most effective strategy. In this respect her stance, while far ahead of her progressive cohorts in so many respects, appeared painfully shortsighted when civil rights became a major liberal aim a generation later.

In the 1930s more dramatic issues than legal segregation highlighted black disabilities in American society. No threat was more menacing than the possibility of physical violence and death through lynching.

Social segregation, disenfranchisement in the South, and lack of economic opportunities everywhere encumbered black Americans. But mob violence was the ultimate assault on the body of the victims and the minds of all those who identified with their fate. The number of these atrocities increased during the early 1930s as economic hardship compounded interracial tension. Leaders of black organizations like Walter White of the NAACP hoped that a new administration would support efforts to criminalize lynching.

White personally gained the support of two Democratic senators, Robert F. Wagner of New York and Edward P. Costigan of Colorado, who agreed to sponsor an antilynching bill. The proposed legislation was introduced in the Senate at the beginning of 1934. The campaign to arouse public sentiment on behalf of the bill included efforts to enlist the backing of the president. Roosevelt was hesitant. He finally agreed to meet with White only because his wife personally intervened to schedule the appointment. Sara joined the three conferees, agreeing with White and her daughter-in-law that they should all stick to the subject whenever her son engaged in good-natured, evasive banter.

But even his mother's uncharacteristic interest could not convince FDR that support for the Costigan-Wagner bill was worth alienating the southern wing of the Democratic party. Whether his position was entirely expedient or reflected, in part, his personal lack of concern is uncertain. The extent to which he used his wife's good standing to deflect criticism in the black community is also difficult to measure. But she continued to act behind the scenes as conduit between White and FDR and in full public view, to move comfortably, if controversially, with and among black citizens. Blacks therefore were convinced that they had at least one friend in high circles, and "at a time when there had previously been neither positive symbol nor substance, the First Lady helped significantly to shape the black response to the New Deal."[42] She was considerably less effective in shaping her husband's attitudes and priorities.

To "My Day" readers, she gave some transparent insight into her relationship with her husband when it came to political issues. "One of the lessons all women need to learn is, that when we are dealing with busy people, no matter how interested we ourselves may be in a subject, we must put what we have to say in the briefest possible form," she wrote. "This is even more important if the person to whom we are talking is listening because of our interest, and not because of his own. We may be able to impart some of our enthusiasm to him if we do not first bore him to death and make him impatient because he is being asked to listen to too many words."[43] Personal experience clearly underlay her counsel. There were limits to Eleanor Roosevelt's skill at negotiating the maze of the growing New Deal bureaucracy and mobilizing public opinion. And there were certainly limits, along with impatience and even antagonism, to her influence in the Oval Office itself.

Franklin Roosevelt respected his wife's opinions. He was not averse to using her position as a highly visible and admired first lady to test the political waters on sensitive issues. She understood that for all her independence of action and frank criticism of shortcomings in New Deal programs as she saw them, there were boundaries beyond which she could not move. FDR made the decisions about political feasibility on the basis of his own judgments, and if his assessments clashed with Eleanor's proposals, her influence was negligible. And if her actions threatened to stir public controversy beyond the scope he would tolerate, then she curtailed them at his request. Bowing to FDR's wishes, she did not attend a rally protesting a particularly brutal lynching although she was appalled at the murder and at the inaction of the government.

When the Daughters of the American Revolution (DAR) barred well-known black singer Marian Anderson from performing at Constitution Hall in 1939, Eleanor Roosevelt resigned from the organization. Her action spoke eloquently about her attitude toward racial discrimination. Her explanation to "My Day" readers was thoughtful and straightforward, for she had pondered her decision carefully. Usually she belonged to organizations in which she could work for ideas and positions with which members might disagree. She might be defeated, but at least she had had her say and perhaps she would prevail in the future. But the inflexibility with which the DAR declared its determination to adhere to its racist policies convinced her that change was impossible. Remaining as a member implied approval of that action, and so she resigned. Secretary of Interior Harold Ickes stepped into the public furor over the DAR prohibition and the first lady's reply and scheduled a free open-air concert at the Lincoln Memorial. It was a moving event. Over 75,000 people gathered to hear the magnificent voice of contralto Anderson and to give some semblance of recognition to the indignities of discrimination. Although she had played a central role in the events surrounding the public uproar, Eleanor Roosevelt did not attend the concert.

The occasions of cautious, imposed reticence were hardly noted by Americans who had grown accustomed to this most energetic and outspoken of first ladies. There seemed to be no end to the causes she espoused or the platforms from which she pronounced her opinions.

She sometimes worried that she might focus on one issue and that her role as publicist for Americans—minorities, tenant farmers, the hungry and homeless—who had no platform or spokesperson of their own would be diminished. On one lecture tour in 1937 she had seen the physical and human toll of the Dust Bowl. Instead of speaking on the prearranged topics, she described what she had seen to her audiences and pleaded for support for programs to address soil erosion. "I have talked about it to so many people," she wrote, "I feel a little afraid they will think I am interested in only one subject."[44] She need not have worried. If there was serious criticism of her wide-ranging interests and outspoken ideals, it centered on the impression she created of a ubiquitous meddler whose activities and postures had no coherent pattern and whose opinions rested on insufficient information and analysis.

Eleanor Roosevelt's actions and visions did have focus and definition. She espoused the basic tenets of American liberalism as it came to be redefined in the 1930s, and she even anticipated planks that would become central to the liberal platform during the decades that followed. She believed that human welfare and social justice should be encouraged and protected under the auspices of an enlightened, caring government. Midway in the first Roosevelt administration, she addressed the issue of the public role in securing a more humane and just society. "The big achievement of the past two years is the great change in the thinking of the country," she told the "press girls" in 1935. "Imperceptibly we have come to recognize that government has a responsibility to defend the weak." In anticipation of contemporary and later attacks on bureaucratic management of programs as well as the programs themselves, she added, "I also think that in spite of criticism, the administration of relief has been a great achievement."[45] Government-supported and administered assistance for those who could not help themselves was the common thread that bound her vision to her seemingly feverish activities.

There were additional issues that she wanted addressed. "I hope that we will have a greater realization of our international interdependence and our responsibility toward the rest of the world," she announced early in 1935. And "I hope we will realize the problem of youth and make a more determined effort to be helpful to the rising generation."[46] In enacting the legislation that created the American welfare state, the Roosevelt administration legislated the social agenda Eleanor Roosevelt's female colleagues had advocated since the turn of the century. Civil rights for minorities and attacks on persistent poverty would become lib-eral priorities in the future. First, however, the president's wife turned her attention and concern toward the special problems of young people in an era of economic depression, problems complicated by the swirling war clouds gathering on the world's horizons.

5

"FIRST MOTHER"
AND WORLD WAR II

"In this world where force is still rampant, one holds one's breath when one looks into the faces of young people," Eleanor Roosevelt told her readers in 1937. "If only they can succeed where we of the older generation have failed," she added hopefully.[1] But she was not at all certain that American youth would live up to her expectations. Like an anxious mother, she worried about the impact of the depression on young lives and hopes. She especially feared that the idealism of some young leaders of student organizations blinded them to the realities of ominous rumblings abroad. Young people wanted to avoid war, she was sure, but how they would go about preserving peace left her confused and uneasy.

The first lady insisted that one avenue to peace lay in the potential of democratic society and the obligation of that society to be responsive to the needs of its citizens. It was imperative, she thought, that young people find out how their government could meet the demands for social justice and economic security at home. They must be committed to democratic values particularly as the threats of European communism and fascism grew. As the war clouds gathered, Eleanor Roosevelt's own concerns for youth and peace intertwined, tangled, and occasionally unraveled. When the war clouds finally burst, she found little support in official circles for keeping the welfare concerns that she shared with the young high on the list of wartime priorities.

Earlier in the Roosevelt administration, however, problems involving youth riveted the attention of Americans in and out of government circles. The depression cast countless young people adrift—out of classrooms to seek jobs, out of family circles when jobs failed to materialize, out of their communities, so that they created a new subculture of wanderers. "I have moments of real terror when I think we might be losing this generation," Eleanor Roosevelt confessed with well-founded anxiety.[2] A permanent underclass of unschooled, unskilled, disillusioned Americans, alienated from family and nation, was a distinct depression-era possibility.

The Civilian Conservation Corps was the initial rapid response to the youth problem, but its net was never cast widely enough. The program transported young men to projects far from their communities, housed and supervised them under army administration and discipline, and neglected to teach them permanent skills. Young women and blacks were almost totally ignored. Eleanor Roosevelt was not alone in her belief that government must enlarge the scope of service to youth. While she worked closely with relief administrators Harry Hopkins and Aubrey Williams, other officials like Secretary of Labor Frances Perkins and Children's Bureau chief Katherine Lenroot were also devising programs to tackle the distress of young Americans.

FDR needed little prodding to mount a major effort. Still it was Eleanor who made a personal appeal on behalf of a special agency, and in June 1935, the president created the National Youth Administration (NYA) by executive order. Charles Taussig, who became head of the National Advisory Council of the new agency, never doubted that the role of the first lady was crucial, that her sympathetic efforts on behalf of youth were a significant force in promoting the government's programs.

She continued to work closely with Aubrey Williams, who directed the NYA along with Taussig. They initiated programs that concentrated on classroom education and vocational training. High school and college students from relief families were eligible for outright grants to keep them in classrooms, delaying their entry into the contracted labor force. For unemployed youth, training programs in job skills were established usually in conjunction with relief projects in their communities. In addition the number of work camps for young women was somewhat expanded. And Eleanor Roosevelt had little difficulty persuading Williams, one of the few administrators in Washington who shared her commitment to racial justice, to address the issue of black youth and to engage the black educator Mary McLeod Bethune. The NYA was that rare New Deal agency which took the plight of blacks seriously.

The National Youth Administration was popular but not without its critics. Southerners opposed aid to black Americans, and conservatives generally fought appropriations for programs they insisted undermined youths' initiative. The first lady took the lead in fending off criticism. "My Day" columns described her visits to projects and praised the young apprentice workers. She invited state administrators to Hyde Park and chaired conferences at the White House. From his vantage point, Williams could understandably believe that she was the greatest person he had ever known.

For all her personal involvement, Eleanor Roosevelt did not believe that the NYA addressed all the dilemmas facing young people nor that only critics on the Right had to be answered. Some young Americans did not believe they were simply passive victims of an economic system in need of repair through the good offices of a democratic, caring government. Rather they were alienated individuals seeking solutions in radical ideologies and foreign models. This was precisely the political stance that Eleanor Roosevelt feared. She felt compelled to build and maintain links with student leaders and organizations on the Left, certain that they could be persuaded that a democratic, reform-minded government was worthy of their faith and allegiance. Historian Winifred Wandersee has concluded that compassion colored the first lady's trust in the young activists and prolonged her tolerance for their positions long after the possibility for cooperation and adherence to democratic principles had vanished. "She was the vital connection," according to Wandersee, "between the Left and the New Deal through her relationship with youth leaders" such as Waldo McNutt, William Hinckley, and Joseph Lash.[3]

The organized youth movement of the 1930s was best represented by the American Youth Congress (AYC) and the American Student Union. The AYC was an umbrella group of sixty varied organizations that gradually came under the direction of a National Administrative Council that was clearly connected to the Young Communist League. The American Student Union, more limited in membership, was directed by young Communists and socialists with the former firmly in control. Eleanor Roosevelt's initial contact with the young leaders of these groups was not cordial. She sought their support for the newly created National Youth Administration, but the American Youth Congress countered with a legislative proposal of its own, far more extensive and expensive than the scope and the costs of the NYA.

Her tactful defense of the government's concern for youth was met with condescending impatience. The mood of the leaders eventually changed, not because the first lady won their trust but because Joseph Stalin shifted his strategy. When Stalin realized the threat presented by fascism, he mandated the Popular Front whereby Communists were to cooperate with liberal forces in the democratic West. The American youth movement obliged. Encountering increasing opposition in Congress that placed liberal proponents on the defensive, the administration was not adverse to welcoming newfound support from the radical Left. Eleanor Roosevelt emerged as the major link between the New Deal and the student organizations. Her presence at conferences and close contacts with the leadership gave the movement legitimacy. In turn, the AYC softened its critical posture toward the administration and heartily supported the NYA and other New Deal programs that were reeling from congressional appropriation slashing.

Budget cutters in Congress countered with accusations that the youth movement was a Communist front and that, by giving student groups respectability, the first lady was the leading culprit in advancing radical causes. She invited AYC leaders to the White House and asked them to be honest with her about their Communist sympathies and ties. They all denied any connections to the Communist party. They deceived her. The signing of the Nazi-Soviet Pact in August 1939 served as the ultimate litmus test of radical loyalties. Overnight American Student Union and American Youth Congress leaders turned against New Deal policies at home and the administration's internationalist stance in the face of mounting tensions abroad. Within one week, Germany and the Soviet Union invaded Poland, Britain and France declared war, and the world was plunged into chaos.

The rapid about-face of the youth movement and the outbreak of war were severe blows to Eleanor's faith in her young friends, but she did not sever her ties to them yet. In November 1939 Congressman Martin Dies of Texas opened the House Un-American Activities Committee hearings into youth organizations' activities and loyalties. Leaders were called to testify about accusations that their groups were Communist controlled. The first lady attended the hearings because she suspected the young people would be harassed by their interrogators. When the questioning did take a hostile turn, "I asked to go over and sit at the press table. I took a pencil and a piece of paper, and the tone of the questions changed immediately."[4] Influence in high places brought results even when the objects of her concern abused her compassion and trust.

The young witnesses denied that their organizations were run by Communists, and that was untrue. Only Joseph Lash of the American Student Union was evasive and hesitant in his replies. He had, like a number of the young activists, disassociated himself from the party line and influence when the nonaggression pact was signed and he was disillusioned with the direction the movement was taking. Still he would not collude in accusations against his colleagues and publicly dispute their policies. His position was tenuous and tense. Eleanor Roosevelt sensed his discomfort. Following the hearings, he joined other witnesses as her personal guests at the White House.

Her unflinching support continued as the American Youth Congress prepared a mass demonstration in Washington the following February. With maternal concern, she housed leaders at the White House and spent hours on the telephone convincing Washington's elite to take in others. At her insistence hotels offered rooms at one dollar a night. She presided at an official reception where young spokespersons met members of Congress and lobbied for their refurbished American Youth Act. But it was the issue of war and American foreign policy that brought the protesters to the nation's capital. To address AYC demands for an explanation of American foreign policy, Eleanor convinced FDR to speak from the rear portico to the young people assembled on the south lawn. She knew that the movement now insisted on American neutrality while the Soviet Union joined Germany in dismembering eastern Europe and that the president had no tolerance for that position. She persisted in her belief, however, that genuine pacifism rather than Soviet manipulation underlay their position.

FDR's speech revealed the impasse that had grown between the administration and organized radical youth. To the first lady's dismay, he kept the crowd waiting in the rain. When he finally appeared he defended New Deal policies and castigated those who assaulted them. Turning to foreign affairs, he attacked AYC opposition to an American loan to Finland, which was then in the midst of repulsing an invasion from its powerful Soviet neighbor. The president minced no words when he told them they were fools or foils if they truly thought that the Soviet Union was the hapless victim of Finnish aggression.

Most of the soaked and sulking audience listened in silence. Some openly booed the president. Even his wife, who did not approve of the tone or all the content of his remarks, was appalled at the behavior of

116

the young people. That day and the next she attended sessions coordinated by the AYC and finally closed the days of demonstrations with a question-and-answer period. For two hours she parried hostile queries with replies that reinforced points made by FDR earlier. One radical student recalled, "She chose instead to defend everything that he had said and done. Her endorsement of him came as a heavier blow than his own speech, for none could question her courage and concern." She faced the students without condescension or impatience. When some responses brought scattered applause or audible boos, she raised her arm to quiet her audience. "I want you neither to clap nor hiss until I have finished and then you may do whichever you like." When she concluded, they gave her a standing ovation, an incredible ending to a unique confrontation that was, according to the *Baltimore Sun*, "a debate between a President's wife and a critical, not to say hostile, auditorium full of politically minded youth of all races and creeds."[5]

In spite of the drama and disillusionment on all sides, Eleanor Roosevelt was still not ready to relinquish the young people as allies. She wrote Anna blaming FDR for losing their support. With persistence bordering on naïveté, she believed that economic security for themselves and social justice for the nation, not radical ideology or foreign loyalties, propelled student activism. She continued her financial contributions and tried to encourage liberal rather than left-wing programs. Her efforts were rebuffed. Her tolerance for their unrelenting isolationism suffered in the face of upheavals overseas. Then in June 1941, Hitler launched his attack on Russia, and young radicals immediately reversed their stance again. Now she refused their support on behalf of immediate American interventionism. In the aftermath of the war, during her service at the United Nations, she looked back on her associations with the youth movement and credited that experience with introducing her to the deceptions and zigzags of Soviet practices. At the time, however, she was a slow and naive learner.

Eleanor Roosevelt had walked her own winding path on issues of war and peace. Having arrived at the point where she believed foreign developments could not be assessed within narrow ideological bounds, she told student leaders in February 1940, that they were not the only ones who did not want war, and that those who knew what war is like felt as they did. Having supported the Allied cause in World War I and then having personally viewed the toll that cause had exacted, she rightly counted herself among those who knew the realities of war.

She had embraced the peace movement of the 1920s, especially those women's organizations like the National Conference on the Cause and Cure of War and the Women's International League for Peace and Freedom, groups that advocated disarmament and American participation in international bodies—the League of Nations and the World Court. These women's groups were antiwar in principle and internationalist in strategy. In 1923, Eleanor Roosevelt had assisted her friend Esther Lape in selecting a winner in a contest sponsored by Edward Bok, publisher of the *Ladies' Home Journal.* A prize of $100,000 had been offered for the best practical peace plan, half to go to the winner immediately upon selection, half to be awarded if the Senate or a national referendum approved the proposal. Because the League of Nations had become such a contentious and divisive issue, plans advocating United States membership in the league were declared ineligible.

More than twenty thousand entries flooded offices staffed by Lape and Roosevelt. A plan proposing American membership in the World Court and cooperation and counsel with the league was chosen; plans were made for a referendum to be conducted in newspapers and magazines. Opposition to the proposal and its administrators surfaced immediately. "Three Women Engineer Bok Prize Contest" the *New York Herald* announced. The headline revealed more than a hint of resentment at women's entrance onto the stage of public policy discussion. The opposition of congressmen whose pacifism was also sincere but who sought solutions in isolationism was more explicit. Progressive in domestic politics, senators William Borah and Hiram Johnson denounced the contest proposal as a cruel hoax to sneak the nation into international organizations. Their attacks doomed the referendum and indicated that peace and disarmament advocates wore many hats in the 1920s and 1930s.

Despite the furor over the Bok contest, Eleanor Roosevelt never wavered in her support for the World Court, combining her lobbying efforts with special calls to women to embrace the movement. Reverting to arguments that played on presumed feminine qualities, she appealed to women to use their intuition, tact, and innate respect for human life to join the great crusade for peace.

As first lady, she addressed peace issues on her radio broadcasts, listed peace as a topic on which she was prepared to speak on her lecture tours, held receptions for delegates to peace organizations' conferences, and lent her name to the prominent antiwar groups of the 1930s. She even urged toymakers to "turn their attention from tin soldiers, cannons, tanks, and battleships and other warlike toys." But toy manufacturers were no more amenable to disarmament proposals than were nations.

The threat of fascist governments in Europe and the reality of Japanese aggression in East Asia caused Eleanor Roosevelt to reevaluate and modify her pacifist values. On the one hand, her internationalism was reinforced. Strict neutrality laws and embargoes enacted by Congress after the mid-1930s implemented isolationist sentiment. The first lady supported the principle of neutrality at first, but events of the Spanish civil war convinced her that refusing aid to victims of aggression as well as the perpetrators was not neutral at all. She defended the Spanish Loyalists and informed her readers that she was not neutral about her commitment to democracy and belief in "the right of people to choose their own government without having it imposed upon them by Hitler and Mussolini."[6] Her outspoken support for the Loyalists and for American volunteers of the Abraham Lincoln Brigade fighting on their side brought the wrath of Catholic organizations, who supported Franco, as well as that of pacifist isolationists down on her head.

Her views on disarmament underwent little change because she had never favored the unilateral approach advanced by many pacifists. She maintained that an "adequate defense is necessary as long as we cannot have simultaneous reductions in armaments." In 1938 she published *This Troubled World,* in which she tried to shake the American people out of their lethargy by sharing her own anxieties over world events. She took issue with isolationists and advocates of unilateral disarmament who insisted that two oceans and a few submarines would protect the country indefinitely. She had redefined her pacifism in what seemed to her the only realistic terms: pacifists do not seek fights and try to prevent fights by aiding threatened nations with all help short of military aid; pacifism also means a nation does not impose its opinions or its demands on another nation. "But if war comes to your own country, then even pacifists, it seems to me, must stand up and fight for their beliefs."[7]

Given her growing alarm over fascist aggression and the lag in American support for a policy that would counter German and Italian policies, she welcomed the internationalist stance of the youth movement until their callous reversal in August 1939. When war erupted one week later, she agreed with FDR that the "neutrality of mind" that Woodrow Wilson had proposed when Europe went to war a quarter of a century earlier was now impossible. Three weeks after the simultaneous German and Russian invasions of Poland, she tried to convince her readers that we "do have to fight with our minds, for this is as much a war for the control of ideas as for control of material resources."[8] She was appalled at the aerial onslaught against civilians and was also dismayed at Hitler's treatment of political opponents and religious minorities, especially German Jews.

The dilemma over Jewish refugees had become acute even before war broke out. Eleanor Roosevelt found *Kristallnacht*, the systematic Nazi attacks on Jews and on their shops and synagogues in November 1938, incomprehensible. She eventually felt the same way about the failure to rescue German and later Austrian Jews clamoring for asylum. Working closely with individuals and organizations, she helped orchestrate efforts to convince Congress to amend American immigration restrictions or, at least, to enact special legislation to admit twenty thousand German refugee children. She counseled the Non-Sectarian Committee formed to marshal support for the bill introduced by Senator Robert Wagner and Congresswoman Edith Rogers. The Friends Service Committee enlisted all the Quaker families needed to guarantee homes for the children. For the first time, she gave the reporters at her press conference permission to write that she firmly supported pending legislation. Writer Jason Berger summarized the outcome: "The Non-Sectarian Committee originally hoped American sympathy would overcome the era's economic insecurity, isolationism, and anti-Semitism. It was wrong."[9]

When war was declared, the refugee crisis became even more critical. FDR initiated a procedure whereby consulates in Europe could issue emergency visitors' visas. But this effort was thwarted by a combination of bureaucratic intransigence and undisguised anti-Semitism. Eleanor Roosevelt met the obstructionist assistant secretary of state Breckenridge Long head on and exerted every effort to schedule appointments for pro-refugee advocates with her husband. FDR's appointment secretary, Pa Watson, was a southerner who had stalled meetings with Walter White of the NAACP. He was also a friend of Long's for whom he provided the same service. On the rare occasions when a meeting did take place, the president charmed the supplicants and evaded the main order of business. As in the case of civil rights, the first lady remained the last conduit between her husband and petitioners for humanitarian principles and actions. That she failed in the end only highlights the extensive racism and anti-Semitism that infected the nation and her exceptional immunity to these pathologies.

A handful of refugees did manage to circumvent intolerance and official barriers. If Eleanor could not actively assist them in reaching safety, she could at least welcome them to their new home. Stella Hershan remembered how she escaped Nazi-occupied Austria with the clothes on her back and a baby in her arms. When her ship finally reached American shores, the mist was so thick she could see only the raised arm of the famous statue in New York harbor. In the months that followed, she created her own version of the massively sculpted face. "She had a kind smile, and her eyes were filled with compassion. She wrote a daily column in the newspapers and called it 'My Day.' Her writing was so simple, even I could understand it. From her I learned about America. One day, I took part in a gathering of newly arrived refugees. The guest of honor spoke the words of welcome." In her unique manner, the speaker told the newcomers that their new circumstances were part of a reciprocal arrangement. In return for safe haven, their new homeland was grateful for the talents, skills, and cultures they had brought. She did not speak of the hostility that had placed countless obstacles in their journeys to safety. Little wonder that almost forty years later, Stella Hershan still remembered that for her, "the Statue of Liberty was personified by that woman, by Eleanor Roosevelt."[10]

More than harried exiles worried the first lady during the two years prior to America's entry into war. As the administration adapted an increasing prodefense posture, she sensed the vulnerability of New Deal principles and policies. As early as October 1939, she shared her concerns with the newspaper women. Making democracy work at home was "one of the ways to keep us out of war. . . . We've got to solve our problems and not get sidetracked into thinking so entirely of other things that we forget we have problems." When asked if the issues of war and peace should take a back seat to domestic affairs, she stressed what to her seemed interrelated: "The war has a great bearing on our domestic problems, and you've got to recognize the fact of the bearing that it has. But we've got to keep a balance."[11] Eleanor Roosevelt did not always analyze issues carefully or state them clearly.

Although FDR often tired of her impatient insistence that he balance reform at home with reaction to threats from abroad, he realized that war provided congressional opponents with a convenient diversion from relief and welfare programs. To counter cuts in social service programs, he created the Office of Civilian Defense (OCD) by executive order.

For a number of women active in the Roosevelt administration, the British Women's Service for Civil Defense was an admirable model for joining home defense with social welfare. FDR's broad-based directive encouraged them to link voluntary morale-building efforts on the home front to federal aid for community needs. New York's feisty, reforming mayor Fiorello La Guardia was named head of the OCD. His focus on the mechanics of civil defense rather than on voluntary participation upset original backers of the agency such as Florence Kerr, who had directed community service projects for the WPA. Although she was reluctant to accept an official post, Eleanor Roosevelt's commitment to community activism and liberal policies overrode her preference for working behind the scenes. She became codirector of the agency.

Deaths in the family delayed assuming her new responsibilities. On 7 September, Sara Delano Roosevelt died. In spite of the emotional barrier Eleanor had constructed between herself and her mother-in-law, she paid tribute to the indomitable woman in her newspaper column. Then within days of the funeral, the first lady was summoned to New York. Her beloved brother, Hall, who had intelligence, grace, and absolutely no self-control, died a physically wrecked, comatose alcoholic. Eleanor kept the agonizing death vigil at the hospital during his last days. Sorrow was mixed with bitterness at the sense of waste and perhaps the replay of her father's shortened, dissipated life as well.

Hall's death left her angry. The lack of discipline that marked his life and hastened his end was beyond her understanding. Eleanor was not unfamiliar with Freudian psychology gaining popularity during the years between the wars, but to her, analyzing the psyche and ferreting out the secrets of the unconscious excused as much as explained human behavior. She did not believe that her whirlwind of public activism and commitment to humanitarian service were compensatory ventures to gain the admiration and love so lacking in her childhood. She harked back to an older, more traditional explanation, a nineteenth-century concept of character. Individuals must develop self-discipline and willpower, have a sense of responsibility and duty. Those were the qualities upon which she fashioned her private as well as her public persona—enduring pain from personal wounds and charting her own course in the public arena. To do less was moral failure, the final verdict on Hall's pitiful last years.

So she threw herself into her new job. "This is no coordinated organization," she wrote Anna, "so I start first on my office, then on channels, which don't now exist."[12]

She worked with her usual energy and determination. Elinor Morgenthau helped. Inviting trusted and experienced social workers and reformers to devise programs, she tiptoed through government agencies jealous of their prerogatives, and she elicited support at the community level. In spite of bureaucratic and political obstacles, she obtained federal backing for maternal and child health, nutrition and physical fitness, and day-care services, just the sorts of programs she feared would vanish altogether in the event of war. On Sunday, 7 December, 1941, she worked all afternoon at the White House with Paul Kellogg, editor of *Survey,* the journalistic Bible of social workers, and with Justine Polier, who directed family welfare programs. The next day everything changed. For the second time in a generation, Congress responded to a presidential request for a declaration of war.

Eleanor and Fiorello La Guardia flew to the West Coast immediately after news of Pearl Harbor. California citizens needed reassurance that fears of bombings and invasion were ill founded. If the first lady had any doubts about her ability to convey tranquillity and assurance, she learned otherwise. Even she admitted, "One thing among others I've learned, if we have trouble anywhere that is where I must go because it does seem to calm people down."[13] The lack of defense measures in virtually all the cities she and the mayor visited, however, did nothing to calm her down. Nor did her presence have a calming effect on local politicians who had little sympathy for voluntary participation programs.

War gave civil defense projects the spurt they needed, but it also undermined the social service aspects of OCD. La Guardia, whose administrative abilities were suspect in many quarters, was replaced. Conservative opponents of New Deal social welfare policies welcomed the excuse to gut programs and defeat their proponents. The House of Representatives voted to give the War Department the funds appropriated for the agency. "Many people still feel that advantage is being taken of the emergency to further socialize America," cautioned a Republican congressman as opponents of the New Deal began a frontal assault on OCD.[14] Some appointees were singled out because they had belonged to radical organizations condemned by Congressman Dies. Southerners were offended at attempts to integrate civilian defense units. Eleanor Roosevelt had unwisely appointed a friend of hers who was a dancer to assist the physical fitness program, and newspapers had a field day over what they presumed were the frivolous activities of her friend. She herself was attacked for being softheaded and for turning personal friends into official colleagues. By association, the Office for Civil Defense was also ridiculed.

The House voted to prohibit OCD expenditures for any physical fitness projects that included dancing or for community efforts that involved theatrical shows. While she laughed off the attacks as purely political, her critics were incredibly vitriolic even by the standards that had become common when the first lady promoted an unpopular cause. Her initial apprehensions over accepting an official post were confirmed. The ambiguous position of even the most politically active and sophisticated of first ladies became more obvious with each passing day. "I realized how unwise it is for a vulnerable person like myself to try a government job," she admitted.[15]

Her friend and biographer Joseph Lash correctly attributed the brutal attacks to political as well as personal causes. She understood that she offered a way for opponents to attack the president in wartime when it is not politically wise to do so. Eleanor Roosevelt resigned. On her next radio broadcast she condemned the privileged few who fought social welfare "under the guise of patriotism and economy." She held tenaciously to her expansive liberal priorities and insisted that the defense of democracy was not simply a matter of war material and military strategy. FDR could loudly proclaim that Dr. Win-the-War now sat in the seat Dr. New Deal formerly occupied, but his wife would not accept the notion that military victory abroad precluded a humane society at home. She believed that national defense could and should subsume better nutrition and housing, better medical care and education, better recreation for all citizens. The OCD had enlisted tens of thousands of volunteers anxious to contribute to progress on the home front. They never received assignments. Within six months of Eleanor Roosevelt's resignation, the voluntary participation program lost its war with official Washington.

Hostilities brought nagging worry on a more personal front. All four Roosevelt sons were in the service even before the attack on Pearl Harbor. The previous March she had brought Anna up to date. James was in the Marines, and Elliott in the U. S. Air Corps. Her youngest son, John, was uncertain "if he should volunteer in the navy supply corps. I'm offering no advice for I hate war & all it does to people's lives even at this distance!" And in a postscript: "I haven't heard yet about F jr's bar exams but he expects to be in the navy April 1st."[16] They all saw active duty in the most dangerous war zones and served with distinction, even heroism. Neither their father's status nor their mother's fears shielded them, although inveterate Roosevelt baiters insisted they were coddled just the same.

A surrogate son and new intimate was an additional source of worry. Joseph Lash was one of the youth leaders whom she had mothered and befriended prior to her break with the student movement. Unlike the others, Lash shed his Communist sympathies and found solace in Eleanor Roosevelt's sympathy and understanding when he was torn between his ideological confusion and his friends' steadfast radicalism. She invited him to the White House, Hyde Park, and her New York apartment, eagerly seeking his company. Within a year she was enjoying a closer relationship and reciprocal affection with Lash than with any of her sons. "I've gotten to depend on you, & my heart sings when I'm going to see you in much the same way as it does when Anna's coming," she wrote him, extending an open invitation to join her for tea, for breakfast, or any other occasion he found convenient.[17] There were thinly veiled romantic as well as explicitly maternal overtones in her almost daily correspondence. Lash, however, was deeply in love with Trude Pratt, a German-born young activist in the process of seeking a divorce. Just as Eleanor encouraged and relished her daughter's earlier affair with reporter John Boettiger prior to their divorces and marriage, so she became involved in the passions and problems of her two young friends.

"I know just the mood of lonely despair you were in, but you have to reach the point where you're sure of Trude," she wrote Lash after the lovers had a serious quarrel. She lectured him on the virtues of trust and indicated how near yet elusive the subject was to her. He would trust Trude when he had confidence in himself. "Sometime I'm going to tell you just how lonely I can be in a crowd & it may help you to overcome the same type of thing which I've had to fight all my life. You don't believe in others because you don't believe in yourself. You have the strength for any self discipline & faith that is required if the objective is worthwhile."[18] Her counsel carried the weight of personal experience and authority.

In spite of her growing closeness to Pratt, whom she mothered too, Lash's radical past and his intimacy with the first lady became fodder for hostile journalists and led to a nasty, bizarre encounter with federal intelligence surveillance. Lash was drafted in April 1942. At the beginning of the following year he was assigned to a weather observer training school at Chanute Field in Illinois. The head of the Counter Intelligence Corps (CIC) at the field jumped at the opportunity to investigate this reputed radical. Lash's mail was intercepted and read, including long, affectionate, and newsy letters from the first lady. When she met him at an Urbana hotel during one of his weekend leaves, their movements were recorded. Several weeks later Lash joined her at the Blackstone Hotel in Chicago where an employee informed her that her room was bugged. Her complaints reached Gen. George Marshall, who confronted officials of CIC. News of the unauthorized surveillance also reached FDR. The president's fury led to the direct dismantling of the CIC. It also led to Lash's hasty dispatch to Guadalcanal in the South Pacific and years of uncertainty for Lash over what the president actually believed had transpired between himself and the first lady.

The incident carried a tinge of vaudevillian caper except for the serious glimpse into the mentality of intelligence officers quick to hunt Communists under beds, suspect illicit sex on top of them, and to associate the two. For Eleanor Roosevelt it revealed the depth of her trusting nature and her capacity for love. Her behavior, however, bordered on foolishness. She had unwittingly jeopardized Lash and brought ridicule to herself at a time when the direction of her public purpose was unsettled.

Her stint with the Office for Civil Defense had been a failure; efforts to salvage relief programs were meeting defeat at the hands of Congress. She was appalled at reports of the treatment of blacks in the armed forces. "What a lot we must do to make our war a real victory for democracy," she wrote Lash after reading a leaflet, "Jim Crow in the Army." It "makes you weep & yet I imagine all of it is true."[19] She also worried about racial tensions at home, especially when they erupted in bloody riots. Because of her outspoken views on racial injustice, she was accused, especially in the South, of fomenting violent confrontations between blacks and whites. In fact, she often tempered her feelings for public consumption at FDR's urging. "He feels he must not irritate the southern leaders as he needs their votes for essential war bills. I am not sure that they could be much worse than they are. The rest of the country seems to me sadly in need of leadership on labor questions and race relations," she complained to Lash.[20] Yet she could also counsel patience to blacks, promising recognition for good performance. Southerners accused her of promoting rebellion, while black leaders found her advice condescending.

She was no stranger to contradictions and controversies, but stalemate on the domestic scene heightened her sense of frustration and lack of concrete goals. For three weeks in the fall of 1942, she toured England ostensibly to examine the British women's war effort and to visit American troops. Women working in defense factories, serving as air controllers, and performing countless other "unfeminine" tasks convinced her that American women could also play a significant role in the war effort. She also visited newly arrived American troops, including segregated black soldiers, covered diplomatic bases by meeting the exiled crowned heads of Europe, and renewed her acquaintance with the British royal family. She charmed and was charmed in return by King George and

Queen Elizabeth, and she bantered and debated with Winston Churchill. Filing her daily columns throughout her stay, she tried to convey the immediacy of the war to her American readers. In a nationwide BBC broadcast to bolster the British, she called on them to fight for a just peace with the same determination they fought the war. She had done more to further Anglo-American understanding "than any other single American who has ever visited these islands," a War Information officer marveled as her plane took off for home.[21]

In spite of her amazing capacity to convey concern and compassion when carrying out stultifying official duties, she demurred when FDR suggested a trip to the South Pacific in 1943. Her serious apprehension conflicted with an undiminished sense of duty to her husband. "This trip will be attacked as a political gesture, & I am so uncertain whether or not I am doing the right thing that I will start with a heavy heart," she confessed to Joseph Lash. But there was always the possibility that she might get to Guadalcanal for a reunion with him, and if not, "where I do see our soldiers I'll try to make them feel that Franklin really wants to know about them."[22]

She reluctantly left Tommy behind and brushed up on her typing. Solving the problem of weight limits on baggage, she traveled as an official representative of the Red Cross in uniforms she purchased herself at prices that appalled her when the bills came later. The hope of a visit with Lash made all else bearable as she began thousands of miles of air travel and countless island landings, greetings, and inspections. Gradually she not only overcame her own hesitations but also the misgivings of her hosts—American commanders and foreign leaders alike.

Admiral Halsey, chief of all operations in the Pacific, resented the intrusion by the perennial "do-gooder" when she arrived. But by the time she completed her visits with wounded servicemen and stops at the Red Cross Club on New Caledonia, he was singing her praises. "I marveled at her hardihood, both physical and mental," he wrote later in his memoirs. "She walked for miles, and she saw patients who were grievously and gruesomely wounded. But I marveled most at their expressions as she leaned over them."[23] She did indeed have the incredible gift of walking endless hospital corridors, chatting with uncounted numbers of wounded men, and treating each as though he were her friend and sole concern. As important to Eleanor as Halsey's hard-won admiration was his consent to reconsider a stop at Guadalcanal after her tours to New Zealand and Australia.

Although she was convinced that her presence in these two countries would cause "much trouble & travail of spirit," her official hosts were immediately captivated by her warmth and informality. Even she had to admit that her radio broadcasts were well received and that she had helped cement understanding with Commonwealth leaders even though everyone seemed to treat her like a delicate flower and kept her far from physical danger. Only the vain and overbearing Douglas MacArthur remained impervious to her presence and sent a skeptical but soon-to-be-converted aide to escort her around army hospitals in Australia.

Ten thousand miles from home, the aide surrendered to the maternal aura that surrounded her. She asked to visit kitchens so she could see how the food was prepared for servicemen. She brought a measure of home to the countless wounded with whom she chatted. "In each [ward] she made a point of stopping by each bed, shaking hands, and saying some nice, motherlike thing," the aide recalled. "Maybe it sounds funny, but she left behind her many a tough battletorn GI blowing his nose and swearing at the cold he had recently picked up."[24] If she wanted to flinch at the most severely wounded, she steeled herself in their presence.

The constant refrains of motherhood were fraught with meaning for Eleanor Roosevelt and American women generally. Women's wartime work took them into nontraditional territory—working night shifts in airplane factories and comforting the wounded in distant field hospitals—but instead of proving women's capacity for expanded roles, their jobs were perceived as supportive, nurturing, and above all temporary. Even female activists from the heady days of the early New Deal fought rearguard skirmishes and met constant defeat. Industrial training schools for youth under the NYA flourished after war was declared, and graduates, including women, found jobs in war factories. But opposition to the NYA mounted, and in 1943 the agency was dismantled. The same fate befell the WPA. Frances Perkins, whose imprint on welfare legislation during the 1930s was unmatched, remained at her Labor Department post but was bypassed by new manpower commissions created to address labor shortages and conditions in the workplace. The sympathetic, maternal presence of the first lady in her Red Cross uniform sent a message about American women far different from the earlier image of the caring but controversial catalyst for social change.

Although the perception of her unconventional public activities gave way to that of a more traditional, comforting mother, Eleanor did have the opportunity to effect one major change. American women made significant contributions to the war effort. They entered the labor force in unprecedented numbers and worked in war industries performing tasks considered far beyond their emotional and physical capabilities. The first lady always explored ways in which women's work could be further expanded when she traveled abroad. Yet when both parties proposed planks in their 1944 platforms endorsing an Equal Rights Amendment, Eleanor came to the aid of her beleaguered reformer-friends who tried unsuccessfully to block action by the Democrats. The first lady admitted she was weary of the issue, but she refused to desert the New Deal women who opposed the amendment. She alone may have been able to reconcile the reformers and the feminists. She alone had the prestige and the influence to convince Congress and a grateful public to reward women with legal equality. American women won the suffrage in the aftermath of World War I. They might have expanded their rights following the second world war. Without the active support of Eleanor Roosevelt those chances were doomed. The ERA was simply not among her reform priorities.

Her stance on the domestic needs and reforms that had emerged in the 1930s remained firm. War demanded a commitment to a just society. Men who served their country should be assured of economic well-being at home and peace abroad after their battle on behalf of democracy and national security was won. As she looked at a sea of young faces at the largest American hospital in Australia, she proclaimed her vision of their future: "Jobs at a living wage and the knowledge that the rest of the world is getting things worthwhile so your children may live in a world of peace."[25] A New Deal expanded at home and exported abroad became the hallmark of her political message even as she performed the maternal duties thrust upon her.

Her vision for the postwar world was constructed on plans for international cooperation that extended beyond an assembly of nations. To the Australian people she broadcast her hopes for a peacetime economy of "abundance and employment for all people with low prices on goods so that the people who are just beginning to struggle upward in the rest of the world and need our goods will be able to buy them."[26] Hers was a call for dismantling trade barriers and also for foreign aid. She hedged, however, on the political status of those people she described as beginning to struggle upward. American's Allies were powers who had lost—temporarily they assumed—many of their colonies. Just as she had modified her call for racial justice with pleas for patient gradualism, so she deplored imperialism but shunned public criticism of British, French, and Dutch postwar intentions. "I would go very slow in this

Gandhi business," FDR replied to her efforts to arrange a meeting between him and the advocate of Indian independence.[27] On a personal
level she could act unselfconsciously. She rubbed noses with a Maori
woman in traditional native greeting when she arrived on the island
during her tour, and the photograph became one of the best known of
the entire trip. Her response to people of color was spontaneous, open,
and genuine. Translating her tolerance into public action, however, gave
way to political and diplomatic expediency.

The trip was a resounding success, but the pace had been grueling.
The indefatigable first lady had lost thirty pounds and even she admitted
she was weary. She had traveled over twenty-three thousand miles. To
her displeasure she had been kept from the most dangerous areas, yet she
flew in great discomfort on a cramped, unheated four-engine Liberator.
Her hosts extended wartime comfort, not luxury. In five weeks, however, she had cemented alliances with finesse, charmed chiefs of staff
with tact, comforted the wounded with warmth, and borne great private
pain over the costs of war and the uncertainty of peace. "Pa asked me
more questions than I expected & actually came over to lunch with me
Saturday & spent two hours!" she wrote Anna upon her return.[28] Her
surprise over FDR's unanticipated interest says less about the extent to
which she served his purposes by going in the first place than whether
he planned or she expected the difficult tour to serve any purpose at all.

Her rave reviews were not universal. Unfriendly congressman and
newspaper publishers sniped at the perennial busybody who hopscotched
around the world at government expense. She responded to the attacks
by curtailing her travels and public speeches, relying on radio broadcasts
to convey her ideas about the postwar world. Her press conferences met
less frequently after her return, but they remained a forum in which to
express her views if reporters' questions gave her the opportunity. The
Wall Street Journal correspondent asked her about ways in which to prevent a surge of unemployment after the war. Americans were not unaware that defense production and the draft, not government policies,
had finally brought the depression to an end. Fears about the economy
once the war was over were widespread. Eleanor Roosevelt responded by
emphasizing the international implications of the issue. World cooperation and world markets dominated her call for planned reconversion.

In spite of the enormity of the economics of reconversion and rehabilitation, she was buoyed by the "enormous sense of the possibilities."
But her optimism was not boundless. She feared that the stranglehold
conservatives held in Congress would continue when peace came, and

she reproached her husband for not placing liberal domestic proposals higher on his list of priorities. He advised patience. If he ran for a fourth term, he vowed to "make a liberal campaign & clean out a lot of people." She repeated the conversation in detail to Joseph Lash, to whom she constantly expressed her hopes and worries for the postwar world and her reservations about FDR's resolve. She entertained maimed soldiers at Hyde Park and ached at the thought they may have suffered needlessly: "They are going to fight their handicaps all their lives"—and for what, if the world were the same cruel, stupid place?[29]

The shape and structure of international relations weighed heavily on her mind. When fifty nations pledged to subscribe to the principles of the Atlantic Charter in the early days of the war, FDR had referred to the countries as the United Nations. Eleanor Roosevelt envisioned the agreement as the core of a cooperative, peacekeeping organization. Franklin shared her vision, but she suspected her husband's compatible relationship with Winston Churchill would lure him into the camp of traditional balance-of-power diplomats. When the president announced his plans to meet the Nationalist Chinese leader Chiang Kai-shek in Cairo and then to fly to Teheran for his first encounter with Joseph Stalin, she wanted desperately to accompany him. He turned her aside with the excuse that no women would attend the conferences. He might seek her advice and share her concerns, but he did not want her pushing him further than he believed necessary in the negotiations. The photographs of Madame Chiang Kai-shek with her husband and Sarah Churchill with her father published after the meetings were only reminders to her of his evasion and deceit.

Duty prevailed in spite of her hurt. She made the third of her wartime trips, this time to the Caribbean. FDR wanted American servicemen stationed in the area to know they were not forgotten while the public was so absorbed with the impending invasion of Western Europe and the dramatic, costly island victories in the Pacific. She hopped among the tropical islands and the South American coast on her own, making the habitual rounds of installations and hospitals and attending official ceremonies as though she had never performed such services before, as though each visit and inspection was a new, exciting experience. Island natives and Brazilian citizens poured into the streets to glimpse the special envoy. Even when her schedule was unannounced, crowds gathered as if some force were drawing them to this human magnet. Like their northern neighbors, Latin Americans seemed to sense that a singular woman moved among them.

At home the pleaders of special causes also believed in her unique qualities and influence. She continued to serve as a conduit for countless messages and for the messengers who sought the president's ear. If she failed to arrange formal meetings, Eleanor served as their voices. Correspondence, some offering suggestions, some petitions, moved through her Greenwich Village apartment or her White House sitting room and into the Oval Office. A young nuclear physicist, anxious over the slow pace of the Manhattan project, solicited her help. Letters from Earl Browder, head of the American Communist party, were channeled through her office. Walter White of the NAACP continued to find her a sympathetic advocate of job opportunities for blacks, and Walter Reuther of the United Automobile Workers shared his plans for postwar industrial reconversion and government policy on employment.

For those matters that captured her imagination, she turned ardent petitioner. More than her own notes and other people's correspondence was directed to the president; personal pleas during the late afternoon cocktail hour in the Oval Office and around the dinner table were incessant. Eleanor's sense of responsibility and urgency made her immune to her husband's desire for periodic escape from official duties. Her approach to issues that concerned her was so intense she failed to understand his need for lighthearted banter and companionship when there was a rare break in his schedule. By early 1944, the state of FDR's health exacerbated their productive, but strained relationship.

After the rigors of the Teheran Conference, Franklin Roosevelt spent Christmas of 1943 at Hyde Park. In spite of the rest and the pleasures of family around him, he returned to Washington ill with what was diagnosed as influenza. From that time on, physical deterioration and growing weariness marked the president. Eleanor reacted to his condition with evasion and denial. Perhaps she sensed his mortality and what the loss of his indomitable qualities of leadership would mean to her postwar dreams. The obsessive nature of her badgering may have stemmed from her fears that time, after all, was the most precious of commodities for people and policies. Her demands for social and economic welfare at home and abroad sometimes resembled harassment, and she completely ignored what family and aides thought was FDR's obvious need for rest and diversion.

Her attitude toward the 1944 election hints at the degree to which her postwar aspirations and confidence in FDR's leadership took precedence over his growing physical limitations and dependency. Genuinely worried friends and aides believed he must forgo the nomination. His wife, who had survived three campaigns with feelings that ranged from private despair to political misgivings, did little to discourage a fourth term. After his nomination, she even persuaded him to campaign more actively than he had planned or felt capable of doing.

Those close to FDR noted an indifference on his part toward the 1944 election that was reminiscent of the first lady's reaction to earlier campaigns. But he succeeded in actively undercutting the renomination of Henry Wallace, whose candidacy, unlike four years before, was vigorously supported by his wife this time. In the years since she had salvaged Wallace's vice-presidential nomination, she had grown to believe that he had earned the right to inherit the mantle of New Deal liberalism. She agreed with the president that Wallace was a poor politician and often behaved like an impractical dreamer, but she had come to share too many of those dreams to renounce the vice president, who had become her friend.

During the darkest days of the war, early in 1942, Wallace had delivered a moving speech in which he called for revitalizing domestic reform, promoting worldwide economic security, dismantling Asian and African colonialism, and establishing an organization to promote the peaceful resolution of international disputes. Neither economic royalists at home nor imperialists abroad would deter the emergence of the "century of the common man," he proclaimed, "for on the side of the people is the Lord."[30] Eleanor Roosevelt shared the idealism if not the religious fervor. To the bombast of publisher Henry Luce, who announced "the American Century," and to Winston Churchill, determined to reconstitute the colonial order, she offered Wallace's words in rebuttal. She had found an ally.

Their radical rhetoric declaring a worldwide people's revolution did little to endear the first lady and the vice president to more cautious Democratic politicians. FDR's pronouncements on the shape of the postwar world were considerably more restrained, and his wife deferred to his wishes when he asked her to tone down her public statements. Reluctantly she also concurred with his decision to throw open the nomination for vice president at the 1944 convention. Anti-Wallace Democrats presented a long brief on behalf of naming a new running mate, and Roosevelt bowed to their arguments. There was little Eleanor could do to change his mind. It was hardly the first time she had supported a candidate or promoted a cause only to bow to political necessity as her husband defined it.

Wallace made a better showing on the convention floor than observers had predicted, but without FDR's formal endorsement, Sen. Harry Truman of Missouri was nominated. After the convention, Eleanor Roosevelt hailed Wallace in her column as a man who "believes in the rights of people—all the people, not just a few . . . At times, to meet existing circumstances, he has had to accept certain modifications of his own objectives, but never has he changed his goal."[31] Her evaluation of Wallace rang truer as self-description and, perhaps, apology.

The demands of war and the flagging health of the president precluded a vigorous campaign. If the polls had not shown impressive gains for the lackluster Republican candidate Thomas Dewey, and had Eleanor Roosevelt not goaded him into action, FDR might have remained sequestered within the White House. But he did emerge, reasserting his mastery of electoral politics and rhetoric. His dog Fala emerged the campaign hero. Republicans accused the president of having sent a plane at taxpayers' expense to pick up the animal supposedly left behind after a conference in the Aleutian Islands off Alaska. With mock seriousness, he told an audience of teamsters that he and his family were used to criticism. But Fala was not and had not recovered from the ridicule. The laughter spread across the country and helped defuse more serious Republican charges of Communist taint and trade union influence. Significant doses of racial and religious slurs were added for good measure. When the campaign was over, Lorena Hickok, who had been working with the Women's Division, wrote her friend, "It was, beyond doubt, the meanest campaign since 1928—and I think it was meaner than that one."[32] Eleanor Roosevelt agreed and even her ailing husband concurred.

At the election night gathering at Hyde Park, the excitement of tabulating victorious returns was tempered by the number of absent faces. Both Louis Howe and Missy LeHand, who one political analyst thought exercised more positive influence on FDR than his wife, had died. Even Sara, who had condescendingly turned over the premises to these outsiders on so many occasions, was missed. The four Roosevelt sons were on active duty; only Anna was present. Change was marked in other ways. When the townspeople marched by torchlight to the home in what had become a quadrennial ritual, the president quietly greeted them from the porch, seated in his wheelchair. The message of an imminent election victory was the same, but the man accepting their good wishes did not put on his leg braces to meet them standing as he had always done in the past. The winning margin was slimmer this time, but a majority of Americans and Eleanor Roosevelt, too, were grateful that his sure, if weaker, hand was still at the tiller.

His fourth inauguration was an austere affair. FDR took the oath of office at the White House, forgoing the traditional ceremony on the steps of the capitol. No parade was held. He spoke, standing with tremendous difficulty, for five minutes. Those who watched at close range were appalled and frightened. The president greeted a few well-wishers in the Green Room; the first lady conducted the official receiving. "12 Inauguration, then lunch which will mean receiving till 3. I begin at 5 & should be home all evening," she outlined the day.[33]

There was one respite for a photograph with the grandchildren. The president, perhaps sensing what others began to see so clearly, wanted them all present. Eleanor and Franklin frame an impressive brood of handsome youngsters, but there is something unusual about the group arrangement. In family portraits adults customarily group together at the center, encircled by younger generations. The Roosevelt grandchildren sit and stand according to size and age like a human barrier between their grandparents. Devotion to family had given purpose to the enduring if not endearing quality of their marriage. Here the camera recorded both the affectionate bonds and the emotional distance that the Roosevelts had constructed over the years.

Two days after the swearing in, Franklin Roosevelt began the secret ocean voyage to Yalta to confer with Churchill and Stalin. "F.D.R. & Anna go tomorrow night & I'm not really happy about this trip but one can't live in fear, can one?" the first lady wrote Joseph Lash.[34] She was as depressed over yet another rebuke as she was apprehensive over the travel and the conference itself. She wanted to accompany her husband, but once again he refused her request. This time he insisted Anna travel with him since Churchill and the American ambassador to the Soviet Union were bringing their daughters. Eleanor's presence would create a fuss but Anna's would not, he insisted.

For little over a year, Anna had lived in the White House and taken over the most personal duties that had once been handled by Missy LeHand. It was an opportune change for Anna, whose problems running a Seattle newspaper had mounted after her editor-husband enlisted in the army. Now John Boettiger was reassigned to the Pentagon, the family was reunited, and Anna had the opportunity to be of great service to her harried father. She served him well, according to her mother, for she "brought to all her contacts a gaiety and buoyance that made everybody feel just a little happier because she was around."[35] She performed secretarial functions and served as hostess when her mother was away, even taking over menu planning.

But Anna, to whom Eleanor Roosevelt felt closer than to any of her other children, also dramatized her mother's inability to meet FDR's need for lighthearted relaxation, for chitchat over a late afternoon cocktail or dinner, for someone who could simply listen. Eleanor was no more able to fill these needs when the pressures of war consumed her enfeebled husband than she could make small talk and dance into the early hours of the morning forty years earlier. Even sympathetic New Dealer Rex Tugwell remembered how the president tried to avoid serious talk at the dinner table. "Eleanor, so humorless and so weighed down with responsibility, made this difficult."[36] The same woman who exuded warmth and understanding, drawing strangers to her like a magnet and putting them at their ease, could not bring the same qualities to the family circle. She knew her shortcomings and appreciated the relief Anna brought to her beleaguered father. Perhaps she was envious too as her distance from the Oval Office and from summit conferences recalled childhood feelings of the perennial outsider.

There was a hectoring, almost obsessive quality to her demands on behalf of causes she felt deeply about. Even as FDR traveled halfway around the world to discuss the contours of the postwar world, she wrote letters appealing for his help in the Senate confirmation battle over his nomination of Henry Wallace as secretary of commerce. The department was then headed by Jesse Jones. Wallace and Jones stood at opposite ends of the Democratic party's ideological spectrum and had fought bitter battles in the past. Congress balked at FDR's choice for a cabinet change. To Eleanor Roosevelt, however, the future of the party was at stake. Victory over the Axis powers would pale in significance if Democrats surrendered to their conservative wing. At home or at Yalta, she never let him forget.

FDR and Anna returned after five weeks abroad. The president was satisfied with the agreements reached, although the conference has been at the center of historical controversy ever since. Although the first lady disapproved of three Soviet Union votes in the new United Nations' General Assembly and at placing the small Baltic states under Soviet rule, she told him, "you must be very well satisfied & your diplomatic abilities must have been colossal!"[37] She drove with him to the Capitol when he reported on the conference at a joint session of Congress. For the first time he spoke while seated. Senators and representatives were aghast at his wasted appearance and the flat tone of the once exuberant voice. His wife, however, wrote Lash he looked well and planned to spend a few days at Hyde Park.

This time the usual soothing effect of the Hudson River Valley did not work. He planned a more extended working vacation at Warm Springs at the end of March, accompanied by two cousins, Laura Delano and Margaret Suckley. Eleanor was glad he would have relaxing companionship. "I knew they would not bother him as I should have by discussing questions of state," she admitted. A letter to an aunt revealed her increased concern over his condition, which as always was combined with her worries about public affairs. "I say a prayer daily that he may be able to carry on till we have peace & our feet are set in the right direction."[38]

FDR arrived in Warm Springs gaunt and exhausted, but after a few days of relaxation, he appeared less weak and indifferent. He worked on a speech to deliver at the founding session of the United Nations Organization to be held in San Francisco later that month. He signed some bills, conferred with aides, chatted with his cousins. There were pleasant diversions. Lucy Mercer Rutherfurd arrived with her friend Elizabeth Shoumatoff. After FDR had sought political office and Mercer had married wealthy widower Winthrop Rutherfurd, their paths seldom crossed. During the war, however, and after Rutherfurd's death, their friendship revived. When FDR was on vacation at Bernard Baruch's estate in South Carolina, Lucy Rutherfurd had driven down from her home in Aiken for an obviously prearranged visit. On several occasions after that, when the first lady was away, Lucy dined at the White House while Anna served as hostess. Now in April 1945, she drove to Warm Springs to join the group.

In the middle of the afternoon of 12 April, the president was posing for the portrait Shoumatoff was sketching. His secretary Grace Tully and his advisers were milling about; Lucy Rutherfurd was seated in an alcove watching the progress of the portrait. Suddenly FDR grabbed his forehead. Complaining of an unbearable headache, he slumped forward in his chair. Aides carried his already unconscious body to his bed as others ran for the cardiologist that his White House physician had asked to accompany him. Rutherfurd and Shoumatoff immediately slipped away.

On the morning of 12 April, Eleanor Roosevelt held a press conference, beginning with the usual list of upcoming engagements. That afternoon she was going to a benefit for the Thrift Shop at the Sulgrave Club and that evening to a fund-raising dinner for the American Friends Service Committee. The next day she would speak at a session of the Foreign Policy Association, lunch with Dean Virginia Gildersleeve of

Barnard College, and entertain New York Democrats at tea before they all went on to the party's Jefferson Day dinner.

The newspaper women asked about the fate of Germany after the surrender that now seemed imminent. The War and State departments, the wartime Allies, and the hoped-for United Nations Organization would address those matters, she told them. She looked forward to the founding session of the international body and planned to accompany the president to San Francisco.

After lunch she was meeting with an adviser to the American delegation to the United Nations when she received a phone call from Cousin Laura in Warm Springs. The president had fainted and was in bed. Admiral McIntire, the surgeon general and her husband's personal physician, thought they should fly to Warm Springs that evening but that the first lady should keep to her schedule beforehand to avoid suspicion. Dutifully she kept her engagement at the Sulgrave Club. In the midst of the testimonials and entertainment, she was called to the phone again. Press secretary Steve Early asked her to return immediately. She apologized for her hasty departure and left, certain of what she would hear when she arrived at the White House. She was right. After hearing the report from McIntire and Early, she sat quietly for a moment and then turned to tackle the duties she knew must be performed.

The first lady sent telegrams to her sons—"HE DID HIS JOB TO THE END AS HE WOULD WANT YOU TO DO"—and an entire nation accepted her message as a comforting and courageous command to carry on. She sent for Harry Truman. When her summons reached him, the vice president was chatting with Speaker of the House Sam Rayburn. Neither had any idea why the invitation sounded so urgent. A shocked Harry Truman learned that he was the president of the United States from Eleanor Roosevelt. She pledged her support, for he was the one in trouble now she told him. Then with McIntire and Early she left for the five-hour trip to Warm Springs.

She was somber and composed when she sat down with her husband's cousins and secretary to reconstruct the day's events. She wanted to know "exactly what happened." Laura Delano complied and told her that Lucy Mercer Rutherfurd had been present. And she also told her about the White House dinners at which Anna served as hostess. For once Eleanor Roosevelt had difficulty controlling her feelings as she painfully absorbed one last hurt at the hands of her husband, this time with her beloved daughter acting as accomplice. There seemed to be no end to those closest to her betraying her, deepening wounds that were never allowed to heal.

She finally rose and walked into the room where the president lay, closing the door behind her. Solemn and dry-eyed, she emerged after five minutes. When conversation resumed, it centered on funeral arrangements.

As she had done for a quarter of a century, Eleanor Roosevelt submerged her private pain and cloaked her public persona with dignity and grace. She accompanied the body on the funeral train from Warm Springs to Washington, lost in her own thoughts but gazing from time to time at the knots of Americans gathered along the tracks and at rural railroad stations. Their faces were etched with disbelief and grief and fearful uncertainty. When the train finally arrived at the station in the capital, the flag-draped coffin was hoisted onto the caisson. Six white horses led the mournful procession to the White House. At the main entrance, Secret Service men lifted the casket and carried it into the East Room with the first lady and her children walking immediately behind.

After the brief funeral service, she called Anna to her room. With only the small gold pin her husband had given her as a wedding gift to relieve her somber widow's black, mother confronted daughter with hurt and anger. Anna defended herself with all the difficulty of any child caught in the crosscurrents of parents' compelling needs and failed expectations. She never doubted that she was a "blameless" bystander as her father and Lucy Rutherfurd revived a friendship that meant a great deal to both of them. But she also knew the grief this discovery caused her mother and that any role, however benign, made her a guilty party in her mother's eyes. Anna Boettiger knew that Eleanor Roosevelt, by her own admission, quickly forgave but never forgot. An unwelcome reserve hovered over their once close relationship for years.

Eleanor Roosevelt faced her own sense of loss after forty years of parenting and politics, partnership and alienation. After the last election, Esther Lape had written to her, urging her to focus and utilize the power and position that were particularly hers. Eleanor's replies dealt instead with clearheaded appraisals of her relationship to Franklin. "There is no fundamental love to draw on, just respect & affection," she wrote her friend. "On my part there is often a great weariness & sense of futility in life but a life-long discipline in a sense of obligation & a healthy interest in people keeps me going. . . . I think FDR's sense of a place in history will keep him on a forward going path." That road was now closed, but she found solace in the hope that their shared goals might be achieved after all. "Perhaps his going will unite the nation & achieve his objectives better than had he lived," she wrote Joseph Lash after the funeral.[39] Perhaps she was simply grateful that the country had been spared a replay of Woodrow Wilson's last infirm years, left with an incapacitated president and dashed ideals. She had no desire to repeat the quasi-presidential role played by Edith Galt Wilson. Instead FDR was rapidly transformed into a symbolic presence supporting her hopes for the postwar world.

Her thoughts also settled on the roles she had played, the ones she had chosen and the ones she had renounced. "Maybe I'd do the most useful job if I just became a 'good wife' & waited on FDR," she had written Lape. "If I did I'd lose value in some ways because I'd no longer have outside contacts. I'd hate it but I'd soon get accustomed to it." Several years later she shared her vacillations, her insight into the disparity between Franklin's needs and her choices with the reading public. Few readers of her second volume of memoirs were aware of the presence of Lucy Mercer that hovered over her frank and painful assessment. "He might have been happier with a wife who was completely uncritical. That I was never able to be, and he had to find it in other people. Nevertheless, I think I sometimes acted as a spur, even though the spurring was not always wanted or welcome. I was one of those who served his purposes."[40]

She had indeed served his purposes, but he had also served hers. Eleanor Roosevelt had become an accomplished and influential political figure before her husband entered the White House. But there he furnished the stage upon which her incomparable abilities and human qualities could gain the widest audience and respect. Few presidents and no other first ladies have ever used that platform to such effect. In less obvious ways he was her spur as much as she was his. Having failed each other emotionally, they both found the intimacy they needed in other quarters. He remained practical, self-assured, circumspect; she became more idealistic and forthright. His cautious realism, unencumbered by ideological constraints or even a clear focus, gave eager young bureaucrats and sympathetic political allies the opportunity to explore new approaches to building a humane society. Her idealism and encouragement gave her social reformer and social worker friends the opportunity to turn their dreams into political reality.

Together Eleanor and Franklin Roosevelt mobilized these forces and created a far different political and social landscape than the one that existed when they entered the White House. Neither had considered supplanting the basic economic order that lay in disarray around them. Instead they planted the seeds of the welfare state, and for almost four decades most Americans approvingly considered themselves the inheritors of their joint "politics of caring."

6

FIRST LADY
OF THE WORLD

Eleanor Roosevelt returned to Washington after the burial at Hyde Park. Although Harry Truman assured her there was no need to hurry her departure from the White House, within a few days she had the accumulated belongings of twelve years packed and readied for shipping. She was so occupied that she had little time to think about new realities, but she did find time among the clutter and fatigue to write to friends.

She suddenly realized that she had never fully appreciated or admitted how much she had leaned on her husband's judgment and leadership. He had provided a firmer anchor than the years of their sparring but spurring each other on had indicated. She revealed her surprising discovery to her friends. To Elinor Morgenthau she explained the difficulty of adjustment, how FDR's absence "leaves one without much sense of backing." With Lorena Hickok she agreed that she had never been aware of the implicit faith she had had in Franklin. For love and companionship to fill the unexpected void, she turned to Joseph Lash: "I want to cling to those I love because I find that mentally I counted so much on Franklin I feel a bit bereft."[1]

Once she returned to Hyde Park, she began the tedious and emotionally difficult chore of sorting through possessions and anticipating their division among the children. Franklin Roosevelt had requested that the big house be turned over to the government, and upon accepting the offer, officials insisted that the mansion be stripped of all its contents by mid-May. So she redoubled her efforts, sorting and packing and distributing and finally confessing that she had never been so exhausted.

There were already offers to speak and to work, but she was determined to settle the estate before deciding upon her future course. Without hesitation she settled on the Val-Kill cottage and surroundings as her home. Since the executors had exempted only the former furniture factory, which she had turned into her home, she resolved to purchase the surrounding farmland and buildings from the estate. She could not bear to see everything pass out of family hands, especially the grounds and woods where for years she had walked and pondered life and her own existence. When Franklin, Jr., counseled against depleting her capital, she refused to listen. Elliott and his family agreed to move into the cottage FDR had built for himself on a bluff above Eleanor's. That made her decision more feasible.

As important as her determination to make the Roosevelt lands a family legacy was her less conscious decision to become the guardian of the Roosevelt political tradition—the liberal tradition as she defined it. Historian William Leuchtenburg has written of the long shadow that the personality and politics of FDR have cast over his successors. Eleanor Roosevelt contributed considerable substance to that legacy. When the Allies received Germany's unconditional surrender just one month after Roosevelt's death, she felt compelled to deliver a radio address on behalf of her husband and for all those Americans saddened that he had not lived to announce V-E Day himself. Dressed in mourning black, looking pale and weary, she thanked those at home and abroad for their contributions to victory and begged her listeners to make the same commitment to securing a permanent peace. "That was the main objective that my husband fought for," she reminded her audience.[2] That was hers as well.

Harry Truman could not and would not ignore her influence. She was both symbol and substance of the gigantic shoes he was working diligently to fill. His first steps were so halting that he telephoned regularly for advice. When she wondered in "My Day" why the Western Allies had announced V-E Day two days before the Russians, Truman sent a long handwritten letter explaining the surrender and announcement schedules that had been agreed upon by the Allies. And he complained about his difficulties with Winston Churchill.

She was overwhelmed by his solicitous correspondence and begged him to at least have his letters typed if he felt he must write to her. Then she launched into her own lengthy impressions of the people with whom FDR had dealt and offered advice on how best to handle them. Let Churchill be as voluble as he wished, she suggested, since he is most amenable to diplomatic maneuvering when he can also display his literary knowledge and his memory. As for the Russians, make them laugh for that "was where Franklin won out."[3]

With deliberation or simply from habit, Eleanor also reopened the dispute over the surrender announcements and added counsel on the internecine rivalries that mark White House politics. "A rumor has reached me that the message from Mr. Stalin to you was really received in plenty of time to have changed the hour but it was held back from you," she wrote.[4] The new president may or may not have welcomed the implicit suggestion that he keep a tighter rein on his aides, but he could not help wondering how the former first lady was privy to a "rumor" of such consequence.

If Harry Truman believed that he could mollify Eleanor Roosevelt with gestures of deference, he soon learned differently. She dispensed advice when she lunched at the White House on one trip to Washington, she wrote him long letters or sent copies of ones written to other prominent Democrats, and she commented on the new administration in her daily column. Although she had not settled on a direction to channel her recovered energy, reticence on public affairs was never an option.

Admirers sent offers of jobs, and friends made countless suggestions. Two well-meaning friends, lawyer Henry Hooker and theatrical producer John Golden, visited her at her Greenwich Village apartment to suggest that they pass on the proposals she received and arrange her schedule. She thanked them graciously and dismissed their offer out of hand. "I love both of you dearly," she told them as she and Tommy swallowed their laughter, "but you can't run my life."[5] She was perfectly capable of doing that for herself.

Without hesitation, she dismissed the possibility of running for public office. Travel, on the other hand, was appealing, especially a trip to the Soviet Union. She began to explore that possibility in the wake of the rapidly deteriorating relationship among the major wartime Allies. For the time being, however, she continued to write "My Day" and a monthly advice column in the *Ladies' Home Journal.* She had long hoped for the time she would be able to express her political opinions openly. The daily column had never been as free of partisan sentiment as she claimed, but now all the inhibiting factors were gone.

The Truman administration discovered her new independence

early. She praised and blamed according to her personal and political convictions. She warned the president that he must not allow Congress to undermine the Fair Employment Practices Commission, established to encourage job opportunities for blacks, if he wished to retain the allegiance of black voters. When he publicly endorsed the FEPC, she commended him for doing "a courageous and wise thing."[6] She believed Truman was sincerely putting his stamp on domestic liberalism and she praised his efforts.

Foreign affairs was another matter. She approved the use of the atom bomb, but she also understood the terrors of nuclear weapons unleashed upon the world. Talk of keeping the bomb secret was disconcerting, she informed her readers. International control was the only way to ensure world peace and prevent a nuclear arms race among nations. Soon, however, her outspoken criticism was tempered, for she became an official appointee of the administration.

At the end of 1945, the president telephoned Eleanor Roosevelt at her New York apartment to ask if she would serve as a delegate to the first meeting of the United Nations General Assembly in London. Franklin, Jr., heard her demur, insisting she lacked experience in parliamentary procedure, not to mention the fine points of foreign relations. Her self-deprecation was sincere and predictable but totally unfounded. She firmly held to the ideals of international cooperation for which the new United Nations Organization held great promise, and she had honed her skills as a parliamentarian decades earlier. Her family and friends urged her to accept, and with great apprehension she did.

Congress agreed almost unanimously that the appointment was inspired. Only the vitriolic racist senator from Mississippi, Theodore Bilbo, voted against her confirmation. Truman had found the means to tie the former first lady closer to his administration and, equally advantageous, had discovered a post that would periodically send her abroad. Like his predecessor, Harry Truman found her counsel was often wise but also unremitting and even irritating. For Eleanor Roosevelt, the appointment, in spite of her initial hesitation, provided just the focus for action she was looking for. As she sailed for London with her fellow delegates, she held a press conference. She was as comfortable and competent as ever with the reporters, but there was also a feeling of new beginnings and opportunities. "For the first time in my life I can say just what I want. For your information it is wonderful to feel free," she told the press in an off-the-record comment.[7]

Several colleagues did not feel wonderful about her presence among them, however. The ranking Republican member of the Senate Foreign Relations Committee was Arthur Vandenberg, as stalwart an isolationist as the Midwest had produced until he became a convert to internationalism in 1940. Neither he nor an alternate delegate, John Foster Dulles, who had been Thomas Dewey's foreign affairs adviser during the 1944 presidential campaign, had much tolerance or respect for their female Democratic associate. Their misgivings were returned in kind. "Vandenburg [sic] is smart & hard to get along with and does not say what he feels," the former first lady wrote to Elinor Morgenthau. "J. Foster Dulles I like not at all."[8] But her criticism was nonpartisan. Her appraisals of Secretary of State James Byrnes, Senator Tom Connally of Texas, and other Democrats were no more flattering.

Days aboard ship were occupied with more than sketches of her fellow delegates. She read reams of documents and attended all the official briefings. By the time the ship docked at Southampton, she had mastered myriad technical details, prepared for the opening sessions, and accepted her assignment to Committee III. Newly established United Nations committees dealt with all conceivable political, legal, and monetary issues. Committee III dealt with humanitarian, educational, and cultural matters. She imagined the decision-making reasoning of her male colleagues: "Ah, here's the safe spot for her—Committee Three. She can't do much harm there!"[9] They were right. What no one foresaw was how much good she could generate from that remote rostrum.

To the surprise of all delegates, one of the session's most divisive issues landed in the lap of Committee III—refugee repatriation. Postwar Europe was inundated by a tide of displaced persons—civilians uprooted by war, handfuls of survivors of concentration camps, prisoners of war far from home. Among these ragged homeless were a million people, primarily from Eastern Europe, who opposed the Soviet regime. Repatriation meant probable death for this "new type of political refugee." The Communists insisted on unrestricted and forced return. After endless meetings, proposed resolutions, and finally a committee recommendation, the head of the Soviet delegation announced his opposition to it.

Andrei Vishinsky had served as prosecutor at Stalin's purge trials of the 1930s. With convoluted, relentless attacks, he had sent many of the founders of the Bolshevik state to their deaths. His oratorical skills were legendary; his political loyalty unquestioned. The committee had recommended tolerance and the right of asylum for refugees. Vishinsky mocked their resolutions, equating tolerance with Western capitulation to Hitler at Munich. Who would reply to his challenges? John Foster Dulles asked Eleanor Roosevelt if she would do so.

As she had done at countless press conferences, debates, and lectures, she mounted the platform and spoke without notes. If Vishinsky wanted to compare tolerance with appeasement, would we also equate forced repatriation with the specific possibility of returning Spanish Republicans to Franco's Spain? In the end, she insisted, governments participating at this historic conclave represented human beings, not abstract political entities. It was imperative that the United Nations adopt principles and practices "which will consider first the rights of man, which will consider what makes man more free: not governments but man!"[10] Vishinsky was defeated on the vote over his amendments. Eleanor Roosevelt had made an unwelcome adversary.

As a result of her stunning performance, she also gained unexpected admirers. "When Mr. Dulles said good-bye to me this morning he said, 'I feel I must tell you that when you were appointed I thought it terrible & now I think your work here has been fine!'" Senator Vandenberg returned home admitting "I want to say that I take back everything I ever said about her, and believe me it's been plenty."[11] She emerged from the London session as an effective spokesperson for human rights and dignity. She did her homework, kept abreast of issues, and held her ground in vigorous debate. But as cracks in Soviet-American relations became wider fissures, Eleanor Roosevelt would gladly have traded Republican praise for her performance for Russian agreement with her principles.

A new year began with the first official meeting of the United Nations Human Rights Commission, which had been created to draft and implement an international bill of rights. Truman appointed Eleanor Roosevelt as the American delegate. She was immediately chosen to chair the committee composed of representatives of eighteen of the fifty-five UN member states. For one and a half years she drove the delegates like a slave driver. When one representative pleaded on behalf of his fellow delegates that they needed periodic reprieves, that they had human rights too, she chided them in return. If their speeches were not so long-winded, their sessions would be shorter.

The members of the Human Rights Commission confronted issues and each other. Differences were philosophical and legalistic, but principally ideological. For Americans, a model document would be patterned on their Declaration of Independence and Bill of Rights with emphasis on political freedoms. The state existed to protect individual rights. For the Soviets social and economic rights predominated. The rights of citizens were subsumed by those of the state. In debate, they tossed American principles in American laps, insisting that the conditions of blacks in the United States be investigated, that economic rights such as guaranteed jobs be spelled out in detail. The Soviet delegate parried and delayed while Eleanor Roosevelt debated and deflected.

Additional conflicts arose and were debated, compromised, resolved. "All men" was rewritten "all people" at the insistence of female delegates from third world nations who feared a literal reading. "All men and women were born" not "created" in deference to the nonreligious. Agreements were reached because the chair of the commission gracefully combined feigned naïveté and cunning, and even hardened State Department veterans were unabashedly awed. The first draft was a singular accomplishment, and "the slave driver" allowed herself a moment of uninhibited celebration. Under the approving eye of a diplomatic adviser, she slid like a skater down the elegant marble floors of the Palais des Nations.

The exuberance was a bit premature. A draft declaration was ready to present to the General Assembly in the fall of 1948, but it was first submitted to Committee III for approval. There it was debated point by point as though for the first time. Muslims had to be persuaded that religious freedom did not countermand the Koran, and the Soviets simply argued and procrastinated. Finally on 10 December, the General Assembly voted. Except for eight Soviet bloc abstentions, acceptance was unanimous. The delegates rose in unison to give Eleanor Roosevelt an ovation. She had truly become the first lady of the world—its foremost humanitarian.

The Universal Declaration of Human Rights was a great personal achievement, but Eleanor was both modest and realistic about the work she had guided and pushed to completion. Written affirmations of human dignity and rights were words, not realities. She knew they were guideposts "to which all men may aspire & which we should try to achieve. It has no legal value but should carry moral weight," she wrote her aunt.[12] A formal covenant was needed to enforce the principles in the international community and give it the force of international law. Although a covenant has never been drafted, the declaration endures as a beacon for all those striving for a world grounded on humanitarian principles. Honored often in the breach by countless governments, human rights has become a moral imperative of American foreign policy, combining with practical geopolitical concerns in policy decisions and their implementation.

By 1949, however, civil liberty at home had become as pressing an issue as human rights in other nations. The American political scene had grown contentious and even ugly during Eleanor Roosevelt's tenure on the commission. Inveterate New Deal haters were sniping at attempts to expand domestic reforms and welfare programs. Americans of many stripes were confused and angry over Soviet–U.S. confrontations abroad and fearful of communist influence at home. Even the former first lady was forced to defend her liberal philosophy and reassess the prospects for international cooperation and goodwill. In light of the growing tensions, "I'm ashamed not to be able to decide what I think we should do but all ways seem equally bad!" she admitted to a friend. [13]

She did not easily relinquish her belief that patience with Soviet demands and understanding of their security needs would yield eventual rewards. The United States must be firm but fair. She disapproved of Churchill's Iron Curtain speech and warned her "My Day" readers that a strong United Nations, not former allies promoting their respective power blocs, was the best hope for a lasting peace. She was apprehensive over direct American aid to Greece and Turkey. When the president pledged American help to any nation whose sovereignty was threatened internally or from abroad, she expressed her reservations that the Truman Doctrine undermined the principle of collective security. At the very least, she wrote, American force should be engaged only at the request of the international organization rather than unilaterally to protect traditional British interests in the eastern Mediterranean.

Signs of continuing militarism alarmed her most of all. With consummate ability to trade on the family name and memory, she let her readers know exactly how she felt about displays of naval power. "I must say it did not fill me with great joy to have the planes from the carrier *Franklin D. Roosevelt* writing the ship's initials in the sky over Greece at a time when many people wondered just what was going to happen in that country." [14]

Still she had directly encountered Russian intransigence and duplicity and had been sorely disappointed when the Soviet bloc abstained during the vote on the Declaration of Human Rights. As historian Blanche Weisen Cook has concluded, cold war developments eventually overwhelmed Eleanor Roosevelt. "Gradually and painfully," she acknowledged that the Grand Alliance of the Second World War was over.

Henry Wallace, who stridently attacked American foreign policy but did not acknowledge Soviet complicity in growing international tensions, alienated her. His open acceptance of support from Communists at home further convinced her that he had taken leave of his political senses. Since he also claimed to speak for all liberal-left forces under the auspices of the newly formed Progressive Citizens of America, she felt some coun-teraction was mandatory to disassociate New Dealers from the Commu-nist taint and influence.

At the start of 1947, liberals like the publisher James Loeb, Jr., and lawyer Joseph Rauh called a conference to explore the possibility of founding such an organization. Eleanor Roosevelt attended the gathering "from 9:30 in the morning till after five in the afternoon," and her pres-ence provided an impetus and legitimacy for what became Americans for Democratic Action (ADA). She spent most of the day quietly listening and knitting, but she did deliver one formal address. Those assembled must "set up a liberal and progressive organization" or the heart and hopes of non-Communist progressives would be dashed all over the world, she admonished the group, described by a founder as the New Deal government-in-exile.

Her words implied a twofold agenda for the new organization. Rauh recalled that it was the conservative thrust of Truman's actions after the Republican congressional victories the previous November more than the Wallace threat from the Left that had galvanized the ADA founders. That the former first lady attended the meeting indicated she agreed the mantle of FDR had slipped from Truman's shoulders. After tired but de-fiant liberals finally agreed on a structure and purpose for their new or-ganization, she calmly wrote out a check for one hundred dollars and pledged to raise additional funds. Ideals were fine, she reminded them, but the financial means to advance them were imperative.[15]

She carried on her political battles on two fronts. Wallace and his supporters made peace offerings, but Eleanor Roosevelt and ADA mem-bers refused to be courted. Remembering her experiences with youth leaders during the late 1930s and their cynical expediency, she was ad-amant. "I learned from them what Communist tactics are. I discovered for myself how infiltration of an organization is accomplished. I was taught how Communists get themselves into positions of importance."[16] Betrayal by AYC leaders prepared her for testing by Soviet delegates at the United Nations and Wallace Progressives at home. Her anti-Com-munism hardened slowly, but she left little doubt where she stood by

1948. She denounced Wallace's Communist backers and denied that Wallace was the true heir of the New Deal.

Truman's policies did not please her either. She did not like his appointments to his cabinet or to the Democratic National Committee—men she felt represented conservative viewpoints. In addition to her misgivings over the direction of American foreign policy, she expressed "a fear of the conservative influence that is being exerted on the economic side," she wrote the president. The importance of urban workers was undervalued; the interests of women were completely ignored. If Democrats cast off their liberal cloak, she warned, Wallace would grab it. Besides, placating conservatives was self-defeating. "The Republicans are better conservatives than we are," she reminded the president, who had not asked for the admonition.[17]

When Wallace announced his presidential ambitions, she did nothing to discourage her sons James and Franklin, Jr., from seeking a "true liberal" to carry on the Roosevelt political tradition. Ironically they created a boomlet for Gen. Dwight D. Eisenhower. Truman and party regulars beat off the attack, and most liberals made pointed statements of support for the president at Wallace's expense. Eleanor Roosevelt was more circumspect during the convention and most of the campaign. Not until party officials realized that an upset victory for Truman over Dewey was possible if only the president could carry New York did they appeal to the former first lady for an unequivocal endorsement. She relented. From Paris she arose in the middle of the night to broadcast a short statement a little over a day before Americans cast their ballots. At a time when pollsters had all predicted a Dewey landslide and stopped polling a week before, the impact of Eleanor Roosevelt's last-minute appeal was impossible to measure. The presumption that she exercised great influence on the public was beyond question. Her partisan loyalty was even more certain. She was surprised and satisfied that Truman and the Democrats had triumphed, but as she wrote the Lashes, "I hope we can keep the President & his advisors really moving on liberal lines."[18]

More than Truman's deviations, however, threatened Eleanor Roosevelt's vision of American liberalism. Alarming signs of mindless searches for domestic radicals menaced the political tolerance upon which she believed democratic ideals and institutions rested. Although she was abroad for long periods of time, she remained well informed of the accusations and fears that were gathering force at home. She understood the postwar anxieties and tensions that fed the Red Scare. But she could not abide individuals who exploited American fear and confusion over Communist expansionism by seeking scapegoats at home and by spreading suspicion of domestic complicity, even treason. She castigated the politicians who swung their Red brushes in ever-widening circles. She defended the accused and pleaded for basic principles of tolerance.

To encounter new ideas, to debate, to disagree were fundamental features of American freedom. "The day I'm afraid to sit down with people I do not know because five years from now someone will say five of those people were Communists and therefore you are a Communist— that will be a bad day."[19] At no time would she ever succumb to such fears, but the situation she deplored had become a daily reality. Some critics of the Communist witch-hunts accused the ADA of unwittingly abetting the panic. The accusations were not altogether displaced. By placing the Communist party beyond the political pale, ADA members, like labor federations that expelled their radical unions and politicians who remained reticent, added to the taint, whose sweep was growing wider and deeper.

Eleanor Roosevelt herself adhered to her calls for political and intellectual reason. Soon after its founding, she had become a trustee for Brandeis University. The new institution laboriously set about building an academic reputation and financial stability. Her hard work, not just her name, were indispensable on both counts. When the trustees met to review faculty hiring, one outstanding applicant for the mathematics department was none other than the son of Earl Browder, head of the Communist party. The Brandeis board deplored the political climate but still feared associating the fledgling university with a Browder. The former first lady threw down the gauntlet. Either her fellow trustees display courage and hire solely on the basis of merit or she would resign. At a time when trustees and administrators at many well-established universities were bowing to pressures and dismissing faculty at the slightest hint of radical associations, Brandeis leadership was sustained by one woman's convictions.

The personal and political havoc caused by congressional investigating committees and Sen. Joseph McCarthy infected private board rooms and public forums alike. Eleanor Roosevelt's contempt for mudslingers and intimidators was equaled by her disdain for honorable men who tolerated them. When Sen. William Jenner of Indiana accused General, later Secretary of State, George Marshall of leading a public life that was a living lie, the accusation dramatized the poison seeping into the nation's political system. In 1952, the refusal of Republican presidential candidate Dwight Eisenhower, whose career had been advanced by Marshall and who had worked intimately with him, to come to Marshall's defense and disassociate himself from the accusers appalled Eleanor. Although she did not campaign actively for Eisenhower's opponent, Adlai Stevenson, she did address a rally in Harlem. There she pointed her remarks directly at Eisenhower: "I know that it must have been terrible to face yourself—to realize that you have been persuaded that you must go out and stand beside men who had said things about someone who had been your best friend, someone who had really given you the opportunity to rise to great position."[20] Eisenhower had stood silent beside Jenner, and she simply could not understand such complicity in this nasty affair. Personal loyalty and democratic principles had both been sacrificed, and this was behavior she could neither comprehend nor countenance.

After Eisenhower's victory, Eleanor Roosevelt, like all appointed officials, submitted her resignation. It was accepted. In spite of her accomplishments as a hard-working delegate and her reputation as a consummate ambassador of goodwill, the new administration could hardly conceal its glee at being rid of her. Eisenhower chafed at her criticism of his handling of McCarthyism; his aides felt compelled to placate Red-baiting senators, especially those attacking the integrity of the State Department.

She was now a private citizen, even freer to speak her mind than she had been as a delegate to the United Nations. She accepted a position with the American Association for the United Nations (AAUN) and undertook an extensive lecture tour to defend the international organization. The same right-wingers bent on ferreting out internal subversives also looked suspiciously on U.S. participation in the UN. Her refusal to abandon the principles of international cooperation was as firm as her pleas for domestic political sanity.

In order to step up the battle against McCarthyism, she agreed to serve as honorary chairman of the Americans for Democratic Action. The sympathetic *New York Post* applauded her stand, for "Mrs. Roosevelt suggests to the reactionaries and to the timid alike that the time for the counter-offensive of decency is at hand." She lectured and wrote about the deleterious impact of the Red scare abroad, the perception that Americans had taken leave of their senses along with their freedoms. She accused the witch-hunters of employing the same tactics as their enemies, creating "an atmosphere akin to that of communist countries, for we are using the very weapon those countries use."[21]

Increasingly she found herself defending the loyalty of friends and former colleagues. Mary McCleod Bethune, Walter White, and other black leaders were suspects. Aubrey Williams, with whom she had worked on the National Youth Administration, came under attack. Accusations against former officials in the Roosevelt administration caused her to question the true basis for the scare tactics. "I am beginning to think, however, that if you have been a liberal, if you believe that those who are strong must sometimes consider the weak, and that with strength and power goes responsibility, automatically some people consider you a Communist."[22] Under these circumstances, Eleanor Roosevelt should have been served a subpoena to appear before the formidable Senate Committee on Internal Subversion. But even the senator from Wisconsin demurred. He challenged the U.S. Army instead, and the army proved to be his match. During televised hearings, the nation watched the senator in action and recoiled. Eleanor Roosevelt had never doubted that day would come, when democratic forces and common sense would prevail.

In October 1954, she turned seventy. In the past she had always discouraged celebration, public or private. This time she relented for a cause close to her heart. She permitted the AAUN to honor her with a gala dinner at the Waldorf Astoria Hotel. In that manner she could reaffirm her faith in the world body and assist the group in badly needed fund-raising. It was a festive affair. United Nations secretary general Dag Hammarskjold attended with his predecessor, Trygve Lie. More than a thousand guests joined them. None of the Eisenhower members of the UN delegation attended. But in an unexpected gesture, Andrei Vishinsky came to pay tribute to a gallant lady and formidable opponent. He would be glad to sit anywhere, he told the stunned dinner organizers. When he posed with the guest of honor afterward, Red baiters added the photograph to their files of incriminating evidence.

The occasion gave Eleanor Roosevelt the opportunity to reaffirm her support for the UN. She credited her years as a delegate as the most satisfying of a lifetime of public activities. "There I was part of the second great experiment to bring countries together and to get them to work for a peaceful atmosphere in the world, and I still feel it important to strengthen this organization in every way."[23] The configuration of world politics had changed considerably since the heady days of the wartime alliance, but her faith in international cooperation remained undeterred.

Her family were all present at the dinner, and she addressed them at the conclusion of her remarks. Whatever her public accomplishments,

"I treasure the love of my children, the respect of my children, and I would never want my children or my grandchildren to feel that I had failed them."[24] It was a moving testimonial to her devotion to family. For she who had experienced such familial upheaval as a child valued the love and bonds of generational ties. If it was a public declaration of the paramount role of her family in her life, perhaps it was also a plea for reciprocity. She would love them and not disappoint them if they did not fail her and returned her affection.

The postwar years had been difficult ones for the Roosevelt children as they tried to stabilize their marriages and find meaningful and productive careers. Their mother was always aware of the momentary crises and the long-range aspirations of each of her children. She offered advice when it was requested, absented herself when independence was demanded, traveled to their sides and gave whatever material and emotional assistance she could when that was needed. The problems of her children were complicated by the competition among them. Family conclaves often degenerated into bitter confrontations and disagreements over matters ranging from how FDR's childhood letters should be edited and published to who should run for what office in which state. Anna and her three brothers always thought their mother favored Elliott. While his politics and social values differed most from his mother's and siblings', Elliott's behavior, both erratic and engaging, may have reminded Eleanor Roosevelt of her father, for whom this special son was named.

No matter how crowded her official calendar, family matters always took precedence. And if she could not keep private peace among them in closed settings, she at least exacted promises that they would display public unity and loyalty. Family also meant a sense of place and renewal of tradition. Hyde Park gave her that feeling. She hoped it could be the one place where her family acknowledged its roots. She was especially grateful that Elliott moved onto and managed the estate when it had seemed everything but her cottage would have to be sold. And later John and his family moved into the cottage built originally with Nancy Cook and Marion Dickerman.

The exchange of gifts at Christmas embodied familial love and devotion. For Eleanor Roosevelt it was always a special time for friends as well. She spent the entire year buying presents for those she loved, gifts she knew family and friends would want or need. She kept a record of what she had given to whom as her closet filled with special purchases over the course of each year. One year James and his wife suggested that the entire family forgo the gift-giving tradition. His mother was furious. "This is the kind of high handed, pompous action which loosens family ties and does not bind them closer," she wrote him in hurt and anger. "One must do things for people one loves or love dies and you are moving in the direction of narrowing your affections, one has less to give that way."[25] She stated her personal testament as admonishment.

The family did unite in the face of personal crisis. Anna's marriage to John Boettiger dissolved, and she encountered serious financial and career problems when she became ill with what was diagnosed as tuberculosis. Her brothers rallied to her side, and her mother hastened preparations for a radio program that would help financially. With Anna written into the contract as producer and Elliott as announcer, Eleanor Roosevelt added a forty-five minute daily radio commentary to her weekly television interview show, her monthly column in McCall's, and "My Day." Elliott, who read the commercials, openly suggested that "Mother uses" the advertised products of the sponsors. Anna had misgivings over the blatant commercialism of the program and the added burden to her mother, but Elliott reassured his sister. He understood his mother as well as she knew each of her children. She thrived on the "feeling of really doing something worthwhile. It makes her feel closer to her own family," he wrote Anna. "Mother would like to knit us all together as a family unit, united in good times as well as bad."[26]

The Roosevelts' ability to close ranks around Anna did not guarantee a lasting truce. Family gatherings became more rancorous. On one occasion sons John and Elliott almost came to blows and then both directed their wrath against their mother. In despair she confessed to a friend that her children would be much better off if she were not alive. From the dais of the testimonial dinner on her seventieth birthday, she may have been extending a public apology for overshadowing them, undermining their independence of action, failing to create the family harmony that constantly eluded them. A year before her death she finally wrote to each of her children that she knew their strengths and weaknesses well and loved them all dearly. She would be loyal in their public ventures and devoted privately. But she would now visit each of them separately, for she could no longer abide their contentious reunions.[27]

When her children were not contending with one another, they were increasingly wary of her friends, especially her "surrogate sons." After their marriage Trude and Joseph Lash distanced themselves from the Roosevelt clan, declining invitations to summer at Hyde Park. They adored Eleanor Roosevelt, but they were aware that her feelings for them were not matched by her children's. When Elliott assured Anna she could accept their mother's help because it "makes her feel closer to her family," he added with more than a hint of resentment: "The truth of the matter is that if Mother didn't do this for you she'd probably do it for someone else like Lash or Gourevitch [sic]. She's just made that way."[28]

David Gurewitsch was the newest star in the Roosevelt firmament. A Russian-born, German-educated, Swiss-trained physician, he was forty-five when Eleanor Roosevelt renewed a casual acquaintance with him on a flight abroad. She was traveling to a United Nations session in 1947, and he was going to a Swiss sanitarium for treatment for tuberculosis. Gurewitsch was a handsome, charming, sophisticated man, physically ill and emotionally distanced from his British wife. He and the former first lady corresponded after going their separate ways in Switzerland. Within weeks the sixty-three-year-old woman was already assuring him that he need not worry that he abused her friendship. She confessed her own lingering reticence, too. "I still have some of my old shyness and insecurity left when it comes to close relationships and that is probably what makes you feel shy. I've really taken you into my heart, however, so there need never be a question of bother again."[29] Their friendship grew in intensity, and the romantic overtones of Eleanor Roosevelt's feelings became increasingly apparent.

Once cured, Gurewitsch returned to New York, where he gave her life new meaning. Yet, like Earl Miller and Joseph Lash before him, he was a much younger man, beyond reach. As she had done so often in the past, she embraced the women and children who accompanied her love object. She entertained his wife until their divorce and drew his young daughter into her orbit. He accompanied her to social events, and she derived great pleasure in the company of this urbane, devoted escort. Insecurity, however, was never far: "I love you dearly David but try to remember to tell me that *you* want to be loved by me now and then because I don't want to be a duty or a bother!"[30] Then when he remarried, to her distress at first, she made her own apartment in the couple's Manhattan town house. Edna Gurewitsch could no more resist the love and solicitude than had others who had joined the charmed circle; she and her new husband played dominant roles in Eleanor's postwar world.

Those years also afforded time to travel in addition to UN assignments, and Gurewitsch often joined her. When the General Assembly adjourned early in 1952, Eleanor took the opportunity to explore. Her beloved Tommy was incapacitated so her new secretary-companion,

Maureen Corr, accompanied her and David. They toured two of the world's developing areas, each holding out promises of the postcolonial era, each embroiled in regional conflicts. Their first stop was Beirut, followed by visits to other Arab capitals. Security was tight, and the famous tourist was greeted with overt opposition for her unabashed defense of Israel. Although she was genuinely appalled at conditions in Palestinian refugee camps, her political and emotional ties to the Jewish state never wavered. "Going from the Arab countries through the Mandelbaum Gate [separating Jordanian from Jewish Jerusalem before the city was united in 1967] into Israel was, to me, like breathing the air of the United States again."[31]

Eleanor Roosevelt had not always reacted so sympathetically to the concept of a Jewish state. She had heard Zionist pleas for a homeland during the war, and while she, like other Americans, was aware of Nazi concentration camps, she was unconvinced that a separate state was the solution to Western anti-Semitism. The former first lady generally responded to people as individuals rather than to elaborate theories. Such was the case when she tramped through the mud at a displaced persons camp during an inspection tour soon after the war. Suddenly an old woman knelt at her feet, threw her arms around her knees, and repeatedly murmured, "Israel! Israel! Israel!" It was the kind of personal encounter to which Eleanor Roosevelt immediately reacted. "As I looked at her weather beaten face and heard her old voice, I knew for the first time what that small land meant to so many people," she recalled.[32]

Although she threw her influential support behind Jewish immigration to Palestine, a year passed before she endorsed partition and the creation of a Jewish state. Once her position was sanctioned by UN vote, she brought all her persuasive powers to bear on reluctant American officials including Harry Truman and his secretary of state. She influenced the decisions to recognize the new nation quickly, to lift the arms embargo during the Arab-Israeli war that ensued, and to appropriate foreign aid in the years that followed. She remained an ardent articulate supporter until her death. Her 1952 trip was the first of three.

She was not oblivious to the economic and military problems, and she deplored the religious influence of Orthodox Judaism on affairs of state, but nowhere did she feel greater kinship. "What astounds me in Israel is that the spirit is like the American spirit," she told "My Day" readers. "There is imagination to accomplish great projects and no fear of undertaking them."[33] She was a constant speaker at Hadassah, the Jewish women's organization that supported the most advanced hospital in the Middle East, and she was a constant presence at fund-raising affairs sponsored by the United Jewish Appeal. Support for Israel remained a divisive force in the American Jewish community until the 1967 war. Her presence at these public occasions was cherished by American Zionists, for any cause with which Eleanor Roosevelt chose to identify gained credibility. When the United States joined the Soviet Union in condemning the British-French-Israeli assault on the Suez Canal in 1956, she was appalled that Republican foreign policy had permitted a wedge to be driven between the Western allies and had condemned the only democratic state in the region as well.

After her first visit to the Middle East she traveled to the troubled Indian subcontinent. She arrived in Pakistan first, where most of her sightseeing and meetings focused on Muslim women. She was intrigued by their attempts to create a network of needed social services as they precariously balanced centuries of traditional closeting with the challenges of postcolonial nationhood. She was optimistic about Pakistan's future, but she held firm to her opposition to American arms aid proposals to shore up the new country's pro-American posture. The newly emerging nations of Africa and Asia, she insisted, needed financial and technical assistance for economic development. Limited resources must not be diverted into military weapons when food was a primary need.

In India she was personally greeted by Prime Minister Nehru, with whom she established immediate rapport. The determination of this complex society to build genuine democracy roused her admiration. She was also sensitive toward Indian apprehensions over American attitudes of racial superiority and their fears of American economic domination. She melted the resistance of skeptical deputies when she addressed Parliament in her singular manner, smiling warmly, speaking without notes, squarely addressing issues that concerned her captive but wary audience. She told the deputies that she understood Indian neutrality in the polarized world of cold war and apologized for the American tendency to equate nonalignment with procommunism. But just as she defended India's right to determine its own course, so she defended Americans against third world charges that they were bent on imperialistic policies. She was sincere and convincing, but Indians drew distinctions between speeches by private individuals and those by public officials. As a Bombay newspaper editorial asked, how many American congressmen shared her view that Indian acceptance of aid from communist countries would not compromise American assistance?

Leftist Indian students were more cynical. Her trip to Allahabad to receive an honorary university degree turned into a confrontation with hostile students. While she met with one group of young people who had signed an open letter denouncing her apologies for American imperialism, thousands of additional students gathered outside the Nehru compound gate protesting her visit. No one could head off what seemed like a riot waiting for an appropriate spark. After her hostess failed to quell the protest, Eleanor Roosevelt climbed on a chair perched on top of a table so that she could be seen over the fence by the hostile crowd. She agreed to leave the compound and meet the students in their hall. She insisted on going alone while the Nehru family, university officials, and David Gurewitsch wrung their hands in concern for her safety.

After reaching the auditorium, she spoke briefly and then answered questions about American policies toward India and Communist China, about foreign aid and American racism. If her answers did not meet with great enthusiasm, her candor created an immeasurable reservoir of goodwill. The students' newspaper in Allahabad did not recant its accusation that she apologized for practices that "prolong colonial rule in non-white countries which are still unfree." But the students also distinguished between official policy and the courage of their visitor. Her encounter years before with the American Youth Congress and her engaging personality served her well.[34]

The Republican administration turned deaf ears to the views she expressed in *India and the Awakening East,* published early in 1953. She pleaded for a foreign aid policy built on economic rather than military aid. She criticized the creation of the Southeast Asia Treaty Organization, which she thought was a counterproductive military alliance that ignored the appeal of communism to hungry stomachs. Marxist ideas did not capture the imaginations of emerging countries, but neither did the potential of political democracy. Individual freedoms are rightfully cherished by Americans, but the "freedom to eat is one of the most important freedoms and it is what the communists are promising the people of India," she warned. The effectiveness of economic aid over military supplies became a constant theme in her speeches. At home and overseas, at formal lectures and spontaneous gatherings, the speeches were beyond count. In 1955 she went abroad in the spring—England, Italy, Israel— and Trude Lash, who accompanied her, wrote home that her friend "does not seem really happy unless she explains something to a crowd of people."[35]

As a private citizen she continued extensive traveling abroad. The Japanese expressly requested that she visit under the auspices of a private

American foundation, and the new administration raised no objections to a nonofficial tour by a private citizen. She was especially interested in the status of Japanese women and discovered that within the patriarchal Japanese family, mothers-in-law held power over the household and younger women second only to husbands and oldest sons. She noted that the older women controlled family finances, directed household management, and were served along with husband and son by subservient daughters-in-law. She wished to promote opportunities for Japanese women as they emerged from the traditional patterns of prewar Japanese society, but on farms and in factories, she found the women had little interest in rights and status. Their ultimate goal was achieving the status of mother-in-law. If memories of Sara Delano Roosevelt surfaced as she made her observations, she failed to note the fact.

At an audience with the emperor and empress, she pressed the issue of women's roles as both preservers of tradition and agents for positive change. The empress was not convinced; the emperor deferred to his government to determine the pace of reform. Her meeting with the prime minister was unsettling on another account. Although he could not say so publicly, he assured her that Japan was going to rearm. She relayed her sense that broad segments of Japanese society opposed such a policy. She could speak with authority for officials admitted that no visitor had ever displayed such openness and been rewarded with such frank responses from the Japanese.

She spoke her mind in other places. Hiroshima was not originally on her itinerary, but she insisted upon a visit to the city and a meeting with some of the bomb victims. Eleanor Roosevelt never questioned the moral or military imperative of the use of the weapon. She answered a flurry of questions frankly, insisting that the causes of war bring about such things as the use of horrendous weapons. The cause, not the effects, of war must be addressed because "if there is another Pearl Harbor, there will be undoubtedly another Hiroshima."[36] She wrote home that she felt as if she was walking on eggs. As she viewed the material and human destruction, she was deeply moved but not sentimental. When some newspapers reported that she wept during a visit to burn patients, she noted that her guide was in tears, not she.

After the party left Japan, there were stops of various lengths at Hong Kong, Delhi, Istanbul, and Athens before they arrived in Yugoslavia. This was the first communist country she had ever visited, although Tito had broken with Stalin in 1948 and made much of his national and ideological independence. She toured the provinces and

Tito entertained her at his seaside resort. She needed little convincing that the United States should cooperate with Yugoslavia since they both opposed Soviet policies. But she knew the difference between international realities and rivalries and internal politics and economics. Tito was an ebullient, charming host, but paeans to his brand of "social democracy" did not convince her that he was a democratic leader of a democratic nation.

Travels abroad expanded her knowledge, feeding her insatiable hunger for new experiences. In spring 1956 she turned her attention to the American political scene and what she hoped would be the renomination of Adlai Stevenson as the Democratic standard-bearer. Sen. Estes Kefauver of Tennessee had done well in several primaries; Truman made no secret of his support for Gov. Averell Harriman of New York. Eleanor took to the campaign trail in several states and was credited with Stevenson's impressive victory in California. The lagging energy that friends had begun to notice was nowhere apparent to the public, even less to herself. During the California campaign her schedule was as frenetic as ever, and she admitted she "was running around so madly speaking for Adlai that I had forgotten I was a grandmother, and a great grandmother at that!"[37]

Although she championed Stevenson's candidacy, she was not without apprehensions over the candidate. His witty, urbane eloquence made liberal principles ring from any platform he mounted. His overseas travels since his 1952 defeat had enhanced his knowledge of foreign affairs and his reputation in diplomatic circles. Still there was an aloofness, a contemplative air that disturbed her. She wished he would mingle more with people so that he would feel as comfortable with the average American voter as he did speaking elegantly from distant rostrums. He weighed courses of action to the point of distraction. Friends and opponents alike wondered if his caution and contemplation did not disguise indecision. And there were ADA stalwarts who insisted that Stevenson's inclinations were considerably more moderate than his liberal rhetoric. Eleanor was familiar with and disturbed by these charges, but her support held firm.

Her political influence and toughness were put to the test at the convention. When Harry Truman arrived in Chicago, he called a press conference where he ticked off Harriman's virtues. The former first lady arrived the next day and undermined Truman's cause during a press conference of her own. Then, with candidate in tow, she visited state caucuses in pursuit of delegate votes. And once more she mounted the convention platform to make an official address. This time she was not heading off a party rebellion but rather propelling Democrats into the future.

The party was the nation's oldest and could indeed be proud of past leaders, traditions, and accomplishments. But the party must also look ahead to young leadership. Democrats "must take into account the advice of their elders, but they must have the courage to look ahead, to face new problems with new solutions."[38] No one had guarded her husband's legacy more fiercely, but neither had anyone more effectively sounded the call to move outside his long shadow and address new challenges—especially the problem of enduring poverty—which the New Deal and the Fair Deal had attacked but not vanquished. Observers hailed her speech as the finest clarion call they had ever heard, although a decade would pass before a president would initiate the war on poverty for which she called with continued mixed results.

Eleanor Roosevelt had the force of personality and authority to swing the convention to Stevenson. Her success was not without sacrifice of principle as she tried to steer a difficult course between political expediency and the compelling demands of black leaders and her ADA colleagues over civil rights. Two years earlier the Supreme Court had struck down the doctrine of "separate but equal" that had institutionalized racial segregation. While southern Democrats issued a manifesto urging resistance, other delegates came to the convention determined to write a strong platform plank pledging full implementation of the ruling. Eleanor Roosevelt chose party unity over principle and supported an ambiguously worded plank. Angry black leaders promised to reexamine their ties to the Democratic party; she threatened to resign from the board of the NAACP. Neither party carried out its threats. On this issue at this time, Eleanor Roosevelt, who once wrote that she was "more careful than I otherwise have been" when she deferred to her husband's political demands, demonstrated that she could also compromise ideals when she was on her own. It was not her finest hour.

After a trip to Europe to show the sights to two grandchildren, she returned to campaign as vigorously for Stevenson's election as she had for his nomination. Her schedule was so full that one newspaper assigned a reporter to cover her activities just to see if she actually did keep to the announced pace. She did. "I have never worked as hard as I have this autumn," she wrote a friend. She also found time for some sage and motherly advice to the candidate: stop agonizing over every word of text, address each crowd as though you were talking to just one person, get more rest, try her special pills to ward off colds and fatigue. Nothing helped and she was bitterly disappointed as the election returns poured in. There was little that could have been done to curb "the love affair between Eisenhower and the American people," she wrote Stevenson in consolation.[39]

One long-sought goal was finally achieved: she visited the Soviet Union. Earlier efforts had encountered logistical and diplomatic snags, but now she departed with an official itinerary and David Gurewitsch. The tour was carefully orchestrated with great emphasis on the museums, circus, and ballets of Moscow and Leningrad. "Getting app[ointments] to see 'services' & not just museums is very difficult," she informed the Lashes. Even Eleanor Roosevelt, who found the size and spontaneity of her "welcome in spots almost embarrassing," also discovered that " 'Intourist' is a reluctant agent."[40]

A seasoned traveler and observer, she managed to circumvent some of the obstacles. On a tour of a collective farm she asked to see the homes of farmers but had to settle for a glimpse of a model house. She flew to Tashkent, where she viewed a hospital and boarding school, and then on to Samarkand, where the once-great Mongol Empire "became quite real & not just a myth." A good part of the trip was spent separating myth from reality, comparing present with past conditions, American standards with Soviet ones. The evaluation process was puzzling. By American levels, the quality of life in the Soviet Union was primitive, yet the "life of the people is enormously improved" compared to conditions fifty years earlier. She noted that only leaders seemed concerned with ideology as distinct from sincere efforts to upgrade the quality of life of the people, who "don't worry about politics." Still she admitted communist propaganda was not so easily separated from social progress: "On every hand 'peace' is preached & we are depicted as the one danger to peace. They have no news that is truthful about the outside world so they believe & are grateful for all the improvements at home." Therefore Russians were incapable of separating myth from reality, a "strange 'Alice in Wonderland world,'" she concluded.[41]

With typical procrastination and inefficiency, Soviet officials informed her that a meeting with Nikita Khrushchev had been arranged. She had just returned to Moscow from the Black Sea resort of Sochi. Since the premier was vacationing with his family outside Yalta, the touring party had to turn around and travel all the way south again. After a night's rest and a brief visit to the palace where the Allied leaders had drawn up the Yalta agreements, she arrived at Khrushchev's villa. What

began as an interview quickly turned into a debate. The canny Ukraini-
an peasant who ruled an empire and the patrician New Yorker whose
influence stemmed from force of personality argued vehemently. They
found little common ground whether they discussed the meaning of the
Yalta Pact and past responsibility for the cold war or current hopes for
Middle Eastern peace and nuclear disarmament. Finally the rest of the
Khrushchev family joined them for refreshments and a farewell. "Can I
tell our papers that we have had a friendly conversation?" the premier
asked. "You can say that we had a friendly conversation but that we
differ," she answered. "At least we didn't shoot each other," he
concluded.[42]

The touring party stopped at Copenhagen after leaving Moscow.
Like other Westerners before and since, Eleanor Roosevelt realized how
somber and strained Russia had been only after departing. Once she
"heard laughter and gay talk and saw faces that were unafraid . . . I
realized how different were our two worlds. Suddenly I could breathe
again!"[43] Still, the delights of freedom only confirmed her belief that
democracy was a luxury that rested on a solid base of full stomachs. She
understood why the planned but brutal economy of the Soviet Union
appealed to developing nations. Food, not arms, technical, not military
training would help guarantee that postcolonial countries could graft political rights onto socially and economically secure systems.

She shared her convictions with everyone who would listen. She
shared her hospitality, too. The cottage at Val-Kill continued to hum
with people and activity. Friends and neighbors chatted around the dining room table stretched to its limits. Unreconstructed New Dealers rem-
inisced in the living room. Grandchildren scampered in and out, often
with bathing suits dripping. Visiting dignitaries picked their way through
the chaos on obligatory stops to pay homage to the world's best known
and admired woman. National holidays were observed with respect for
historical origins and past events. On the Fourth of July she or one of
her sons would read the Declaration of Independence. At her last
Thanksgiving gathering, she read the proclamation FDR had issued in
1933 during the depths of the depression. She welcomed what would be
the last year of her life with his traditional White House toast: "To the
United States of America." One could not meet the challenges of change
at home and upheavals abroad without firm rooting in the past.

For all the bustle of people and expressions of love and respect,
however, self-doubt and loneliness were unremitting. The constant presence of family and friends and the bulging schedule book could not mask

despondency. She admitted as much when she corresponded with Joseph Lash during the war. Referring to Trude Lash, who was engrossed in frenzied activities for a student service organization, Eleanor wrote him, "When one isn't happy it is hard not to live at high speed." Lash thought it was an apt description for a woman with four sons in the military, but it applied to her entire adult life. "For the first time I feel she is driven by some inner compulsion that will never let her come to rest," an adviser at the UN wrote.[44] He may or may not have gained insight into the ties between the obsessive nature of her frantic pace and her unyielding personal unhappiness. What was truly remarkable was her ability to live on two planes simultaneously, one marked by private pain, the other by public activity.

She claimed her closest friends made it possible for her to carry on in the public arena, that those dearest to her were all that really mattered, that she could easily renounce the hectic activism and bask in the comfort of her personal relationships. Yet for all the left-over demons of a love-starved childhood and the unremitting sense of unworthiness, there was a zest to Eleanor's activities during the postwar years that belied somewhat the underlying depression. As Lash notes perceptively, "It was Franklin's death that was changing her—she no longer had to fight him and pretend to herself that it was his life she was leading, not her own." On occasion she finally confessed that "she enjoyed the things she did."[45]

At the age of seventy-five, she also admitted she had reached a milestone, a time when she was entitled to look back and engage in a bit of introspection. Whatever her public acclaim and renown, she did not think she was an exceptional person. She insisted she possessed only three assets: "I was keenly interested, I accepted every challenge and every opportunity to learn more, and I had great energy and self-discipline." She was not an intellectual nor was she enticed by elaborate ideologies. "My interest or sympathy or indignation is not aroused," she continued, "by an abstract cause but by the plight of a single person whom I have seen with my own eyes."[46] One malnourished child illuminated the terrors of world hunger; one distraught refugee dramatized the need for a Jewish homeland.

Her path of caring and coping carried her in ever expanding circles from the personal, to the community, to the nation, and to the world. In the end, her willingness to seek out and do battle with problems at all levels stemmed from a personal victory. She admitted in the most general terms to loneliness and grief. But harking back to the frightened, insecure child that she had described in her first memoir a quarter-century earlier, she now wrote with justifiable pride and confirmation that "having learned to stare down fear, I long ago reached the point where there is no living person whom I fear, and few challenges that I am not willing to face."[47] Victory was not complete, but it was no small achievement for an emotionally scarred woman.

She could be feisty as well as fearless. Although she continued to shun celebrations when the spotlight was on her, she allowed the Democratic Advisory Committee to use the occasion of her seventy-fifth birthday for a party fund-raiser. Harry Truman acted as master of ceremonies and all the current crop of presidential hopefuls used the event to present themselves to fellow Democrats by toasting the guest of honor. Adlai Stevenson was the most eloquent; John Kennedy, the most effusive. Five other would-be nominees praised the woman the New York Times featured as "Mrs. Democrat." Only Sen. Lyndon Johnson was missing.

After all the appropriate praises, Truman rose to speak. He called for party unity, for it was imperative that Democrats send one of their own back to the White House. And then he directed his remarks to "those self-appointed guardians of liberal thinking who have become rather vocal lately." Where did these "hot-house liberals get their mandate to dictate to the party?" he asked. He preferred practical working liberals to the pretentious kind who "distort the objectives of the Democratic Party."[48]

Eleanor Roosevelt rose to respond to the toasts and to the former president. It was the end of a long day that had begun early that morning when she testified before the Senate Subcommittee on Migrant Labor on the deplorable conditions of agricultural workers. She had visited with friends and filed her newspaper column. With her habitual graciousness she thanked everyone for the tributes. With her usual self-effacing tone, she credited the praise heaped upon her to the work her husband had done and to the heritage he had left. And with the tenacity and certainty that had become increasingly apparent during the years she was on her own, she undertook to guard that legacy as she interpreted it. She announced she was going to differ with Harry Truman. The first lady of the world calmly turned a celebration into a confrontation.

The former president "doesn't like certain kinds of liberalism," she began. "I welcome every kind of liberal that begins to learn by coming into our party what it is to work on being a liberal." The world was changing, she reminded her listeners. It was a different place with different problems than it had been when the war ended, and it was still changing daily. New ideas from new people to address new issues were necessary, and the Democratic party must embrace these "liberals that are younger, even if they are older in age, younger in coming into the party, because they may be conscious of new things that we have to learn."[49] So the seventy-five-year-old matriarch of the party responded to the seventy-five-year old former president.

Political analysts buzzed over the exchange. Commentators thought that Truman had singled out ADA members who were promoting tough measures on civil rights, federal aid to education, and a government program on health care at the expense of "practical" officeholders holding the line while Republicans occupied the White House. ADA leader Joseph Rauh thought so, too, and marveled at Eleanor Roosevelt's retort.

Ironically her call for new faces and voices did not extend to her preference for the presidential nomination. In spite of two defeats and his insistence that he was not a candidate, Eleanor Roosevelt backed Adlai Stevenson in 1960. The more momentum the Kennedy campaign gained, the greater her support of Stevenson. Her opposition to the young senator from Massachusetts was complex and deep-seated.

In 1956, Kennedy had vied for the vice-presidential spot on the Democratic ticket. His backers approached her for support, and she refused outright. Although Kennedy had been in the hospital during the Senate's vote on the censure of Joseph McCarthy, he had waffled in his reply when asked to clarify his position afterward. She would not accept the pleadings of his aides that all that was "old news." To Eleanor Roosevelt principle was involved, and she had little patience with politicians who refused to take a stand on basic issues. Four years later JFK's attitudes toward McCarthy and McCarthyism were even older news, but she had neither forgotten nor forgiven. To his friends and advisers, Kennedy complained that she simply did not realize that he represented a large Catholic constituency with a pro-McCarthy bent. She would not have been impressed with that reasoning either.

His Catholicism, not just his constituents, caused her concern too. Eleanor Roosevelt had overcome religious prejudice. She had worked hard for Al Smith and had seen the ugliness of religious intolerance joined to political opposition. But she never fully overcame her suspicions about the power and authoritarianism of the church hierarchy. She had encountered that authority firsthand and had not enjoyed the experience.

After Sara Delano Roosevelt died, FDR was anxious to sell the twin town houses in Manhattan. Abram Sachar, later president of Brandeis

University and then an administrator at Hunter College, thought the buildings would make an ideal student center. He and the president met as two amiable businessmen and, in short order, agreed that the college assume the mortgage on the property and name the proposed project the Sara Delano Roosevelt Interfaith Student Center. By the time the refurbished facility was ready for dedication, the president was on a wartime trip. The first lady filled in. At the last moment, however, Francis Cardinal Spellman, archbishop of the diocese of New York, refused all support if the term *interfaith* were used. There was, after all, only one faith, according to the cardinal. At Eleanor Roosevelt's insistence, the ceremony proceeded, and the building was named the Sara Delano Roosevelt Center. She assured the dismayed Sachar that her husband would be delighted that the facility carried his mother's name and the students would know exactly what functions the center provided.

Her next encounter with the cardinal was not so easily or quietly resolved. Like many liberals, she had long supported federal aid to primary and secondary schools. In 1949 a bill was introduced into Congress calling for appropriations to public schools. The Catholic church lobbied for parochial assistance in the form of textbooks and transportation. Eleanor Roosevelt informed "My Day" readers that she was adamantly opposed to the use of any public funds for the support of any functions of private schools, especially those of religious denominations. She stood irrevocably for the separation of church and state.

Cardinal Spellman issued a public letter. He accused her of misrepresenting the church's position and of personally attacking him. He insisted that her position was consistent with her history of anti-Catholic activities. "And even though you may use your column to attack me and accuse me of starting a controversy," he wrote, "I shall not publicly acknowledge you." All her stands were "documents of discrimination unworthy of an American mother!"[50]

The cardinal's denunciation of her "long record of anti-Catholicism" indicated that more than just aid to education lay at the root of his diatribe. Eleanor Roosevelt had indeed taken several positions that ran contrary to church policy. Her sympathy to Loyalists during the Spanish civil war and her unwavering support for the United Nations resolution that called on member states to sever ties with Franco's Spain infuriated the Vatican. Her lukewarm concern for the imprisoned Hungarian Cardinal Mindszenty, whose wartime activities had been controversial, angered Spellman, too.

In a private letter to the cardinal which she published one week later, she responded point by point, sounding the constant theme that too often the church overlooked the famous dictum concerning the respective spheres of God and Caesar. Then she concluded with a rebuff that was "devastating" according to the Catholic mayor of New York. "I assure you that I had no sense of being 'an unworthy American mother,'" she wrote. "The final judgment, my dear Cardinal Spellman, of the worthiness of all human beings is in the hands of God."[51]

A public storm broke over the exchange of letters. Mail flooded Hyde Park, overwhelmingly in her favor. Catholic political leaders rallied to her side, too, but many were apprehensive about the impact of this confrontation on a sizable bloc of Democratic voters. Ed Flynn, former party head, arranged a reconciliation with quiet encouragement and orchestration from the Vatican.

Spellman telephoned her; he and Eleanor Roosevelt wrote and revised two "clarifying" letters for publication; he then drove to Hyde Park for tea, chatting as though the bitter controversy had never occurred. Actually, he was incensed at the forced apology implied by his visit. And his hostess did not let him depart unscathed. He had threatened to bar Catholics from voting for the New York senatorial candidate because of his stand against aid to parochial schools. Without veiling her threat, the former first lady bade her guest good-bye with the warning that if Herbert Lehman failed to get the usual level of Catholic support that Democrats expected, liberal New Yorkers would see to it that Catholics in public office in the future would be few and far between.

The confrontation reaffirmed her fears regarding church influence in secular affairs. And the letters that poured into her cottage endorsed her stand in language that betrayed prevalent if latent anti-Catholicism among disturbingly large segments of the American community. A decade later, lingering apprehensions over official church policy and power as well as doubts over the ability of a Catholic to gain the presidency colored her views toward Kennedy and his drive for the party's nomination. In a television appearance she chided him for his lack of courage in evading the McCarthy issue, and in a column she expressed her distrust of John Kennedy's father, Joseph, whom she suspected of buying the presidency for his son. Her sons, in the meantime, all jumped on the Kennedy bandwagon.

As the probability of a Kennedy nomination grew, her determination to absent herself from the convention and state no preference of her own crumbled. She announced support for a Stevenson-Kennedy ticket and forced Stevenson into a reluctant, ambiguous statement of availability. She encouraged a "draft Stevenson" movement, discouraged pro-Stevenson forces from jumping ship, and flew to the convention in Los Angeles. "I doubt very much whether I can do anything," she wrote a friend before beginning whirlwind activities in which she tried her best to do everything.[52] She was superb at a press conference where one columnist reported that she "hatcheted" the senator with the steely sweetness of a grandmother. She visited eleven state caucuses pleading Stevenson's cause and attended an emotionally charged rally.

Nothing stemmed the Kennedy drive for a first-ballot victory. Her own call for the party to turn to a new, younger generation was heeded despite her own best efforts. Disappointed with Stevenson's evasive behavior and her own abortive performance, she left Los Angeles immediately after the balloting. Reluctantly she took a phone call from Kennedy at the airport and spoke in unaccustomed harsh and brusque terms. After arriving at Hyde Park, however, she extended an invitation to visit. Kennedy was both delighted and apprehensive about making the obligatory pilgrimage to this fount of party influence. Eleanor Roosevelt could no longer control the outcome of a convention, but she was still a force to be reckoned with.

Their meeting crystallized her inward discipline and commitment to public duty. The day before the scheduled lunch, her granddaughter Sally fell from a horse and was killed. "I find it hard to realize even now that I'll never see that child running thro' my house again," the devastated grandmother wrote Anna.[52] But personal tragedy never interfered with political obligations. Kennedy offered to postpone the visit, but she insisted that he come as planned.

The seventy-five-year-old guardian of the party's soul and the young man who carried its hope of reclaiming the presidency made peace. They sat at a small table in front of the far window of the comfortable living room. They discussed the need for Democrats to close ranks, especially the Kennedy and Stevenson camps. Although she hoped he would name Adlai Stevenson his secretary of state, she assured JFK that his cabinet choices were his alone. "I liked him better than I ever had before," she told a friend afterward, "because he seemed so little cocksure." On Kennedy's part, he left the hour-long lunch "absolutely smitten by this woman."[54] If true, he was not the first to anticipate disagreement with Eleanor Roosevelt only to succumb to her personal magnetism and political acuity. Still, a hint of strain remained in both camps.

She agreed to make campaign appearances and relished his victory, narrow as the margin was. Stevenson was not named to head the State

Department. Her disappointment may have influenced her decision to view the inauguration from the stands, bundled in blankets on a blustering January day, rather than accept an invitation to sit on the platform. But if there was pique, she listened to the inaugural address with an open mind. She thought she heard the tone of self-confidence, optimism, and delight in meeting challenges that marked a strong president.

Adlai Stevenson accepted appointment as ambassador to the United Nations and suggested that Eleanor Roosevelt serve on the delegation to the General Assembly. Only perfunctory appearances would be necessary, for it was obvious that the vagaries of age were catching up with the former first lady. Increasingly the woman who always kept her myriad engagements, and punctually at that, missed sessions. She tried to dismiss the aches and pains; otherwise "the first thing you know you're an invalid." She apologized to Stevenson for her absences because of flu, but then admitted, "Actually, I don't have the 'flu but phlebitis! I didn't want to talk about it and thought the 'flu a good excuse."[55] Excuses were more frequent, but still she accepted several new appointments.

At the end of 1961, Kennedy created a presidential commission on the status of women. The groundwork had been carefully laid by Esther Peterson in the Labor Department. She was firmly opposed to an Equal Rights Amendment to the Constitution, pressure for which had resurfaced. She also believed it was economically and diplomatically expedient to tap unutilized female resources in the cold war competition with the Soviet Union. Besides, the administration was embarrassed by constant questions at news conferences about what the "New Frontier" was doing for women. May Craig, a veteran of the press conferences of the 1930s, was the irritant, complaining about the paucity of female appointments in the new administration. Peterson expected a study on women's status generally to deflect criticism over lack of concern at the same time it concluded women's rights were always constitutionally guaranteed. She scored a coup by channeling an invitation to Eleanor Roosevelt to chair the proposed commission through the White House. Roosevelt accepted what would be her final official role, giving the commission—like other organizations to which she lent her name—immediate recognition.

Without hesitation, she prepared for the new assignment. The former first lady had, after all, promoted opportunities for women, especially women in politics, for four decades. During the early 1950s when a publisher suggested a written history and tribute to female activists, she convinced Lorena Hickok to undertake the effort. "Please consider it, it is needed, but I can't give the time to consultation with [publishers], research & basic writing."[56] Both their names, however, appeared on *Ladies of Courage*, a compendium of praise for women of both parties at all levels of government, dedicated to Molly Dewson, and critical of the loss of stature of the Women's Committee of the Democratic party. Eleanor Roosevelt's eagerness to promote women was unflagging, but as her delegation of *Ladies of Courage* to Hick indicated, her efforts were diluted by her expanding activities in other areas. But along with Emma Guffey Miller, she wrote to Kennedy to point out the lack of women in visible political positions.

Ironically, political women were singularly absent from the commission handpicked by Peterson, whose background lay in organized labor. The group was dominated by women from trade unions and from voluntary organizations. Working-class leaders and community activists provided the backbone of opposition to the ERA, succeeding the social reformers of earlier decades in that capacity. Eleanor Roosevelt had actually modified her resistance to the amendment, believing that women in trade unions could take collective action on their own behalf, which made protective legislation increasingly obsolete. Still she never turned her altered stance into open advocacy of the ERA, and Peterson must have believed she could still be counted on to stem the growing popularity of the amendment.

Eleanor Roosevelt played host to a major gathering for commission members at Hyde Park in February 1962. Afterward her health deteriorated rapidly. The various subcommittees conducted their studies and wrote their conclusions under Peterson's supervision. The final report was formally presented to Kennedy on the anniversary of the former first lady's birth in 1963. *American Women* was a coda to forty years of weakened feminist consciousness as well as the opening salvo of a reborn women's movement. The report endorsed the primacy of women's roles in their homes and their communities but also noted the growing numbers of women in the labor force. Commission members underplayed discrimination in the workplace, but they did propose equity in hiring in the civil service and proposed legislation to mandate equal pay for equal work. Admitting past gender-based inequities that should be addressed by federal legislation was novel, but at the time the proposal was designed as a tactical device to circumvent the blanket amendment. If an equal pay act were passed and survived judicial review under the guarantees of the Fifth and Fourteenth Amendments, both women's rights and the special legislation that protected female workers could be safeguarded.

The cautious thrust of the report would not have disappointed Eleanor Roosevelt, if she had lived to read it. Although she constantly monitored and tried to open opportunities for women, she always stressed immediate personal examples of achievement rather than vast social change. She did not extrapolate her own experiences as wife, mother, and public figure onto a wider stage. The female generation with whom she came of age was even less likely to do so. Usually single, educated, and professionally productive, these women achieved as individuals and were willing to serve as positive models, but they ignored the cultural and institutional impediments that blocked the paths of the next generation.

Liberals generally, and liberal women in particular, were absorbed with issues of class during the middle third of the twentieth century. They constructed the welfare state, designed to smooth the ragged edges of industrial society, to guarantee a modicum of protection and security for farmers and workers—and even middle-class citizens during truly hard times—buffeted by economic winds over which they had no control. In the postwar period, liberals added race and civil rights guarantees to their priorities. Gender was simply not high on the liberal agenda. If Eleanor Roosevelt held a narrow vision of women's rights and status in society, she merely reflected the blind spot of American liberalism in its heyday.

Contemporary issues and long-range programs received less attention from her after the spring of 1962. Her energy flagged; aches were transformed into constant pain. She ran a persistent fever that occasionally spiked to dangerous levels. At the beginning of July, she was hospitalized. David Gurewitsch not only remained "the one to whom my heart is tied above all others,"[57] but was also her physician. After a summer of periodic remissions and resumed activity alternating with growing debility, she was readmitted to the hospital at the end of September. Her children and dear friends gathered at her bedside in the hospital and then at her uptown apartment for the final vigil. But nerves were frayed and years of resentments exploded.

Anna came to New York and took over the management of her mother's apartment, giving orders to Maureen Corr. Corr, as faithful and competent as her predecessor, Tommy, now found she was dispensable. Gurewitsch disputed Eleanor's diagnosis, treatment, and the role of consultants with Jim Halstead, Anna's physician husband. Anna monitored visitors including the Lashes and even her brothers. Anna and David Gurewitsch could barely conceal their mutual hostility; they argued over medical measures once a definitive diagnosis of rare bone marrow tuberculosis replaced the earlier belief that Eleanor suffered from aplastic anemia. They gave conflicting reports to competitive newspapers.

The sorry scene was probably inevitable. Eleanor Roosevelt loved these people passionately, but she could not make them love, even respect, each other when she was well and vigorous. Now, desperately ill, she had no control over the anger and exasperations swirling around her. Even worse, she was powerless to act against the heroic medical attempts that were being made to prolong a life she was ready to surrender. She welcomed death, yet she was sentenced "to suffer every human indignity, every weakness, every failure that she had resisted and conquered so daringly during her whole life," Trude Lash wrote movingly. It seemed "as though she were being punished for being too strong and powerful and disciplined and almost immune to human frailty."[58] But at long last, on 7 November 1962, after a severe stroke, Eleanor Roosevelt suffered no more degrading punishment. At seventy-eight, the first lady of the world died.

The public who paid their respects to the gallant woman knew little of her last physical plight or the stormy family battles. The mayor of New York ordered the city's flags flown at half-staff, and President Kennedy followed suit. Political figures at home issued moving tributes, and so did foreign leaders. Average Americans felt suddenly bereft. One woman called a newspaper to verify the time of her death. "She couldn't have died at 6:15," she woman sobbed. "We were eating dinner then and we were happy."[59]

After a simple service at the Episcopal church at Hyde Park, Eleanor Roosevelt was buried next to her husband. Presidents Truman, Eisenhower, and Kennedy watched somberly. One would-be president, Adlai Stevenson, represented the UN mission. Lyndon Johnson, who would occupy the Oval Office in a year's time, stood nearby. Sandwiched between the reminiscence of the man from Lubbock, Texas, who remembered Eleanor Roosevelt speaking in a Panhandle town while a sandstorm raged outside, and the official condolences sent by the Queen of England was a short statement by Jim Farley, former postmaster general and chairman of the Democratic party. "Her devotion to duty was truly unselfish, and as long as the memory of American woman is recorded in our country's annals, the name of Anna Eleanor Roosevelt will be enshrined." Few people disagreed, and the editorial writer for the *New York Times* wrote, "We shall not soon see her like again."[60]

CHRONOLOGY

1884	Born in New York, 11 October
1892	Death of mother
1894	Death of father
1901–1903	Education at Allenswood School, England
1905	Marriage to Franklin D. Roosevelt, 17 March
1906	Birth of Anna Eleanor
1907	Birth of James
1909	Birth and death of Franklin Jr.
1910	Birth of Elliott Election of FDR to New York Assembly, move to Albany
1913	Appointment of FDR as Assistant Secretary of the Navy, move to Washington
1914	Birth of Franklin, Jr.
1916	Birth of John
1917–1918	Volunteer work during World War I
1920	Return to New York, joins New York League of Women Voters
1922	Joins New York Women's Trade Union League and Women's Division of the Democratic Party
1924	Chairs women's subcommittee on the platform at the Democratic party convention
1926	Builds cottage at Val-Kill, co-founds Val-Kill Industries, begins teaching at Todhunter School

1928   Co-chairs women's division campaign for Al Smith
FDR elected governor of New York

1933   FDR inaugurated president, 4 March
First press conference for women reporters, 6 March

1936   Begins "My Day" newspaper column

1937   THIS IS MY STORY published

1940   Addresses Democratic national convention, 16 July

1941–1942   Appointed to and resigned from the Office of Civilian Defense

1942   Trip to Great Britain

1943   Tour of southwest Pacific

1945   Death of FDR, 12 April
Appointed to United Nations Delegation

1947   Founding of the Americans for Democratic Action

1948   United Nations Declaration on Human Rights

1949   THIS I REMEMBER published

1952   Trip to Israel and India

1953   Trip to Japan and Yugoslavia

1956   Campaign for Adlai Stevenson

1957   Trip to the Soviet Union

1958   ON MY OWN published

1961   Chairs President's Commission on the Status of Women

1962   Died in New York, 7 November

GENEALOGY

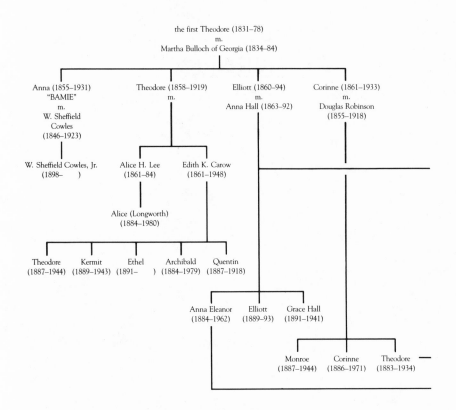

the first Theodore (1831–78)
m.
Martha Bulloch of Georgia (1834–84)

Anna (1855–1931)
"BAMIE"
m.
W. Sheffield
Cowles
(1846–1923)

Theodore (1858–1919)
m.

Elliott (1860–94)
m.
Anna Hall (1863–92)

Corinne (1861–1933)
m.
Douglas Robinson
(1855–1918)

W. Sheffield Cowles, Jr.
(1898–   )

Alice H. Lee
(1861–84)

Edith K. Carow
(1861–1948)

Alice (Longworth)
(1884–1980)

Theodore
(1887–1944)

Kermit
(1889–1943)

Ethel
(1891–   )

Archibald
(1884–1979)

Quentin
(1887–1918)

Anna Eleanor
(1884–1962)

Elliott
(1889–93)

Grace Hall
(1891–1941)

Monroe
(1887–1944)

Corinne
(1886–1971)

Theodore
(1883–1934)

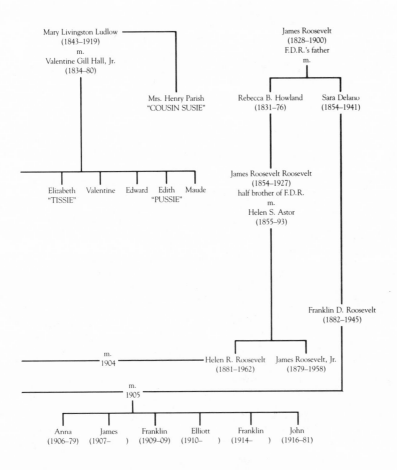

Mary Livingston Ludlow
(1843–1919)
m.
Valentine Gill Hall, Jr.
(1834–80)

James Roosevelt
(1828–1900)
F.D.R.'s father
m.

Mrs. Henry Parish
"COUSIN SUSIE"

Rebecca B. Howland
(1831–76)

Sara Delano
(1854–1941)

Elizabeth
"TISSIE"

Valentine

Edward

Edith
"PUSSIE"

Maude

James Roosevelt Roosevelt
(1854–1927)
half brother of F.D.R.
m.
Helen S. Astor
(1855–93)

Franklin D. Roosevelt
(1882–1945)

m.
1904

Helen R. Roosevelt
(1881–1962)

James Roosevelt, Jr.
(1879–1958)

m.
1905

Anna
(1906–79)

James
(1907–   )

Franklin
(1909–09)

Elliott
(1910–   )

Franklin
(1914–   )

John
(1916–81)

NOTES AND REFERENCES

PROLOGUE: CHICACO, 1940

1. Quoted in Joseph P. Lash, *Eleanor and Franklin* (New York: W. W. Norton & Co., 1971). 618n.

2. Frances Perkins, *The Roosevelt I Knew* (New York: Viking Press, 1946), 132.

3. *New York Times*, 19 July 1940.

4. Lash, *Eleanor and Franklin*, 620.

5. *New York Times*, 19 July 1940.

6. Nathan Miller, *FDR: An Intimate History* (Garden City, N. Y.: Doubleday & Co., 1983), 452.

7. *New York Times*, 19 July 1940.

8. Lash, *Eleanor and Franklin*, 623.

9. *New York Times*, 19 July 1940.

10. *The Autobiography of Eleanor Roosevelt* (Boston: G. K. Hall, 1984), 218. This book combines abridged versions of Eleanor Roosevelt's three volumes of memoirs and a fourth section, "The Search for Understanding." Citations from her memoirs all come from this single volume.

11. Lash, *Eleanor and Franklin*, 624.

12. Lash, *Love Eleanor: Eleanor Roosevelt and Her Friends* (Garden City, N.Y.: Doubleday, 1982), 308.

13. Bernard Asbell, ed., *Mother and Daughter: The Letters of Eleanor and Anna Roosevelt* (New York: Coward, McCann & Geoghegan, 1982), 121.

14. *Autobiography*, 218.

1. COMING OF AGE

1. Quoted in Lash, *Eleanor and Franklin*, 7.

2. Ibid., 20.

3. Ibid., 28.

4. Ibid., 32.

5. Edmund Morris, *The Rise of Theodore Roosevelt* (New York: Coward, McCann, & Geoghegan, 1979), 438.

6. Ibid., chap. 17.

7. *Autobiography*, 9, 10.

8. Lash, *Eleanor and Franklin*, 49.

9. *Autobiography*, 13.

10. Lash, *Eleanor and Franklin*, 61.

11. Ibid., 73.

12. Ibid., 61.

13. *Autobiography*, 12.

14. Lash writes about Souvestre with detailed sensitivity in *Love, Eleanor*, chap. 2.

15. Ibid., 31.

16. Lash, *Eleanor and Franklin*, 86, 73.

17. Lash, *Love, Eleanor*, 36.

18. *Autobiography*, 36.

19. Ibid., 37.

20. Ibid.

21. Lash, *Love, Eleanor*, 33, 34.

22. *Autobiography*, 40.

23. Ibid.

2. MATRON AND MOTHER

1. Geoffrey C. Ward, *Before the Trumpet: Young Franklin Roosevelt, 1882-1905* (New York: Harper & Row, 1985), chap. 6.

2. *Autobiography*, 50.

3. Ibid., 51.

4. Ibid.

5. Ibid., 53.

6. Ibid., 55.

7. Ibid., 61.

8. Ibid., 62–63.

9. Ibid., 63.

10. Ibid.

11. Ibid., 62.

12. Ibid., 65.

13. Ibid., 68.

14. Ibid.

15. Ibid., 71.
16. Ibid., 75.
17. Ibid., 75–76.
18. Ibid., 74.
19. Ibid., 86.
20. Ibid., 86, 87.
21. Quoted in Lash, *Eleanor and Franklin*, 210, 211.
22. *Autobiography*, 89.
23. Lash, *Love, Eleanor*, 69.
24. *Autobiography*, 91.
25. Lash, *Eleanor and Franklin*, 191.

3. POLITICAL APPRENTICE

1. Lash, *Eleanor and Franklin*, 237.
2. *Autobiography*, 105.
3. Lash, *Eleanor and Franklin*, 241.
4. Ibid., 256.
5. Lash, *A World of Love: Eleanor Roosevelt and Her Friends, 1943–1962* (Garden City, N.Y.: Doubleday & Co. 1984), 101.
6. Lash, *Love, Eleanor*, xiv.
7. Lois Scharf, "The Women's Movement in Cleveland," in *Cleveland: A Tradition of Reform*, ed. David D. Van Tassel and John J. Grabowski, (Kent, Ohio: The Kent State University Press, 1986), 85–86.
8. *Autobiography*, 120.
9. Asbell, *Mother and Daughter*, 136.
10. *As Equals and As Sisters: Feminism, Unionism, and the Women's Trade Union League of New York* (Columbia: University of Missouri Press, 1980), chap. 7.
11. Lash, *Love, Eleanor*, 84.
12. *New York Times*, 15 April 1924.
13. *Autobiography*, 125.
14. Ibid.
15. Quoted in Abigail Q. McCarthy, "ER As First Lady," in *Without Precedent: The Life and Career of Eleanor Roosevelt*, Joan Hoff-Wilson and Marjorie Lightman, eds. (Bloomington: Indiana University Press, 1984), 217.
16. Lash, *Love, Eleanor*, 97.
17. Lash, *Eleanor and Franklin*, 296.
18. Lash, *Love, Eleanor*, 96: Lash, *World of Love*, 303.
19. Lash, *Love, Eleanor*, 109; *Autobiography*, 148.
20. Lash, *Eleanor and Franklin*, 319.
21. M. K. Wisehart, "What Is a Wife's Job Today?" *Good Housekeeping*,

August 1930, 10; Wisehart, "Ten Rules for Success in Marriage," *Pictorial Review*, December 1931, 4, 36.

22. Lash, *Eleanor and Franklin*, 336.

23. Helena Huntington Smith, "Noblesse Oblige," *New Yorker*, April 1930, 25.

24. Ida Tarbell, "Portrait of a Lady," *Delineator* October 1931, 19, 48.

4. THE FIRST LADY AND THE GREAT DEPRESSION

1. *Autobiography*, 163.

2. Lash, *Eleanor and Franklin*, 355.

3. Ibid., 358.

4. Lash, *Love Eleanor*, 154.

5. Lash, *Eleanor and Franklin*, 358.

6. *Autobiography*, 171.

7. McCarthy, "ER As First Lady," 222.

8. *The White House Press Conferences of Eleanor Roosevelt*, ed. Maurine Beasley (New York and London: Garland Publishing, 1983), 7.

9. *Autobiography*, 176.

10. *Press Conferences*, 9.

11. Ibid.

12. *Autobiography*, 132.

13. *Press Conferences*, 19.

14. Martha H. Swain, "ER and Ellen Woodward: A Partnership for Women's Work," in *Without Precedent*, 152.

15. *Press Conferences*, 28–29.

16. Eleanor Roosevelt, *My Days*, (New York: Dodge Publishing Company, 1938), 130.

17. *Press Conferences*, 13.

18. *My Days*, 125.

19. Lois Scharf, "ER and Feminism," in *Without Precedent*.

20. Marie Manning, "Keeping Up with Mrs. Roosevelt." *Delineator*, March 1935, 10.

21. *My Days*, 101.

22. *Press Conferences*, 25.

23. Asbell, *Mother and Daughter*, 61.

24. *Autobiography*, 130.

25. Asbell, *Mother and Daughter*, 177–78.

26. *My Days*, 3, 4.

27. Asbell, *Mother and Daughter*, 95.

28. *My Days*, 91–92.

29. *Press Conferences*, 9.

30. *My Days*, 110.

31. *Press Conferences*, 61.

32. Ibid., 20.

33. Ibid., 115.

34. *Down and Out in the Great Depression: Letters from the Forgotten Man*, ed. Robert S. McElvaine (Chapel Hill: University of North Carolina Press, 1983), 58.

35. Ibid., 75, 57, 77.

36. *My Days*, 118.

37. Ibid., 190–91.

38. Ibid., 83, 86.

39. *Farewell to the Party of Lincoln: Black Politics in the Age of FDR* (Princeton, N.J.: Princeton University Press, 1983), especially chap. 6.

40. *My Days*, 126–27.

41. *Press Conferences*, 44.

42. Weiss, *Farewell to the Party of Lincoln*, 135.

43. *My Days*, 180–81.

44. "My Day," 24 March 1937.

45. *Press Conferences*, 29.

46. Ibid., 28.

5. "FIRST MOTHER" AND WORLD WAR II

1. *My Days*, 91.

2. Quoted by John Salmond in "National Youth Administration," *Franklin D. Roosevelt, His Life and Times: An Encyclopaedic View* (Boston: G. K. Hall, 1985), 278.

3. Winifred D. Wandersee, "ER and American Youth: Politics and Personality in a Bureaucratic Age," in *Without Precedent*, 73.

4. *Autobiography*, 209.

5. Ibid., 83; Lash, *Eleanor and Franklin*, 606.

6. Quoted in Jason Berger, *A New Deal for the World: Eleanor Roosevelt and American Foreign Policy* (New York: Columbia University Press, 1981), 15.

7. Ibid., 14.

8. Ibid.

9. Ibid., 26.

10. Letters to the Editor, *New York Times*, 4 July 1986.

11. *Press Conferences*, 136.

12. Asbell, *Mother and Daughter*, 138.

13. Lash, *Eleanor and Franklin*, 648.

14. Ibid., 649.

15. Ibid., 652.

16. Asbell, *Mother and Daughter*, 130.
17. Lash, *Love, Eleanor*, 334.
18. Ibid., 338.
19. Lash, *World of Love*, 14.
20. Ibid., 38.
21. Lash, *Eleanor and Franklin*, 668.
22. Ibid., 682.
23. Ibid., 685.
24. Ibid., 687.
25. Ibid., 686.
26. Berger, *New Deal for the World*, 37.
27. Ibid., 39.
28. Asbell, *Mother and Daughter*, 169.
29. Lash, *World of Love*, 136.
30. Berger, *New Deal for the World*, 35.
31. Ibid., 34.
32. Lash, *World of Love*, 151.
33. Ibid., 164.
34. Ibid., 165.
35. Asbell, *Mother and Daughter*, 176.
36. Ibid.
37. Lash, *World of Love*, 168.
38. Asbell, *Mother and Daughter*, 184; Lash, *World of Love*, 179.
39. Ibid., 150, 186.
40. *Autobiography*, 279.

6. FIRST LADY OF THE WORLD

1. Lash, *World of Love*, 188.
2. Joseph P. Lash, *Eleanor Roosevelt: The Years Alone* (New York: Norton, 1972), 23.
3. Quoted in William E. Leuchtenburg, *In the Shadow of FDR: From Harry Truman to Ronald Reagan* (Ithaca and London: Cornell University Press, 1983), 10.
4. Lash, *Years Alone*, 29.
5. Ibid., 33.
6. Ibid., 31.
7. Lash, *World of Love*, 209.
8. Ibid., 214.
9. *Autobiography*, 302–3.
10. Lash, *Years Alone*, 53, 54.
11. Lash, *World of Love*, 221.

12. Ibid., 294.
13. Ibid., 262.
14. Leuchtenburg, *In the Shadow*, 11.
15. Interview with Mr. Joseph L. Rauh, Jr., on 31 January 1978 for the Franklin D. Roosevelt Library, Hyde Park, New York.
16. *Autobiography*, 210.
17. Lash, *Years Alone*, 142.
18. Ibid., 154.
19. Ibid., 234.
20. Ibid., 213.
21. Berger, *New Deal for the World*, 104, 106.
22. Ibid., 107.
23. Lash, *World of Love*, 418.
24. Ibid.
25. Asbell, *Mother and Daughter*, 261; Lash, *World of Love*, 307–8.
26. Asbell, *Mother and Daughter*, 368–64.
27. Lash, *World of Love*, 537.
28. Asbell, *Mother and Daughter*, 264.
29. Lash, *World of Love*, 243.
30. Ibid., 330.
31. *Autobiography*, 326.
32. Ibid., 310.
33. Berger, *New Deal for the World*, 94.
34. Ibid., 98–99.
35. Lash, *World of Love*, 426.
36. Lash, *Years Alone*, 225.
37. Lash, *World of Love*, 442.
38. Lash, *Years Alone*, 257.
39. Ibid., 263, 264.
40. Lash, *World of Love*, 473.
41. Ibid., 472.
42. *Autobiography*, 383.
43. Ibid., 384.
44. Lash, *World of Love*, 7, 282.
45. Ibid., 319.
46. *Autobiography*, 410, 413.
47. Ibid., 412.
48. *New York Times*, 8 December 1959.
49. Ibid.
50. Lash, *Years Alone*, 158.
51. Ibid., 159.
52. Ibid., 292.
53. Asbell, *Mother and Daughter*, 342.

54. Ibid., 297, 298.
55. Lash, *World of Love,* 535.
56. Ibid., 382.
57. Ibid., 548.
58. Ibid.
59. *New York Times,* 8 November 1962.
60. Ibid.

BIBLIOGRAPHIC ESSAY

Joseph Lash describes Eleanor Roosevelt's mission to Chicago in *Eleanor and Franklin* (New York: W. W. Norton & Co., 1971) and in *Love, Eleanor: Eleanor Roosevelt and Her Friends* (Garden City, N.Y.: Doubleday & Co., 1982), volumes upon which this biography depends heavily. The first lady's own recollections can be found in her second volume of memoirs, *This I Remember* (New York: Harper & Bros., 1949). Frances Perkins recounted her role at the convention in *The Roosevelt I Knew* (New York: Viking Press, 1946). Jim Farley contradicts the sequence of events described by others in *Jim Farley's Story: The Roosevelt Years* (New York: McGraw-Hill Book Co., 1948). FDR's proposed nomination refusal is quoted from Nathan Miller, *FDR: An Intimate History* (Garden City, N.Y.: Doubleday & Co., 1983). A different version, but with the same thrust, can be found in Edward L. and Frederick H. Schapsmeier, *Henry A. Wallace of Iowa: The Agrarian Years, 1910–1940* (Ames: Iowa State University Press, 1968). Anna Boettiger's letter to her mother is printed in *Mother and Daughter: The Letters of Eleanor and Anna Roosevelt,* ed. Bernard Asbell (New York: Coward, McCann, & Geoghegan, 1982).

Eleanor Roosevelt's childhood and adolescence are based on Lash's *Eleanor and Franklin,* pt. 1, and *Love, Eleanor,* chaps. 1 and 2. Quotations by Eleanor Roosevelt draw on her first volume of memoirs, *This Is My Story* (New York: Harper & Bros. 1937). The description of the family of Theodore Roosevelt, Sr., and the relationship between his two sons derive from Lash and from Edmund Morris, *The Rise of Theodore Roosevelt* (New York: Random House, 1979). The classic study of female intimacies remains Carroll Smith-Rosenberg, "The Female World of Love and Ritual in Nineteenth-Century America," *Signs* 1 (1975). On young women's crushes in colleges, see Nancy Sahli, "Smashing: Women's Relationships before the Fall," *Chrysalis* 8 (1979).

Before the Trumpet: Young Franklin Roosevelt, 1882–1905 by Geoffrey Ward (New York: Harper & Row, 1985) presents an insightful portrait of FDR to the time of his marriage. Ward includes two sensitive chapters on Eleanor Roosevelt and the young couple's courtship and wedding. In Part 2 of *Eleanor and Franklin* and chapters 3, 4, and 5 in *Love, Eleanor*, Lash covers the years of courtship, marriage, and childbearing through the discovery of the Lucy Mercer letters. Eleanor Roosevelt's recollections of these years are included in *This Is My Story* which concludes in 1920. The family version of the Mercer affair is recounted by Joseph Alsop in *FDR: A Centenary Remembrance* (New York: Viking Press, 1982).

Lash describes the growing independence of Eleanor Roosevelt in *Eleanor and Franklin*, pt. 3, and in *Love, Eleanor*, chaps. 6, 7, and 8. These crucial years are just beginning to receive the study they deserve. Elisabeth Israels Perry and Susan Ware have begun with "Training for Public Service: ER and Women's Political Networks in the 1920s" and "ER and Democratic Politics: Women in the Postsuffrage Era," respectively. Both articles are printed in *Without Precedent: The Life and Career of Eleanor Roosevelt*, ed. Joan Hoff-Wilson and Marjorie Lightman (Bloomington: Indiana University Press, 1984). Eleanor Roosevelt understates her increasing autonomy and expertise in *This I Remember*.

On female bonding among women activists during the early twentieth century, see Blanche Weisen Cook, "Female Support Networks and Political Activism: Lillian Wald, Crystal Eastman, Emma Goldman," *Chrysalis* 3 (1977). Basing his description on the recollections of Marion Dickerman, Kenneth S. Davis tells of the private relationships and the political work of Dickerman, Cook, and Roosevelt in *Invincible Summer: An Intimate Portrait of the Roosevelts* (New York: Atheneum, 1974). Histories of the League of Women Voters and the Consumers' League at the national level and in New York are sorely lacking, but Nancy Shrom Dye details the history of the New York WTUL in *As Equals & As Sisters: Feminism, Unionism, and the Women's Trade Union League of New York* (Columbia and London: University of Missouri Press, 1980).

By the mid-1920s, the *New York Times* covers the varied activities of Eleanor Roosevelt. Magazine articles and interviews include "Ten Rules for Success in Marriage" by Mrs. Franklin D. Roosevelt as told to M. K. Wisehart, *Pictorial Review* 33 (December 1931); M. K. Wisehart, "Wife's Job?" *Good Housekeeping* 91 (August 1930); Ida Tarbell, "Portrait of a Lady," *Delineator* 119 (October 1931); and Helena Huntington Smith, "Noblesse Oblige," *New Yorker* (April 1930).

Lash covers the first two Roosevelt terms in *Eleanor and Franklin*, chaps. 36 through 50, and in *Love, Eleanor*, chaps. 9 through 15. The first lady's perspective on these years can be found in *This I Remember*. Her early newspaper columns were edited and published as *My Days* (New York: Dodge Publishing Co., 1938). Transcripts of her press conferences that have survived are edited by Maurine Beasley, *The White House Press Conferences of Eleanor Roosevelt* (New York: Garland Publications, 1983). Scripts of radio broadcasts and texts of speeches, newspaper and magazine columns, and articles are part of the massive Eleanor Roosevelt manuscript collection at the Franklin D. Roosevelt Library at Hyde Park.

Eleanor Roosevelt's emotional turmoil over entering the White House is described by Lorena Hickok in *Eleanor Roosevelt: Reluctant First Lady* (New York: Dodd, Mead & Co., 1962). Their intense intimacy is documented by Doris Faber, *The Life of Lorena Hickok: Eleanor Roosevelt's Friend* (New York: William Morrow & Co., 1980). Part of the distraught letter Eleanor Roosevelt sent to Cook and Dickerman at the 1932 convention was quoted by Davis in *Invincible Summer.* Davis added her threat to run off with Earl Miller in *FDR: The New York Years, 1928–1933* (New York: Random House, 1979).

The scope of the first lady's social and political concerns was admirably outlined by Tamara Hareven in *Eleanor Roosevelt: An American Conscience* (Chicago: Quadrangle Books, 1968) before the vast collection at Hyde Park was open, but the volume remains a fine study. James R. Kearney's *Anna Eleanor Roosevelt: The Evolution of a Reformer* (Boston: Houghton Mifflin Co., 1968) was written under the same limitations. It concludes in 1940 and is much more critical of the first lady as social thinker.

Martha Swain looks at the first lady's concern for women's relief needs in "ER and Ellen Woodward: A Partnership for Women's Relief and Security"; Lois Scharf criticizes those efforts in "ER and Feminism." Both articles can be found in *Without Precedent.* The network of women reformers in Washington during the 1930s is the subject of Susan Ware, *Beyond Suffrage: Women in the New Deal* (Cambridge: Harvard University Press, 1982).

Joanna Schneider Zangrando and Robert L. Zangrando discuss "ER and Black Civil Rights" in *Without Precedent,* balancing her pace-setting stance with her compromises. The crucial role played by Eleanor Roosevelt in shifting political loyalties of blacks is defined by Nancy J. Weiss, *Farewell to the Party of Lincoln: Black Politics in the Age of FDR* (Princeton: Princeton University Press, 1983). Letters that poured into the White House and other relief offices have been edited by Robert S. McElvaine, *Down & Out in the Great Depression: Letters from the "Forgotten Man"* (Chapel Hill: University of North Carolina Press, 1983).

The youth movement and Eleanor Roosevelt's involvement is detailed in an early work by Joseph Lash, *Eleanor Roosevelt: A Friend's Memoir.* A more recent examination of that period is Winifred D. Wandersee's "ER and American Youth: Politics and Personality in a Bureaucratic Age" in *Without Precedent.* Stella K. Hershan, who collected anecdotal impressions of the first lady in *A Woman of Quality* (New York: Crown Publishers, 1970), associated Eleanor Roosevelt with the Statue of Liberty in a letter to the *New York Times,* 4 July 1986. Jason Berger presents a dry but important account of Eleanor Roosevelt's shifting positions toward issues of war and peace in *A New Deal for the World: Eleanor Roosevelt and American Foreign Policy* (New York: Columbia University Press,

1981). Blanche Wiesen Cook looks at these years and beyond to post–World War II developments in "Turn toward Peace: ER and Foreign Affairs" in *Without Precedent*. The war years conclude Lash's *Eleanor and Franklin*. *Love, Eleanor* ends with a long detailed account of Lash's attempt to explain his imbroglio with intelligence agents and his hasty assignment overseas. Fully one-third of *A World of Love: Eleanor Roosevelt and Her Friends, 1943–1962* by Lash (Garden City, N.Y.: Doubleday & Co., 1984) covers the war years. As in other chapters of this biography the letters in *Mother & Daughter* shed light on both the private and the public worlds of the first lady.

The material on the years of widowhood draw extensively on Lash's *Eleanor Roosevelt: The Years Alone* (Garden City, N.Y.: W.W. Norton & Co., 1972) and *A World of Love* as well as on her final volume of memoirs, *On My Own* (New York: Harper & Bros., 1958). An abridged version of her memoirs, *The Autobiography of Eleanor Roosevelt*, includes an additional update that is useful. "The Search for Understanding." William E. Leuchtenburg clearly illustrates the impact of Eleanor Roosevelt as caretaker of the Roosevelt legacy in *In the Shadow of FDR: From Harry Truman to Ronald Reagan* (Ithaca and London: Cornell University Press, 1983). Berger's *A New Deal for the World* continues the story of her involvement with foreign affairs to the time of her death. Oral interviews with Abram L. Sachar, Joseph L. Rauh, and Pauli Murray from the Franklin D. Roosevelt Library were extremely helpful. Cynthia Harrison examines the Commission on the Status of Women in "A 'New Frontier' for Women: The Public Policy of the Kennedy Administration," *Journal of American History* 67 (1980). Personal memories and tributes are published by David A. Gurewitsch, *Eleanor Roosevelt: Her Day* (New York: Interchange Foundation, 1973) and Edna P. Gurewitsch "Remembering Mrs. Roosevelt: An Intimate Memoir," *American Heritage* 33 (December 1981).

SELECTED BIBLIOGRAPHY

PRIMARY SOURCES

Franklin D. Roosevelt and Hyde Park: Personal Recollections of Eleanor Roosevelt.
    Washington, D.C.: U.S. Government Printing Office, 1949.
If You Ask Me. New York: D. Appleton-Century Co., 1946.
India and the Awakening East. New York: Harper & Bros., 1953.
It's Up to the Women. New York: Frederick A. Stokes Co., 1933.
It Seems to Me. New York: W. W. Norton & Co., 1954.
Ladies of Courage. With Lorena Hickok. New York: G. P. Putnam's Sons, 1954.
The Lady of the White House. London: Hutchinson & Co., 1938.
The Moral Basis of Democracy. New York: Howell, Soskin & Co., 1940.
My Days. New York: Dodge Publishing Co., 1938.
On My Own. New York: Harper & Bros., 1958.
This I Remember. New York: Harper & Bros., 1949.
This Is My Story. New York: Harper & Bros., 1937.
This Troubled World. New York: H. C. Kinsley & Co., 1938.
Tomorrow Is Now. New York: Harper & Row, 1963.
United Nations: Today and Tomorrow. With William DeWitt. New York: Harper
    & Bros., 1953.
The White House Press Conferences of Eleanor Roosevelt. Edited by Maurine Beas-
    ley. New York: Garland Publications, 1983.
You Learn by Living. New York: Harper & Bros., 1960.

SECONDARY SOURCES

Asbell, Bernard., ed. *Mother and Daughter: The Letters of Eleanor and Anna Roo-
    sevelt.* New York: Coward, McCann, & Geoghegan, 1981. A collection of
    revealing letters with insightful commentary by the editor.

Beasley, Maurine H. *Eleanor Roosevelt and the Media: A Public Quest for Self-Fulfillment.* Urbana: University of Illinois Press, 1987. A new study of the evolution of Eleanor Roosevelt's use of mass media for personal and political goals.

Berger, Jason. *A New Deal for the World: Eleanor Roosevelt and American Foreign Policy.* New York: Columbia University Press, 1981. A dry but fine study of Eleanor Roosevelt's developing views on foreign affairs and policies.

Black, Ruby. *Eleanor Roosevelt: A Biography.* New York: Duell, Sloan & Pearce, 1940. The first biography of the first lady by an admiring member of her press corps.

Davis, Kenneth S. *Invincible Summer: An Intimate Portrait of the Roosevelts Based on the Recollections of Marion Dickerman.* New York: Atheneum, 1974. A revealing look at the close relationship among Eleanor Roosevelt, Marion Dickerman, and Nancy Cook from the early 1920s to the death of FDR.

Faber, Doris. *The Life of Lorena Hickok: Eleanor Roosevelt's Friend.* New York: William Morrow & Co., 1980. The biography of the Associated Press reporter who became the first lady's most intimate friend during the 1930s.

Gurewitsch, David A. *Eleanor Roosevelt: Her Day.* New York: Interchange Foundation, 1973. A personal memoir by Eleanor Roosevelt's close friend and physician that covers the years after FDR's death.

Hareven, Tamara K. *Eleanor Roosevelt: An American Conscience.* Chicago: Quadrangle Books, 1968. An early and still extremely thoughtful account of the political development and public career of the first lady.

Hershan, Stella K. *A Woman of Quality.* New York: Crown Publishers, 1970. A collection of reminiscences of people from all walks of life who were touched by their association with Eleanor Roosevelt.

Hickok, Lorena A. *Eleanor Roosevelt: Reluctant First Lady.* New York: Dodd, Mead & Co., 1962. An intimate and revealing biography of the first lady by the journalist who knew her best during the depression years.

Hoff-Wilson, Joan, and Marjorie Lightman, eds., *Without Precedent: The Life and Career of Eleanor Roosevelt.* Bloomington: Indiana University Press, 1984. Twelve scholarly essays that trace the political growth of the first lady, her views on vital issues, and her political friendships.

Kearney, James R. *Anna Eleanor Roosevelt: The Evolution of a Reformer.* Boston: Houghton Mifflin Co., 1968. A critical exploration of the first lady's political development and activities during FDR's first two terms.

Lash, Joseph P. *Eleanor Roosevelt: A Friend's Memoir.* Garden City, N.Y.: Doubleday & Co., 1964. An early memoir by ER's close friend and biographer that focuses on her relationship with the youth movement during the late 1930s.

———. *Eleanor and Franklin: The Story of the Relationship Based on Eleanor Roosevelt's Private Papers.* New York: W. W. Norton & Co., 1971. The definitive biography of the first lady from family background to the death of FDR. The first work to make use of the ER collection at the presidential library.

———. *Eleanor Roosevelt: The Years Alone.* New York: W. W. Norton & Co., 1972. The second volume of the most complete biography to date. Covers her years at the United Nations, world travels, and final days.

———. *Love, Eleanor: Eleanor Roosevelt and Her Friends.* Garden City, N.Y.: Doubleday & Co., 1982. Collection of ER's personal letters through 1943 with extensive commentary by Lash. Intended to give insight into her private life and counteract the speculation that followed in the wake of the Faber biography of Hickok.

———. *A World of Love: Eleanor Roosevelt and Her Friends, 1943–1962.* Garden City, N. Y.: Doubleday & Co., 1984. The second volume of personal letters focuses on her relationships with Lash and Gurewitsch.

Roosevelt, Elliott, and James Brough. *An Untold Story: The Roosevelts of Hyde Park.* New York: G. P. Putnam's Sons, 1973. A son's memoir of the family prior to FDR's presidency.

———. *Mother R: Eleanor Roosevelt's Untold Story.* New York: G. P. Putnam's Sons, 1977. An exploration of the Roosevelt family that focuses on Eleanor in critical fashion.

———. *Eleanor Roosevelt, with Love: A Centenary Remembrance.* New York: Dutton Publishers, 1984. A more straightforward and less critical tribute to his mother.

Roosevelt, James, with Bill Libby. *My Parents: A Differing View.* Chicago: Playboy Press Book, 1976. A poorly written but insightful look at the Roosevelts' relationship by their eldest son.

Sandifer, Irene Reiterman. *Mrs. Roosevelt—As We Knew Her.* N.p.: Privately published, 1975. An outsider's view of the private and public life of ER by the wife of her State Department adviser during her years at the United Nations.

Youngs, J. William T. *Eleanor Roosevelt: A Personal and Public Life.* Boston: Little, Brown & Co., 1985. A concise, extremely readable biography of the first lady.

BIBLIOGRAPHIES

Eleanor Roosevelt Centenary Bibliography. Prepared by Barbara H. Kemp. Washington: National Museum of American History, 1984.

First Lady: A Bibliography of Selected Materials by and about Eleanor Roosevelt. Compiled by David Myers et al. Washington: Library of Congress, 1984.

INDEX

ABOUT THE AUTHOR

Lois Scharf received her doctorate from Case Western Reserve University where she teaches twentieth-century American history as well as American labor and sports history.

Scharf is the author of *To Work and To Wed: Female Employment, Feminism, and the Great Depression* (1980) and is coeditor of *Decades of Discontent: The Women's Movement 1920–1940* (1983). Among her recently published chapters in anthologies are "The Great Uprising in Cleveland: When Sisterhood Failed," in *A Needle, A Bobbin, A Strike: Women Needleworkers in America*, edited by Joan M. Jensen and Sue Davidson (1984) and "ER and Feminism," in *Without Precedent: The Life and Career of Eleanor Roosevelt*, edited by Joan Hoff-Wilson and Marjorie Lightman (1984).

Scharf is also the executive director of National History Day. History Day programs across the country encourage secondary school students to engage in historical research and to enter their papers, projects, and live and media presentations for judging by professional historians at local, state, and national competitions.